Education, Equality and Human Rights

To what extent has the twentieth century created equality for all? What has been and what could be the role of education in this?

Education, Equality and Human Rights addresses the issue of human rights and their relationship to education in the twenty-first century. Each of the five equality issues of gender, 'race', sexuality, special needs and social class are covered as areas in their own right as well as in relation to education. Written by experts in their particular field, the chapters trace the history of the various issues up to the present and enable readers to assess their continuing relevance in the future.

This comprehensive book provides an important educational perspective on world-wide equality issues for student teachers and teachers at all stages. It is an accessible and thought-provoking text for all those studying or interested in education, equality and human rights issues.

Contributors: Maud Blair, Viv Ellis, Simon Forrest, Richard Hatcher, Tom Hickey, Jane Kelly, Jane Martin, Richard Rieser, Satnam Virdee.

Mike Cole is senior lecturer in education, and research and publications mentor in the School of Education at the University of Brighton. He has written extensively on equality and education and in more recent years he has engaged in critiques of postmodernism, globalization and education.

Education, Equality and Human Rights

Issues of Gender, 'Race', Sexuality, Special Needs and Social Class

Edited by Mike Cole

ROUTLEDGE / FALMER · Taylor & Francis Group

London and New York

First published 2000 by RoutledgeFalmer
11 New Fetter Lane, London EC4P 4EE

Simultaneously published in the USA and Canada
by RoutledgeFalmer
29 West 35th Street, New York, NY 10001

RoutledgeFalmer is an imprint of the Taylor & Francis Group

© 2000 Selection and editorial matter Mike Cole;
individual chapters to their contributors

Typeset in Times by Keystroke, Jacaranda Lodge, Wolverhampton
Printed and bound in Great Britain by Biddles Ltd, Guildford and King's Lynn

British Library Cataloguing in Publication Data
A catalogue record for this book is available from the British Library

Library of Congress Cataloging-in-Publication Data
Education, equality, and human rights / edited by Mike Cole.
    p.   cm.
  Includes bibliographical references and index.
    1. Educational equalization – Great Britain. 2. Discrimination in education – Great
  Britain. 3. Human rights. 4. Critical pedagogy – Great Britain. I. Cole, Mike, 1946–
LC213.3.G7 E335 2000
370.11′5 – dc21   99-055456

ISBN 0–7507–0876–x (hbk)
ISBN 0–7507–0877–8 (pbk)

Contents

Illustrations

Figures

Tables

Contributors

Maud Blair is a lecturer in the School of Education at the Open University. She has written and published widely in the areas of 'gender' and 'race' and is co-author of the 1998 Department for Education and Employment study, *Making the Difference: Teaching and Learning Strategies in Successful Multi-ethnic Schools*. Her current research interests include the over-representation of black students in school exclusions, and the relationship between school exclusion and the criminal and juvenile justice systems.

Dr Mike Cole is Senior Lecturer in Education, and Research and Publications Mentor in the School of Education at the University of Brighton. He has written extensively on equality and education. In more recent years, he has engaged in critiques of postmodernism, globalization and education. His most recent publications include the co-written (with the Hillcole Group) *Rethinking Education and Democracy* (1997), the edited collection *Professional Issues for Teachers and Student Teachers* (1999), and the co-edited collections *Promoting Equality in Primary Schools* (1997), *Promoting Equality in Secondary Schools* (1999), *Postmodernism in Educational Theory and the Politics of Human Resistance* (1999) and *Migrant Labour in the European Union* (1999).

Viv Ellis is a lecturer in English in Education at the University of Brighton. He has written about teachers' responses to pupil writing, the relationship between the English curriculum and children's lives, and ICT, culture and pedagogy. Previously he was Curriculum Manager for English and the Expressive Arts at an 11–18 community school in the West Midlands.

Simon Forrest is a research fellow in the Department of Sexually Transmitted Diseases, University College, London. He is currently working on research into young people's experience of different kinds of sex education in English secondary schools. He has written about young people and sex education, gender and sexuality for teachers and has contributed to resources on sex and relationships for young people.

Richard Hatcher is Director of Research in the Faculty of Education at the University of Central England in Birmingham. He has written widely on issues of equality and social justice in schools, with special reference to government education policy.

Tom Hickey is a principal lecturer in the School of Historical and Critical Studies at the University of Brighton. Course Leader of a masters programme in critical social and political philosophy, he also teaches at undergraduate level on options in philosophy, aesthetics, international relations and political economy. He is currently working on the relationship between political theory and early twentieth-century British politics. He can be contacted via http://www.brighton.ac.uk/schacsweb/

Jane Kelly is a principal lecturer in the School of Art and Design History at Kingston University. She has written on postmodernism and feminism, feminist art history and contemporary art practice. At present she is writing on the relationship between Marxism and feminism. She has been actively involved in the Women's Liberation Movement since the 1970s.

Jane Martin is a senior lecturer in sociology at University College Northampton, with a special interest in gender and policy making in British education. She has been working on women pioneers in education for a number of years and recently published a well-received original study *Women and the Politics of Schooling in Victorian and Edwardian England*. She is presently writing a co-authored book with Dr Joyce Goodman on *Women and Education 1800–1980*. This features the work of Shena Simon both as a member of the Spens committee on education in the 1930s and Manchester local education authority until 1970, among others. She is currently book reviews editor for *Gender and Education* and member of the editorial board of *History of Education*.

Richard Rieser is a disabled teacher who has taught in higher education, further education secondary, primary and nursery, and who has also written widely on inclusion. He is currently Advisory Teacher for Inclusion in Hackney. He is also Co-ordinator of Disability Equality in Education, a training charity which is developing training for inclusion. He is a member of the National Advisory Group for SEN, which advises the government on inclusion and SEN and is Chair of the Alliance for Inclusive Education, Vice-Chair of the Council for Disabled Children and Vice-Chair of the NUT Disabled Teachers Working Group. He has been an active campaigner for equality through the National Union of Teachers for the past twenty-one years.

Satnam Virdee is a lecturer in sociology in the Department of Government at the University of Strathclyde. His main research interests include racist and anti-racist collective action in trade unions; the political economy of racism; and racist violence. He is the author of several monographs including *Racial Violence and Harassment* (PSI, 1995). He is currently undertaking an ESRC-funded ethnographic study of the racialization of school life and is writing a book on racism and resistance in English trade unions.

Introduction

Human Rights, Education and Equality

Mike Cole

Instituted in England and Wales in 1988, the National Curriculum is nearing the end of its shelf-life. Since the election of the New Labour government in 1997,[1] a new core curriculum has been designed to take effect in September 2000. Citizenship education from August 2002 will be a compulsory part of the core curriculum at Key Stages 3 and 4, and there will be a non-statutory element in the form of Personal, Social and Health Education and Citizenship at Key Stages 1 and 2. As a result, equality, equal opportunities and human rights are about to become firmly on the educational agenda.[2] In *Education for Citizenship and the Teaching of Democracy in Schools* (QCA, 1998), the Crick Report,[3] it is recommended that 'Citizenship Education' take up to 5 per cent of curriculum time across all stages. 'Equality' and 'human rights' are two of the essential key concepts to be reached by the end of compulsory schooling, with a 'belief in human dignity and equality', a 'commitment to equal opportunities' and a 'concern for human rights' being 'essential values'. Essential knowledge includes 'human rights charters and issues' (*ibid.*, p. 44).

With respect to the key stages: at KS 1, pupils should be able to 'reflect on issues of social and moral concern' and 'recognise how the concept of fairness can be applied . . . to their personal and social life' (*ibid.*, p. 46); and at KS 2, they should 'know about . . . ethnic cultures' and 'understand the meaning of 'fairness, justice . . . and human rights' (*ibid.*, p. 48).

At KS 3, students should 'understand the meaning of . . . human rights' (*ibid.*, p. 50) and should 'understand, at a basic level, the legal rights of young people with particular reference to the UN Convention on the Rights of the Child' (see below). They should 'also understand the meaning of . . . discrimination [and] equal opportunities' and 'understand . . . rights and responsibilities . . . with particular reference to the European Convention on Human Rights' and 'know about the Universal Declaration of Human Rights' (*ibid.*, p. 49; see below). Finally, at KS 4, students should 'understand the significant aspects of topical and contemporary issues and events' and 'the meaning of terms such as civil rights[4] [and] natural justice', along with an understanding of the 'world as a global community, including issues such as . . . heavily indebted countries, and the work of the United Nations organisations' (*ibid.*, p. 52).[5]

As currently formulated, the concept of 'human rights' is a comparatively recent phenomenon. The President of the United Nations General Assembly, Dr E.H.

served at the proclamation of the Universal Declaration of Human Rights mber 1948 that this was 'the first occasion on which the organised world nity had recognised the existence of human rights and fundamental freedoms ending the laws of sovereign states' (Laqueur and Rubin, 1979, cited in Osler and Starkey, 1996, p. 2).

Article 1 of the United Nations Universal Declaration of Human Rights states: 'All human beings are born free and equal in dignity and rights. They are endowed with reason and conscience and should act towards one another in a spirit of brotherhood' (cited in *ibid.*, p. 173).[6] One might respond charitably to the exclusion of women in the affirmation of brotherhood, when one reads Article 2, which affirms: 'Everyone is entitled to all the rights and freedoms set forth in this Declaration, without distinction of any kind, such as race, colour, sex, language, religion, political or other opinion, national or social origin, property, birth or other status' (*ibid.*). However, although Article 2 stresses 'without distinction of any kind', I would want to cite 'disability' and 'sexuality' specifically, in addition to the other examples given.

As far as education is concerned, Article 26 declares:

> Everyone has the right to education. [It] shall be free, at least in the elementary and fundamental stages. Elementary education shall be compulsory . . . [and] shall be directed to the full development of the human personality and to the strengthening of respect for human rights and fundamental freedoms. It shall promote understanding, tolerance and friendship among all nations, racial or religious groups and shall further the activities of the United Nations for the maintenance of peace.
>
> (*Ibid.*, p. 174)

Forty years later, in November 1989, the United Nations adopted the UN Convention on the Rights of the Child. Defining a 'child' as anyone under 18, 'unless by law majority is attained at an earlier age' (*ibid.*, p. 175), the Convention reiterated the principles enshrined in the United Nations Charter and stated that

> the education of the child shall be directed towards . . . respect for the child's parents, his or her own cultural identity, language and values [and] the preparation of the child for responsible life in a free society, in the spirit of understanding, peace, tolerance, equality of sexes, and friendship among all peoples, ethnic, national and religious groups and persons of indigenous origin . . . [C]hildren of minority communities and indigenous populations [have the right] to enjoy their own culture and to practise their own religion and language.
>
> (*Ibid.*, pp. 178–9)

In addition, 'children with disabilities' have the right to 'special care, education and training designed to help them to achieve the greatest possible self-reliance and to lead a full and active life in society' (*ibid.* p. 177). I would want to add to this Convention the right, when this becomes apparent, of children to their own sexuality.

With respect to the UK, on 9 October 1998, the Human Rights Act 1998 received Royal Assent in the House of Lords. As Plimmer put it, referring to the Bill's earlier introduction there, this marked

> a recognition by the Labour Government that the traditional freedom of the individual under an unwritten constitution to do that which is not prohibited by law gives inadequate protection from misuse of power/acts/omissions by the state/public bodies in a manner which is incompatible with human rights under the [European Convention of Human Rights]
>
> (Plimmer, 1998, p. 2)[7]

Given that rights under the European Convention are being brought into domestic law, it is more urgent than ever to implement Recommendation R (85) 7 of the Council of Europe, adopted by the Committee of Ministers in May 1985. The Recommendation encourages 'teaching and learning about human rights in schools' (Osler and Starkey, 1996, p. 181). The Council of Europe recently adopted another recommendation (Recommendation 1346). This called on member states to 'review curricula from primary school to university to eliminate negative stereotypes, highlight positive aspects of different cultures, and promote tolerance'. It also stressed the need 'to include human rights education in all school curricula and in the training of all officials dealing with the public'. The Assembly further recommended that human rights education should be considered as a priority for the intergovernmental work of the Council of Europe (Amnesty International, 1998, p. 9).

Recommendation R (85) 7 has a specific section on 'teacher training' which states that future teachers should 'be encouraged to take an interest in national and world affairs' and should 'be taught to identify and combat all forms of discrimination in schools and society and be encouraged to confront and overcome their prejudices' (Osler and Starkey, 1996, p. 183).

Now that human rights is set to become part of the curriculum, this European Recommendation should be an essential requirement for student teachers, teachers and others involved with the education of children and young people. (QCA, 1998, is well aware of the need to amend the role of teacher education, including in-service education, in the light of the proposed changes (pp. 30–1).)

The purpose of this book is to address this requirement.[8] In order 'to identify and combat all forms of discrimination in schools and society' and 'to confront and overcome prejudices', it is necessary to understand equality issues *per se* as well as being able to apply them to education. Hence the chapters of this book introduce the issues of gender, 'race' and racism, sexuality, disability and social class in their own right, before specifically relating each to education.

With respect to these five equality issues, five important points need to be made.[9] First, they are all social constructs, which reflect particular social systems; they are not inevitable features of any society, but rather crucial terrains of struggle between conflicting social forces in any given society. In other words, I do not believe that societies *need* to be class-based, to have 'racialized' hierarchies, to have one sex dominating another. I refuse to accept that people are *naturally* homophobic or prone to marginalizing the needs of disabled people. On the contrary, I believe that, in general, we are socialized into accepting the norms, values and customs of the social systems in which we grow up, and schools have traditionally played a major part in that process. Where these social systems exhibit inequalities of any form, those at the receiving end of exploitation, oppression or discrimination have, along with their supporters, historically resisted and fought back in various ways, as the various chapters of this book bear witness. Schools do not have to be places where pupils/students are encouraged to think in one-dimensional ways. Indeed, were this the case, there would be no point in this book. They can and should be arenas for the encouragement of critical thought, where young people are provided with a number of ways of interpreting the world, not just the dominant ones.

Second, each of the issues under consideration in this book has a material and institutional parameter (differences in wealth and power, laws which disfavour certain groups) and a socio/psychological parameter (modes of thinking and acting both by the exploiters and discriminators and those on the receiving end of exploitation and discrimination).

Third, these inequalities are interrelated and need to be considered in a holistic way. Every human being has multiple identities. To take a case in point, there are, of course, lesbians, gays and bisexuals in all social classes, among the Asian, black and other minority ethnic communities and among the white communities. There are gays, lesbians and bisexuals with disabilities and with special needs.

Fourth, while recognizing the interrelation of various inequalities, at the same time, their separateness must also be acknowledged. As will become clear in the chapters of this book, people are not only exploited and oppressed in similar ways, they are exploited and oppressed in different and specific ways.

Since each chapter is introductory in its own right, I do not propose to discuss each equality issue here. However, there is one final point to make in this Introduction. It is necessary to make a distinction between equality and equal opportunities. Equal opportunities policies, in schools and elsewhere, seek to enhance social mobility within structures which are essentially unequal. In other words, they seek a meritocracy, where people rise (or fall) on merit, but to grossly unequal levels or strata in society – unequal in terms of income, wealth, lifestyle, life-chances and power. Egalitarian policies, policies to promote equality, on the other hand, seek to go further. First, egalitarians attempt to develop a systematic critique of structural inequalities, both in society at large and at the level of the individual school. Second, egalitarians are committed to a transformed economy, and a more socially just society, where wealth and ownership is shared far more equally, and where citizens (whether young citizens or teachers in schools, economic citizens in the workplace or political citizens in the polity) exercise democratic controls over their lives and over the structures of the societies of which they are part and to which they contribute. While equal opportunity policies in schools and elsewhere are clearly essential, it is the view of the contributors to this volume that they need to be advocated within a framework of a longer-term commitment to equality. It is in this spirit that the book is written.

Acknowledgement

I would like to thank John Clay and Dave Hill for their helpful comments on this Introduction.

Notes

1 For a critical analysis of New Labour and education policy, see, for example, Cole (1998); Hatcher (1998); Allen *et al.* (1999); Hill (1999); Power and Whitty (1999).
2 For suggestions as to how equality can be promoted under the existing National Curriculum, see Cole and Hill (1997) and Hill and Cole (1999).
3 For a critical analysis of this report, see Clay et al. (1999).
4 *The Concise Oxford Dictionary* defines 'civil rights' as 'the rights of citizens to political and social freedom and equality'.
5 Time and space do not permit a detailed consideration of the new government guidelines on Citizenship. Suffice it to say that within it there are clear opportunities for promoting human rights and social justice.
6 This citation from the *Universal Declaration of Human Rights* and the following citations from the *Universal Declaration of Human Rights*, the *Summary of the UN Convention on the Rights of the Child* and Recommendation R (85) 7 of the Council of Europe are taken from Osler and Starkey (1996), Appendices 1, 2 and 3, respectively. I have indicated the page number of Osler and Starkey's book on which each citation occurs.
7 The Institute of Public Policy Research has suggested that the Act might fail in its aims, however, because of the lack of an official body to ensure that it works (*Guardian*, 12 October 1998).
8 The book does not deal specifically with human rights in their more extreme manifestations, such as freedom from torture, from inhuman or degrading punishment or freedom from slavery. However, I believe such issues are appropriate for schools, with appropriate safeguards relating to age.
9 The rest of this Introduction draws on Cole and Hill (1999).

References

Amnesty International (1998) *Teachers and Academics Network Newsletter*, London: Amnesty International (Summer)

Clay, J. et al. (1999) *Citizenship and Education: The Third Way?* London: Tufnell Press

Cole, M. (1998) 'Globalization, Modernization and Competitiveness: A Critique of the New Labour Project in Education', *International Studies in Sociology of Education*, 8 (3), pp. 315–32

Cole, M. and Hill, D. (1999) Introduction in P. Hill, and M. Cole (eds), *Promoting Equality in Secondary Schools*, London: Cassell

Cole, M. and Hill, D. (eds) (1997) *Promoting Equality in Primary Schools*, London: Cassell

Hatcher, R. (1998) 'Social Justice and the Politics of School Effectiveness and Improvement', *Race, Ethnicity and Education*, 1 (2), pp. 267–89.

Hill, D. and Cole, M. (eds) (1999) *Promoting Equality in Secondary Schools*, London: Cassell

Osler, A. and Starkey, H. (1996) *Teacher Education and Human Rights*, London: David Fulton

Plimmer, M. (1998) 'Standing in Someone Else's Shoes', *New Law Journal*, 10 July

Qualifications and Curriculum Authority (QCA) (1998) *Education for Citizenship and the Teaching of Democracy in Schools*, London: DfEE

1 Gender and Equality

One hand tied behind us

Jane Kelly

Introduction: Women's liberation or post-feminism?

Although some women claim that we are in a post-feminist era, we have only to look at the demands of the first Women's Liberation Conference, held at Ruskin College, Oxford, in 1970, to recognize that we are still far from having achieved equality. The 1970 conference demanded equal pay, twenty-four-hour childcare,[1] free contraception and abortion on demand. Later, other demands were added – the right to determine one's own sexuality; the rights of black women, including the right to determine their own demands autonomously; reproductive rights; and the right to education.

If we look at just the first three, none of these has been achieved. Despite the Equal Pay Act of 1973, women still only earn 72.7 per cent of the male wage, and 4 million women earn less than £4 an hour.[2] Provision for pre-school childcare is the lowest in Europe, despite the fact that the proportion of women working is among the highest in Europe, and cuts in local government over the last eighteen years have led to nursery and crèche closures and increased fees; the few high-profile and expensive workplace nurseries have done little to fill the gap. In 1998, of the top five hundred companies, only 5 per cent contributed towards the childcare costs of their employees. The New Labour government's policy of a nursery place for every four-year-old is scarcely an adequate response to the needs of mothers for pre-school childcare, whether raising children on their own or not.

As for free contraception and abortion on demand, while contraception is now available, there are threats to charge a fee for the contraceptive pill. Abortion rights continue to be under threat, either directly or through cuts in the NHS, while reproductive rights for ordinary women seeking fertility treatment are continually curtailed, also as a result of cuts in funding, and are anyhow non-existent for single and lesbian women, as a result of the Human Embryology and Fertilization Act, passed in 1990, unless you are rich enough to pay for private treatment.

Postmodern Feminism

The current fashion for postmodern theory is quite incapable of explaining why, twenty-five years after the founding of the modern Women's Liberation Movement and the achievement of several pieces of equal rights legislation, such as the Equal Pay Act of 1973 and the Sex Discrimination Act of 1975, the original demands have not been met. The adoption of various postmodern frameworks by many feminist writers and theorists has not helped us to understand why this should be the case. Postmodernism's refusal to analyse society as an entity and its determination to concentrate on the local situation means it is unable to understand women's oppression. Some feminists who have adopted postmodernism even encourage the use of distinct and often contradictory theories to look at different elements (e.g., Fraser and Nicholson, 1990, p. 26) which leads to incoherence and an inability to understand the interrelation between these different elements of the oppression of and discrimination against women.

Since the 1980s, the writings of the French female psychoanalysts Luce Irigaray and Julia Kristeva, who had been students of Jacques Lacan, have been increasingly adopted by feminists, along with the writings of Michel Foucault, Jacques Derrida and Roland Barthes. The stress these writers put on the place and role of the individual in society leads to real difficulties in analysing the position of women. They argue that individual consciousness is in a state of constant change, unstable and in flux; that the female subject enters the conscious world of male-dominated language and is thus inevitably discriminated against, forced to speak an alien language; that power is not centralized, for example in the state, or some other recognizable authority, but located within the individual herself. Consequently, the acquisition of knowledge or the ability to judge truth from falsity is an impossible ideal, best forgotten.

Despite the recognition of the need for strategic thinking when dealing with something as pervasive as women's oppression, feminist writers who have adopted such a framework flounder in the incoherent and contradictory character of these theories. For example in the article by N. Fraser and L. Nicholson, first published in 1988, the writers, trying to construct a social theory that is adequate to the task, catalogue a range of sociological methods, but ultimately produce an incoherent and contradictory list,

> an array of different methods and genres . . . large narratives about changes in social organisation and ideology, empirical and socio-theoretical analyses of macrostructure and institutions, interactionist analyses of the micro-politics of everyday life, critical-hermeneutical and institutional analyses of cultural production, historically and culturally specific sociologies of gender . . . The list could go on.
>
> (Fraser and Nicholson, 1990, p. 26)

Mainly notable for its use of long words to disguise the appalling lack of understanding of the role and place of theory, this is a sort of 'pick an' mix' method, which might be all right when choosing sweets in Woolworths, but is hardly adequate when faced with the task of achieving the liberation of women. The authors seem to suggest that we can adopt one way of looking at the realm of institutions, another method to analyse everyday life (as if the two were unconnected), and as for gender – 'historically and culturally specific sociologies' will be the means. We could use a bourgeois feminist framework to discuss legal rights such as equality, a radical feminist theory to analyse pornography and socialist feminism to look at women and work.[3] Suitably postmodern in its variety it might be, but incoherent and chaotic if you are trying to link together different elements of women's oppression in order to understand them and so be in a position to develop strategies for change.

Their article accepts that feminism is, by its very nature, political and therefore inevitably about change, making strategic ideas a necessity, yet adopts versions of postmodernism which, because of their adherence to the local, the contingent and the specific, disallow precisely that necessary strategic thought.

Postmodernism's refusal to think about the whole world and its relationships is thoroughly pessimistic and totally inadequate when it comes to changing the lives of half the world's population – namely women. Rather than using postmodern theories I want to suggest that Marxist theory is much better placed to explain why women have not been able to achieve equality over the last twenty-five years.

Against those who say that Marxist and socialist theory is gender- and colour-blind, that it 'has used the generalising categories of production and class to delegitimise demands of women, black people, gays, lesbians, and others whose oppression cannot be reduced to economics' (Fraser and Nicholson, 1990, p. 11), I want to argue for a return to the ideas of socialism and Marxism, to reject the criticism that it ignores and is ignorant of the position of women (and other oppressed groups), in order to discuss the position of women today in Britain. I think it is important to relate the ideological offensive against women, carried out by the Tory governments since 1979 and continued by New Labour, to the real position of women, at home and in the paid workforce, and to sketch out some areas of fruitful campaigning activity for the development of feminism and to fight for equal rights (see, for example, Kelly, 1992, 1999).

In this chapter I am going to look first at some examples of discrimination against women in the nineteenth century, as well as various struggles resulting in legislative gains for women's rights, including for both middle- and working-class women. Second, I will discuss some issues relating to women, work and the labour market today. I will explain why equal rights legislation has failed to alter women's position at work, and ask whether discrimination and inequality are direct results of biology – in the famous phrase: is biology destiny? – or whether the social position of women, especially the role played by women in the family, is more influential. Finally, I want to to suggest one or two theories based on Marxism which may help us understand these problems, to put us in a better position to continue the struggle for equality.

Gendered Divisions: Women in the Nineteenth Century

While we should continue to press for the demands made in the early 1970s, we should not assume that nothing has been gained. If we look back to the position of women in nineteenth-century Europe, we can see just how many gains have been made since then. The Industrial Revolution, which moved production out of the home into the factory, had profound effects on both middle- and working-class women. It resulted in different spheres of influence and a gendered division, at least for middle-class women, between the domestic or private space of the home – the woman's world – and the public world of men.

In Victorian Britain, sexual hypocrisy meant that middle-class women were not supposed to enjoy sexual contact, while their husbands, partners in promoting the family values of thrift, sobriety and piety, used prostitutes in their thousands. The secondary position occupied by both middle- and working-class women in Britain in the nineteenth century is symbolized by the so-called 'rule of thumb'. Nowadays this means a more or less accurate measurement; then it meant that a man was legally entitled to hit his wife or partner, as long as the stick was no thicker than his thumb!

These changes were not confined to Britain. Women were in a similar position in France, for example. Berthe Morisot, an impressionist painter, was unable to help organize the impressionist exhibitions, despite the fact that she showed in all but one of them, because the organizers (Monet, Pissarro, Renoir – all men) met in cafés which were out of bounds to middle-class women. One of the reasons middle-class women were barred from so many public places in the French cities was because working-class women *were* present: as barmaids, laundresses, salesgirls and especially prostitutes, on the streets and in cafés. So this private/public division was not only gendered but divided by class (Lipton, 1987; Pollock, 1988; Garb, 1993). The barring of middle-class women from the sights and sounds that constituted modernity, which was the subject matter of impressionism, meant that female artists like Morisot, Mary Cassatt and Eva Gonzales painted different and more restricted subjects, such as domestic interiors, views from balconies: the street, the café, backstage at the theatre were barred to them. As a result, until the recent development of a feminist art history, many books on impressionism omitted the women artists from the history altogether, refusing to recognize that discrimination led them to different subjects; despite the fact that in Morisot's case her style was classically impressionist.

In Austria, too, Freud's discovery that many middle-class women suffered from what he described as 'hysterical symptoms', including temporary paralysis of limbs, has also been partially explained by reference to their seclusion within the home. Oppressive domesticity, daily unchanging routines, complete economic and social dependence on men led some women to rebel in the only ways open to them. Whether such hysterical symptoms were the result of real sexual abuse by their fathers, other male relations or close family friends or whether the experiences had been fantasized is open to question; that the women experienced extreme physical symptoms for which there were no physiological explanations cannot be denied.

While the Industrial Revolution constructed a norm of oppressive domesticity for middle-class women, it also led to the growth of a new class, the proletariat, or working class, which included men, women, and initially children as well. The contradiction between the ideal of a genteel, domestic femininity for women and the reality of working women's lives, fulfilling the needs of the capitalist economy, produced a number of struggles for women's rights, fought for by both middle- and working-class women, most notably for female suffrage – the right to vote.

The demand for women's suffrage in Britain, fought for on and off during the whole of the second half of the nineteenth century and the first decades of the twentieth, saw the British labour movement divided. The Chartist demands in the 1840s for annual parliaments, proportional representation and universal suffrage did not include the vote for women: they were opposed to female suffrage, as were many in the Independent Labour Party (ILP) during the last decade of nineteenth century and the first of the twentieth, and the Labour Representation Committee (LRC), the early form of the modern Labour Party.

The following quotes give a flavour of these debates:

> In 1841 the Rochdale Social Missionary, William Spier, debated the Manchester Chartist James Leach, in Rochdale. In the course of his speech Spier reminded the audience that although the Charter claimed to stand for 'the principle of universal suffrage . . . women were excluded from its benefits – this was one half of the population: how could it be called universal suffrage?'

> In reply, Leach stated that 'he did not think that such a wide difference existed between men and women as to make it necessary for women to enjoy the suffrage: he thought that men, as fathers, husbands and brothers, would secure the best interests of women.' Many of his fellow radicals agreed, with the additional proviso that even if women *thought* their political interests were different from those of their menfolk, this was just a further reason for denying them the vote since then they might 'arrive at political conclusions adverse to those of their husbands . . . and then there is one more . . . subject of domestic discord . . . !' Or in the words of Feargus O'Connor, an adamant anti-feminist, 'IT WOULD LEAD TO FAMILY DISSENSIONS . . . ' Even men who supported voting rights for widows and spinsters balked at the idea of giving the franchise to married women.

> (Taylor, 1983, p. 271)

Conversely, at the turn of the century Kier Hardy, a supporter of women's right to vote and a radical member of the ILP, said that:

> he valued the zeal of middle and upper class suffragettes, but felt that 'without the active support and cooperation of working women they will have no chance whatever of being successful.' Much of his speech [in 1902 to suffragettes at Chelsea Town Hall] was devoted to countering the arguments against women's suffrage he had come across on the Labour Representation Committee. Socialists were fearful of the influence of the priest and the parson if women got the vote: Hardie said he preferred that to the influence on men voters of the publican (usually Tory) and the bookmaker. Trade unionists sometimes argued that votes for women could lead to domestic discord: what

sort of domestic peace is it, Hardie asked, if it is based on the wife being treated as an 'inferior domestic animal'?

(Liddington and Norris, 1978, p. 153)

The vote for women aged thirty years and over was eventually won in Britain in 1918 and in 1928 for those over twenty-one, but it should be remembered that in France women only gained suffrage in 1944.

Other feminist campaigns in Britain produced reforms such as the Married Women's Property Acts, in 1870, which gave women the right to keep their inheritance and earnings; the Custody of Infants Act of 1886, which gave widowed mothers rights over their children, previously the responsibility of a male guardian after the husband's death; and in 1888 maintenance for deserted wives as long as the husband was at fault.

There were changes in education too, especially with regards to middle-class women. In 1850 North London Collegiate School, the first academically oriented day school for the daughters of the middle class was opened, and in 1873, along with a number of general changes in education, Girton College, Cambridge, the first college for women, was founded. The setting up of mass education in the last decades of the nineteenth century is a telling example of the institutionalization of inequality. Always related both economically and ideologically to the needs of the state, mass education was set up with class and gender divisions structured in. From the 1870s to the end of the century, working-class girls' education was dominated by training in domestic economy, in cookery and laundry – education for motherhood. In the early twentieth century, childcare was added.[4] In this same period the majority of middle-class girls were educated at home or in small private boarding schools, apart from the few more academic schools like North London Collegiate School and Cheltenham Ladies College (1854). These two had a broader educational content than schools for working-class girls, but like other middle-class girls' education, it too was primarily a training for marriage and homemaking.[5]

Until the end of the nineteenth century most changes pertained solely to middle-class women, for working-class women could afford access to neither education nor the law. However, legislation was passed which altered the lives of working-class women. In the 1870s and 1880s laws restricting the conditions of work for women were gradually introduced; for example, women (and children) were banned from working in the mines and from night work. This latter was a double-edged sword: women were only barred from night work where men were also employed, and this was usually better-paid work; they were allowed to work at night in the caring professions – nursing – and in places of entertainment, for example, bars and music halls. The exclusion from better-paid night work was achieved in the name of reform with the connivance of the male-dominated trade union movement which used the argument that a man was entitled to a 'family wage', enough to keep his wife and children so that the former should not have to take paid work.

In trying to emulate the middle-class ideal, the working-class wife and mother was made dependent on the male wage earner and the man was made responsible for his whole family. In practice, of course, women continued to take paid work, but in the less well-paid and less protected areas.

This contradictory reform was not accepted without a fight. For example, in 1874 the Women's Protective and Provident League (WPPL) was formed to oppose both restrictive legislation for women as well as their exploitation at work. Launched by Emma Patterson, who was a bookbinder from Bristol, with the help of Mrs Mark Patterson (later Lady Dilke), the WPPL sought:

> 'the protection afforded by combination', thereby avoiding exploitation by employers and the hostility of working men who, fearful 'that the employment of women . . . [would] lower their wages', were 'forbidding their members to work with women' and agitating 'to limit the hours of women's work in factories and workshops'. To Patterson, such legislation was offensive because it both reduced female earning power and put women on a par with children, for whom protection was also sought.
>
> (Bolt, 1993, p. 175)

But the legislation was passed anyhow.

This is not merely a matter of historical debate, for as recently as the 1970s, trade unionists at the Cowley car plant in Oxford fought a long battle for the right of women to work nights, alongside men and for better wages than daytime work offered. This debate is part of the equality versus difference debate: do you fight for women's rights on equal terms with men – for example, making pregnancy and childbirth a temporary disability akin to breaking your leg – or do you argue that women's lives are fundamentally different from men's so that they need different rights and legislation to men, including protection from certain types of work, and in particular circumstances, during pregnancy, for example? Alexandra Kollontai a leading member of the Bolshevik Party, took the latter view. In the period after the 1917 revolution in Russia she took up these issues and wrote a number of papers on them. As Alix Holt writes in her introduction to Kollontai's writings:

> Some of the first laws prepared by the commissariat related to the protection of maternity: women were given a legal equality that took their reproductive function into consideration. Women were not to be employed in various jobs harmful to their health, they were not to work long hours or night-shifts, they were to have paid leave at childbirth.
>
> (Holt, 1977, p. 117)

Kollontai had been discussing the needs of women in pregnancy and after childbirth well before 1917, including in a 1914 pamphlet entitled 'Working Woman and Mother'. Some of the demands she developed here included maternity insurance schemes to provide benefits for women for sixteen weeks, or longer if the doctor thought necessary, both before and after the birth of a child. These were to be given directly to the mother, whether there was a live birth or not, and were to be one and a half times the woman's normal wage, or of the average wage if the woman was not employed. She was also to be entitled to benefits, equalling one-half of the normal wage, for the whole period of breast feeding, and for at least nine months (Holt, 1977, pp. 137–8). For Kollontai, the reproductive capacity of women had to be taken into account as a special circumstance, not only for the sake of the mother, but for the child's health.

Compared to nineteenth-century legislation in Britain, framed by the demand for a 'family wage', and leading to the exclusion of women from well-paid work, the changes introduced into the new Soviet Union were based on the equality of women, and their right not to be discriminated against because of reproduction.[6]

Women and Work

Economic independence, paid work outside the home, has been seen by many as a prerequisite of freedom for women. The ability to take paid work depends on the control of fertility. From the outset the modern Women's Liberation Movement recognized the centrality of choice in matters of reproduction in the fight for equality for women. The development and introduction of the contraceptive pill, while it carried some unacceptable health risks, was still the first contraceptive method that could be relied upon to be effective, and meant that women could increasingly control their fertility: sexual intercourse did not any more lead inevitably to pregnancy and childbirth. The Abortion Act of 1967 also helped women in their right to choose whether, when, where and how to have children.

The control of fertility was an important development in the process of the incorporation of women into the workforce from the 1960s onwards. Women had been drawn into the workforce during the Second World War but were moved out of heavy industry and munitions afterwards. Although immigration from the Caribbean and from the Asian subcontinent was initially used to fill the labour gap, by the early 1960s this immigration was being restricted, and women were once again drawn into the workforce in increasing numbers.[7]

The percentage of women at work has increased over the last twenty-five years or so, from less than 40 per cent in 1973 to nearly 50 per cent today, and women, including a larger number of married women than ever before, work for a greater part of their lives. However, in the main, women's work is different from men's work, within the so-called segregated labour market, in worse conditions and for less pay. The suggestion made by some who adopt a post-feminist agenda that women have achieved equality at work is far from the truth. Some middle-class women may have achieved an apparent equality in some professions, but this is a tiny percentage compared to the overall numbers of women working. It represents a drop in the ocean.

The majority of women at work today are segregated both *horizontally*, in different jobs to men, for example, in nursing and primary school teaching where the majority of workers are women, and *vertically*, in jobs that men do as well, but where women are usually lower down the scale or career ladder. Women's work is confined to several key sectors. In 1997 just over half (52 per cent) of working women were in three major occupational groups: clerical/secretarial, personal and protective services, and sales, areas where only 18 per cent of men worked (Sly, Price and Risdon, 1997). This segregation leaves women in less important, poorly paid areas, in the service sector, in the caring professions, replicating expectations of women's work at home. In their majority women work in jobs which enable them to care for children as well as take paid work. In addition, taking a break for childbearing – euphemistically called a career break – also interrupts work patterns, affecting work and career prospects. Jobs normally carried out by men are also undervalued when women are the majority of the workers. For example, in the ex-USSR most doctors were women and were very badly paid compared to industrial workers.

Where women work in sectors alongside men, they work in the lower grades with less pay. For example, the majority of teachers are women, but the majority of head teachers are men. This is replicated in the teaching unions: the National Union of Teachers has a majority of women members but the General Secretary has always been a man.

The Dual Labour Market thesis (Barron and Norris, 1976) describes this segregated labour market, pointing to the way women workers are segregated into areas of work associated with their domestic roles and responsibilities, but it does not explain why women are in this situation, why they have accepted this secondary position, why it is seen as normal, nor what employers gain from hiring women, rather than men.

Women now represent around 50 per cent of the workforce, and the right to work and the right to choose both seem firmly embedded in contemporary thinking, yet women still only earn 72.7 per cent of the male wage. Why have the Equal Pay Act and the Sex Discrimination Act of 1975 not eradicated inequality?

To understand this we need to look at the history of the past twenty years. The political shift to the right after 1979 with the election of the Thatcher government led to cuts in welfare provision, worsening working conditions and attacks on the rights of trade unions during the 1980s and 1990s. Women have been hit especially hard. Cuts in maternity leave, reductions in the rights of part-time workers, loss of childcare provision, as well as the continuing current attacks on the welfare state, have left women worse off at work, and responsible for more caring at home than in the past – caring for under-school-age children, the sick and the elderly.

Despite the election of a Labour government in May 1997, cuts in the welfare state continue, in part necessitated by the need to meet the Convergence Criteria for the Single European Currency:[8] these cuts are also hitting women especially hard. Women are the majority of workers in the public sector, where conditions are worsening – in the National Health Service, in education, in social services – and women are the carers in the family where they will be expected to pick up the pieces left by a disintegrating welfare system.

Dramatic and startling changes in employment have taken place in Britain since 1980. There has been a massive loss of traditional jobs in engineering, mining and manufacturing. These were jobs with high status, good conditions and pay, full time and unionized, with trade unions that fought to improve conditions, such as the installation of pit-head baths for miners, and they were jobs for men.

There has been a parallel increase in the service sector, jobs with flexible hours, part-time and short-term contracts, poorly paid and non-unionized: these are women's jobs.[9]

These structural changes go some way to explaining why women have not achieved equal pay: there is both horizontal and vertical segregation between men and women at work. Women work in the segregated labour market and in jobs at the bottom of the ladder. Assumptions about women's wider roles of responsibility for home and children make their paid work secondary. This not only includes women with husbands or partners but single women and female single parents.

Does this mean, therefore, that the oppression of women is based on biological difference? Does the biological fact of women's procreative capacity inevitably lead to this position of inequality? Is this position unalterable? Or is it rather a result of the particular ways in which our society operates, and therefore would another type of society have different solutions? I will now turn to elements of Marxist theory to offer some possible explanations for women's inequality which suggest that this is not simply a function of biology, but is fundamentally determined by the economic and social demands of capital, which uses biology to reinforce the secondary role of women and sustains gender divisions to maintain its rule.

Divide and Rule: Production, Reproduction and the Reserve Army of Labour

Capitalist society not only divides by class, but takes advantage of other divisions, including sex and 'race', to maintain its rule. Recognizing that women's oppression had been used by the ruling class to maintain power in all societies, Engels linked together the production of goods for use or sale and the reproduction of life. 'The decisive element of history is pre-eminently the production and reproduction of life and its material requirements' (Engels, 1978 [1884], p. 4). In *The Origin of the Family, Private Property and the State*, Engels shows that the way in which a society reproduces itself (makes things, provides food and shelter, and so on) will affect everything about that society. Thus he argues that where the capitalist mode of production predominates, where the law of value reigns, where production for profit supersedes production for use, the same ideas also influence such intimacies as marriage and family life. Within the family, he says, women are oppressed as a secondary partner, used to reproduce both the present and future labour force cheaply, as well as providing a source of cheap labour outside the home.[10]

Women are expected to reproduce the future labour force, by childbearing. In addition they are expected to 'service' the other members of the family for free: shopping, preparing food, cooking, cleaning, giving emotional support; all these are the responsibility of women, to such an extent that women often find themselves without any knowledge or understanding of their own emotional and practical needs.

Marx and Engels gave insufficient weight to the way in which women's entry into the workforce is determined by her role in the family; instead they analysed the family and paid work separately.

> Marx's analysis of the general tendencies within capitalism provides the foundation for the analysis of female wage labour, but . . . his specific, and extremely fragmentary, allusions to the position of women are unsatisfactory because he, like Engels, does not adequately analyse the relationship between the family and the organisation of capitalist production.
>
> (Beechey, 1987, p. 56)

Domestic roles played by women clearly influence the way they work and the kinds of jobs they do. Putting women's reproductive and domestic roles first, women's paid work outside the home is less valued than male work. Even when the woman is in fact the sole wage earner and where women make up half the workforce, it is assumed that their work is secondary to a male wage. This devaluing of women's work is based on the idea of the 'family wage' referred to above, a wage earned by the man, enough to cover the cost of housing and feeding the wife and family so that when a woman works, this cost is assumed to have already been paid – whatever the actual situation – so that she can be paid less. Thus women's work is seen as less important than men's and is paid at a lower rate.

Alongside the analysis of the oppression of women in the family, the Marxist concept of the reserve army of labour is also relevant. In the nineteenth century, Marx identified young people and agricultural workers who had been replaced by machinery, as well as the unemployed, as 'the industrial reserve army of surplus-population' (cited in Beechey, 1987, p. 46). More recently feminists have located women, too, as a social group used in the same way (Bruegel, 1986, pp. 40–53; Beechey, 1987, pp. 45–50, 87–8). The use of women as part of the reserve army depends on existing, in this case sexual, divisions in the working class.

The reserve industrial army is necessary to capital in at least two ways:

> it provides a disposable and flexible population . . . labour power that can be absorbed in expanding branches of production when capital accumulation creates a demand for it, and repelled when the conditions of production no longer require it . . . It is also seen as a condition of competition among workers, the intensity of which depends on the pressure of the relative surplus population. This competitive pressure has two consequences. It depresses wage levels: Marx argues that the general movements of wages are regulated by the expansion and contraction of the industrial reserve army, which in turn corresponds to periodic changes in the industrial cycle. Competition also forces workers to submit to increases in the rate of exploitation through the pressure of unemployment.
>
> (Beechey, 1987, pp. 47–8)

The first point is best exemplified by the way in which women were drawn into engineering and munitions factories during the World War II to replace the male population who were fighting. Nurseries were provided for children to facilitate this. With the return of soldiers into civilian life in 1945, women were encouraged to go back to their domestic roles, or into the caring and service sectors.

The second point, the ability of the reserve army to depress wages (and conditions), partly explains what has taken place during the 1980s and 1990s. These two decades have seen a massive growth of women's jobs, alongside a loss of male ones, but it has not been an equal swap. Male jobs in engineering, steel, mining, manufacturing, jobs which were unionized, with decent wages and security, have been lost. Work normally associated with women and young people, in the service sector, in sales, and so on, jobs which are predominantly non-unionized, poorly paid, often part time, sometimes on short-term, even zero-hours contracts – the infamous 'Mc Job'[11] – have been created. In the process women, and young people, have been brought into the workforce and are being used to undermine the conditions and wages of traditional, male work and to introduce and normalize to the whole workforce such notions as part-time working and short-term contracts. This is the so-called 'flexible workforce'.

This change in the composition of labour is evidenced by reports on the make-up of today's labour market. According to *Labour Market Trends*, March 1997, 71 per cent of women between the ages of sixteen and fifty-nine were economically active at the start of 1996, of whom 44 per cent were working part time (compared to 8 per cent of men). This represents 82 per cent of the 5.8 million people working part time (Sly, Price and Risdon, 1997). However, the 8 per cent of men working part time has doubled between 1986 and 1996, while the number of part-time women has gone up by only 1 per cent in the same decade. Even more striking, the number of women in temporary jobs has increased by 23 per cent while the increase for men is 74 per cent. We can be sure not only that these figures are underestimates, but that the trend is continuing, despite an upturn in the economy in 1996–7 (*ibid.*, p. 99).

It seems to be the case that the work of women, defined by their expected domestic roles, has been used to undermine both the level of wages and the conditions of work in the late twentieth century. While there have been a number of other factors in this process, including economic stagnation, de-industrialization, high levels of general unemployment and attacks on trade union rights, women's position as part of the reserve army of labour is at least one element in the process.

Conclusion

While formal equality may seem to have been achieved by equal pay laws and legislation outlawing sexual discrimination, capital works in devious ways to outwit and undermine such reforms. Formal legal equality within a capitalist society can never be real equality. Even though campaigning for such legislation is important in raising consciousness on these issues, we cannot depend on the legal process alone to achieve it. Underlying, structural reasons, the way in which capital operates, at both economic and ideological levels, make real equality more or less impossible to achieve under capitalism. However many women are in work, it is unlikely that we will be given equal pay, access to all levels and grades of work, adequately paid maternity leave (to say nothing of paternity leave), free childcare, equal rights in practice, without a complete change in the system. But fighting for changes now is not a waste of time. The achievements of the Women's Movements in the nineteenth and twentieth centuries put us in a better position than ever before to fight for equality with men. However, without realistically assessing our actual situation, that fight will take place with 'one hand tied behind us'.

Thirty years after the first Women's Liberation Conference in Oxford, women remain unequal – at work, in the home, in legal and social institutions. Achievements in some areas such as divorce, reproductive rights and legislation on equal pay and against sex discrimination are open to reversals and are often unenforceable. Capitalists and their supporters gain from social division and will always impede genuine equal rights for all, for capitalism is a system *premised* on inequality and the right of the rich to exploit the poor.

Notes

1 This should not be misunderstood as care for each child for twenty-four hours, but the availability of childcare for women at all times, thus allowing women to choose when to work and to have some leisure time without childcare responsibilities.
2 In 1997 women earned 72.7 per cent of male full-time pay. If part-time workers were included this percentage would fall (*The New Review*, November/December 1997).
3 Bourgeois feminism works within a bourgeois, democratic framework, seeking legislative changes to end inequality and discrimination against women at work, in education, and so on. Examples include nineteenth-century campaigns in Britain and the USA for suffrage, women's rights to inheritance, education, etc. Bourgeois feminism is still the main political organizing principle in the USA, despite radical feminist rhetoric – for example, NOW (National Organization of Women) who organized the Equal Rights Amendment campaign.

   Radical Feminism rests on the idea that all known societies are/have been patriarchal, that is, dominated by men, and thus power rests in their hands and is used in their interests. This power is expressed in every aspect of life and culture from rape and sexual violence to authoritarian male hierarchy in government, the armed forces, education and culture. Therefore, the division between men and women is the first and primary division (some even call it the first class division) and therefore men, all men, are the main enemy. This analysis ignores the role of class (and 'race') in society. It leads to separate forms of organization, which exclude men, as at Greenham where the slogan 'Take the toys from the boys' ignored the role of the female Prime Minister! However, some radical feminist campaigns have been vigorous and successful, especially in Britain, on issues like rape (Rape Crisis Centres), rape in marriage, battered women's refuges and domestic violence, including campaigning for the release of women who have killed violent partners.

   Socialist feminism analyses women's liberation as a process intertwined with the liberation of all oppressed groups, including and led by the working class. The slogan 'No socialism without women's liberation! No women's liberation without socialism!' sums up the framework. It argues that the oppression of women is the result not of biology on its own but of the social and economic circumstances in which women are the reproducers of the future labour force. Thus women's role, which is assumed from their reproductive capacity, includes caring and looking after people first and foremost and the rest of their role in society is determined by this.

   Socialist feminists have campaigned and written about the role of women in the family, at work, in trade unions, on reproductive rights, as well as many topics taken up by bourgeois and radical feminists. Alliances are sought from within the labour movement – for example, getting the TUC to call the big anti-Corrie demonstration in 1979 in defence of abortion rights.

4   This was in response to fears of a decline of the 'race' in the face of the growing Empire, and more particularly the discovery of the poor health of working-class recruits in the Boer War 1899–1902 and World War I in 1914. There was also a falling birthrate and rising infant mortality rates (see Chapter 3 of this volume).

5   While it will not come as a surprise to anyone that in the nineteenth century education was oppressively gendered, it may come as more of a shock to discover that as late as 1963 the Newsom Committee Report, *Half Our Future*, published by the Central Advisory Council for Education, 1963, argued that for girls of average or less than average ability (whatever that is): ' . . . their most important vocational concern [is] marriage', and therefore domestic science, as it became known, remained high on the curriculum agenda, with girls given the chance to run a flat for a week. Incidentally the mothers of these same girls were by this time almost certainly working outside the home! (Open University, 1984; for a detailed discussion of gender and education, see Chapter 2).

6   It is of course true that the appalling economic plight of the Soviet Union in the years following the revolution meant that, as Holt tellingly states, 'the collective was unable to do its duty towards women' (Holt, 1977, p. 120).

7   The percentages of women in work show an upward curve from around 30 per cent in 1918 to around 50 per cent today, but the sharpest increase is from the 1960s.

8   Governments who wish to enter the Single Currency within the European Union have to meet the Convergence Criteria of the Maastricht Treaty, later developed at Amsterdam. This means reducing their national debt to 60 per cent or less of Gross Domestic Product (GDP), and their Public Sector Borrowing Requirement (PSBR) to 3 per cent or less of GDP.

9   Income Data Services Ltd (1993) shows women as 49 per cent of workforce, with a rise between 1973 and 1993 of 2 million women's jobs and a loss of 2.8 million male jobs. But this was not a straight swap for at least 45 per cent of women in the 1990s are working part time. In 1993, 35 per cent of all workers were not in full-time, permanent jobs.

10   The costs of rearing children, shopping for and cooking for a family, if paid at a going rate, would be astronomical.

11   This term comes from the employment practices of fast-food outlets, which include zero-hours contracts and employees clocking on and off dependent on the level of custom. Most of the employees are young.

References

Barron, R.D. and Norris, E.R. (1976) 'Sexual Divisions and the Dual Labour Market' in D.L. Barker and S. Allen, *Dependence and Exploitation in Work and Marriage*, London: Longman

Beechey, V. (1987) *Unequal Work*, London: Verso

Bolt, C. (1993) *The Women's Movements in the United States and Britain from the 1790s to the 1920s*, London: Harvester Wheatsheaf

Bruegel, I. (1986) 'The Reserve Army of Labour, 1974–1979', in Feminist Review (ed.), *Waged Work: A Reader*, London: Virago

Central Advisory Council for Education (England) (1963) *Half Our Future: A Report of the Central Advisory Council for Education*, London: HMSO

Engels, F. (1978 [1884]) *The Origin of the Family, Private Property and the State*, Peking: Foreign Language Press

Fraser, N. and Nicholson, L.J. (1990) 'Social Criticism without Philosophy: An Encounter between Feminism and Postmodernism', in L.J. Nicholson (ed.), *Feminism/ Post-modernism*, New York and London: Routledge

Garb, T. (1993) in F. Frascina, et al., *Modernity and Modernism: French Painting in the Nineteenth Century*, New Haven and London: Yale University Press

Holt, A. (1977) *Alexandra Kollontai: Selected Writings*, London, Allison & Busby

Income Data Services Ltd (1993) *IDS, Management Pay Review, May*, London

Kelly, J. (1992) 'Postmodernism and Feminism', *International Marxist Review*, 14, Winter, Paris: Presse-Edition-Communication (PEC)

Kelly, J. (1999) 'Postmodernism and Feminism: The Road to Nowhere', in D. Hill, P. McLaren, M. Cole and G. Rikowski (eds), *Postmodernism in Educational Theory: Education and the Politics of Human Resistance*, London: Tufnell Press

Liddington, J. and Norris, J. (1978) *One Hand Tied Behind Us: The Rise of the Women's Suffrage Movement*, London: Virago

Lipton, E. (1987) *Looking into Degas: Uneasy Images of Women and Modern Life*, Berkeley, Los Angeles and London: University of California Press

Low Pay Unit (1997) *The New Review*, November/December, London

Open University (1984) *Conflict and Change in Education: A Sociological Introduction*, Block 6: Gender, race and education; Unit 25: 'Women and Education', Milton Keynes: Open University Press

Pollock, G. (1988) *Vision and Difference: Femininity, Feminism and the Histories of Art*, London and New York: Routledge

Sly, F., Price, A. and Risdon, A. (March 1997) *Labour Market Trends*, London: Government Statistical Office

Taylor, B. (1983) *Eve and the New Jerusalem*, London: Virago

2 Gender, education and the new millennium

Jane Martin

Mapping change in relation to girls' improved examination participation and performance, Linda Grant states:

> Only feminism, I'm afraid, can explain the complex social and psychological forces which condition the expectation that their success is derived from something other than their ability, and that their presence at the highest levels means that the barbarians are at the gates (Grant, 1998, p. 12).

Introduction

This chapter will focus on gender equity issues in education. It has only been relatively recently that gender has come under scrutiny in British sociology of education. Until the 1970s the bias was towards the analysis of class differentials of educational achievement. This led to a simplification of the issues but a growing amount of historical and sociological research has now been published, much of which points to the fact that boys and girls experience schooling differently. At the same time, it is important not to ignore the differences that exist among groups. The interacting dynamics of class, gender and 'race' relations are crucial, as are sexuality, disability and individual biographies. So, the chapter begins with a discussion of historical perspectives on gender and education, before moving on to relate the theoretical understandings of Chapter 1 to more recent concerns, considered in their policy context.

Historical Perspectives on Gender and Education: 1800 to 1944

The education of children in the nineteenth century was organized along the lines of social class. Elementary education was associated with the working classes and secondary education, which was not simply confined to the three Rs, was associated with the middle classes. Girls rarely feature in general histories of mass schooling and the historiography of the gender dimension has been marred by an assumption that girls and boys experienced an identical education. Among historians of women's education this assumption manifested itself in a focus on separate accounts of middle-class schools. For example, there are a number of histories documenting women's struggle to secure access to secondary and higher education (Bryant, 1979; Kamm, 1965; McWilliams-Tullberg, 1975), as well as more recent accounts of the lifestyle and occupational culture of women teachers in girls' secondary schools and in higher education (Edwards, 1990; Vicinus, 1985). Yet the history of women's education has not neglected working-class girls' schooling. Gomersall (1988, 1994) and Horn (1988) contributed to our knowledge of the early period and a growing body of evidence points to gendered experiences. First, there were fewer school places for girls (Hurt, 1979). Second, girls were less likely to be sent to school (Martin, 1987). Third, the two sexes did not have access to a common curriculum. Girls lost out on all the academic subjects save reading, and concern about value for money led the government to introduce payment by results in 1862 when needlework became compulsory for girls. Each pupil earned the same amount for successful examination performance, but girls were permitted a lower standard of achievement in arithmetic because of the time they spent sewing (Weiner, 1994; Digby and Searby, 1981).

The 1870 Education Act was a watershed in English and Welsh education history. For the first time, locally elected, single-purpose educational authorities were empowered to raise and administer a school rate to plug the gaps in the elementary sector (Simon, 1980). Gender differences were extended and increasingly formalized after the passage of the Act. Ostensibly co-educational, in urban areas the new board schools sometimes had different entrances for the sexes, as well as separate playgrounds and separate departments for older children (Turnbull, 1987). This period also saw the promotion of a sex-differentiated curriculum. In 1878, for example, theoretical domestic economy became a compulsory specific subject for girls; four years later the government gave grants for the teaching of cookery. By the 1890s, a significant expansion in the curriculum prescriptions for working-class girls saw the inclusion of laundry work and housewifery. Despite the addition of manual teaching, Turnbull (1987, p. 86) concludes that working-class boys 'did not receive practical instruction equivalent to the girls' needlework, cookery, laundry work and so on'. Further, when national efficiency became a priority in the aftermath of military failures and deficiencies highlighted by the number of recruits declared unfit for call up in the Boer War (1899–1902), the Board of Education favoured *more* domestic instruction, with lessons in the practicalities of housework and mothering for working-class girls (Attar, 1990; Dyhouse, 1981; Turnbull, 1987). Hurt (1979) suggests military drill as the masculine equivalent to the separate sort of education given to the girls, but fails to acknowledge the proportion of time filled by domestic subjects' instruction. From 1870 onwards, the four features of curriculum thinking – selection, differentiation, functionality and social advancement – were clearly visible within the state-aided elementary sector (Weiner, 1994). Family culture was used as a rationale for the kinds of education offered to working-class girls and the training in domesticity linked with erratic school attendance. Girls were frequently expected to fulfil the roles of 'good wives' and 'little mothers' on wash days, or if their mother was ill or having a baby (Dyhouse, 1981; Davin, 1996). Elsewhere, Davin (1979) argues the purpose of mass schooling was to impose an ideal family form of a male breadwinner and an economically dependent, full-time wife and mother. As Gomersall (1994, p. 238) has summed up:

> This was an ideal that came broadly to be shared by the bourgeoisie and men and women of the working classes alike, each for their own particular economic, political, cultural and social reasons. That it was unattainable for most outside the ranks of skilled and unionised labour was seen as unproblematic; it integrated the goals of the powerful men of the working classes with those of the dominant social and economic groups and served as an aspirational ideal to the unskilled, unorganised work-force
>
> (Gomersall, 1994, p. 238)

Although Mary Wollstonecraft applied ideas of equality to women in a *Vindication of the Rights of Women* (1792), her vision did not find much favour in Victorian Britain. Unlike their male counterparts, middle-class girls were largely educated for the marriage market and Wollstonecraft did not consider the frivolous education they received as any education. In the words of the suffragette leader Emmeline Pankhurst (1979, pp. 5–6): 'My parents, especially my father, discussed the question of my brothers' education as a matter of real importance. My education and that of my sister were scarcely discussed at all.' Likewise Emily Davies (who led the campaign for access to secondary and higher education), resented the fact that whereas her three brothers all went to well-known public schools followed by Trinity College, Cambridge, she only received a limited education. This included a brief spell at a day school supplemented by occasional paid lessons in languages and music (Caine, 1992). Divisions within the education of the middle class and the working class reveal a dichotomy between the experience of girls and boys in terms of expectations and opportunities.

Both working people and women members of the school boards had much to lose from the educational reorganization that followed the 1902 Education Act (Hollis, 1989; Martin, 1999; Turnbull, 1983) – working people because the division between elementary and secondary schooling was more firmly defined; women because they were disqualified by sex for election to the new education authorities. The Act abolished the school boards and made subcommittees of county councils responsible for the board schools, now called public elementary schools. For the first time the local education authorities were permitted to establish rate-aided secondary schools whose form and curricula were to follow those of the élitist, public schools. Secondary school fees were set at £3 per annum and this excluded all save the high-ability working-class child who won a free place on the basis of an attainment test. Purvis (1995, p. 14) has suggested those who benefited were highly likely to be lower-middle-class males.

As I have already mentioned, the intentions in educating boys and girls were different. Increasingly a similar policy was pursued in elementary and secondary schools. For instance, both the 1905 Code of Regulations for Public Elementary Schools and the Regulations for Secondary Schools imposed practical training in the female role. Policy guidelines incorporated a set of linked assumptions advocating separate but complementary adult roles for men and women. On the one hand, the female curriculum was discussed in terms of girls' biology and what this meant for their future after school. On the other, the principle of male-as-norm meant the teaching of other subjects was informed by the assumption that boys were breadwinners and secondarily fathers (Hunt, 1991). This was approved school practice by the 1920s and a report on the differentiation of the curriculum in secondary schools concluded that there were two main aims for education: to prepare children, first, to earn their own livings and, second, to be useful citizens. However, ideologies of femininity dictated that girls also needed to be prepared for family life and motherhood, since their primary vocation was to be 'makers of homes' (HMSO, 1923, cited in Hunt, 1991, p. 119). This one role was seen to supersede all other social principles, both inside and outside school.

State policy endorsed the view that women were different from men; not only biologically but socially, intellectually and psychologically. Within the school girls were more likely to be taught by women, while the men tended to teach the boys, especially older boys (Purvis, 1995). This was crucial to the National Association of Schoolmasters (NAS), formed in 1923, who deplored the influence of female teachers on male students (Littlejohn, 1995). Only male teachers could reinforce 'normal' masculinity. As a writer in the union journal the *New Schoolmaster* put it:

> in the matter of managing and instructing young children the sex of a person may matter but little . . . in the great task of educating children the sex of the teacher is of paramount importance. The character of children is the essential consideration, and the essentials of character lie in the sex of the person.
> (*New Schoolmaster*, November 1936, cited in Littlejohn, 1995, p. 50)

By the 1920s approximately three-quarters of elementary school teachers were women. In these circumstances the NAS continued to press their demands for men teachers for all boys over seven, and headmasters in mixed schools. Indeed, they did not relinquish the first objective until 1976. Clearly this insistence on the importance of gender in teaching has implications for the construction of patriarchal relations in teachers' work. Littlejohn (1995, pp. 53–4) claims, 'the most volatile and explosive issue of all was the appointment of women to the inspectorate with special responsibility for handicraft and physical education'. To subject men teachers to the authority of women passing judgement on the teaching of technical crafts and sports was more than they could bear. It was emasculating.

Overall, education policies remained tailored to processes of class formation in the interwar years. Beyond that, there was evidence of gender-based asymmetries in terms of access to schooling, curriculum content and years of education attained.

Historical Perspectives on Gender and Education II: 1944 to 1975

The 1944 Education Act encouraged intense speculation about the potential impact of free secondary education for all. Many saw the reform as primarily about the realization of class equality and the production of a new type of society. But this did not mean 'that all children now received what had before the Act been described as secondary education' (Thom, 1987, p. 131). Scarcity of grammar school places necessitated selection procedures on the lines of 'age, ability and aptitude', as recommended in the Norwood Report (1943). However, the official ideology for girls' education still assumed a homogeneity of female interests. Thus, for example, while Norwood interspersed the word 'child' with 'boy', criteria particular to girls' schooling featured in a lengthy chapter on domestic subjects. Different social roles were taken for granted and the question of gender was perceived very differently from that of class. Little had changed, as Thom (1987, p. 125) makes clear:

> Gender was raised, but it was raised as a general social question, that is, the issue of whether girls and boys should receive a different sort of education from [one] another. No one asked what the implications were for equality in this; rather, whether boys and girls required a fundamentally different organisation of education.

Throughout the 1940s and 1950s (when selection through the 11+ examination predominated); girls had to do much better than boys to obtain a place at a grammar or technical school (Deem, 1981; Thom, 1987). This was justified on the grounds that girls' academic superiority in the early stages made it necessary 'to tilt the balance in the favour of those late-developing boys' (Grant, 1994, p. 37). The accepted theory was that boys would catch up by the age of fourteen. Gender stereotypes about male superiority were reinforced earlier by medical practitioners who warned female students of the risks evoked by too much intellectual work (Dyhouse, 1981). As late as the 1930s, it was professed that a girl who worked hard might get brain fever (Rendel, 1997, p. 56). So, when it came to male–female 11+ result patterns, common sense and social observation suggested the difference 'is not real because it does not last, it is not a phenomenon produced by the test, it is a phenomenon produced by "nature"' (Thom, 1987, p. 141). The fact that girls frequently scored better marks than boys prompted some local authorities to set up different norms; others added new tests to level up the sexes (Thom, 1987). Technical adjustment was necessary to balance the numbers of successful girls and boys; there was also a historic shortage of girls' grammar school places. It has to be accepted 'that there is no such thing as a fair test' (Gipps and Murphy, 1994, p. 273), but this went unremarked in 1940s and 1950s Britain.

More recent analyses redress the balance. Examining the education policy context after the Labour Party came to power in July 1945, Dean (1991) discusses the gendered nature of education policies and the impact of those policies on practice. In particular, he develops the argument that the victorious politicians saw the domestic role of women as crucial for the construction and rehabilitation of social harmony and cohesiveness. For the young female population leaving school at fifteen, the Ministry of Education continued to point to that special curriculum for girls, organized around familial concerns. Further, the influential school inspector John Newsom attacked the academic grammar schools for ignoring domestic skills and placing too much emphasis on public examinations and obtaining professional careers. Yet even here the cult of motherhood and domesticity was still prevalent. Two-thirds of those who went to university were men; more women trained as teachers. In 1958 there were 100 teacher training colleges for women, as opposed to 18 for men and 18 mixed-sex colleges (Heward, 1993, pp. 23–4). Class and gendered concepts of adult destiny were similarly evident in the curriculum recommendations of the 1959 Crowther Report on the education of fifteen–eighteen-year-olds. In the secondary modern schools (virtually synonymous with working-class schooling), this report suggested that: 'The prospect of courtship and marriage should rightly influence the education of the adolescent girl . . . her direct interests in dress and personal experience and the problems of human relationships should be given a central part in her education' (Crowther Report, p. 124, cited in Riley, 1994, p. 37). However, there is evidence of female disaffection with schooling in this period. Early leaving generated attention in the Gurney–Dixon Report of 1954 and Crowther commented on the fact that grammar school girls were more likely to leave school at the statutory age (Deem, 1981). Imputing motivation is difficult, but it is conceivable that early leaving was prompted by fear of failure. More recent research into female truancy found this was the main reason given for 'bunking' lessons (Le Riche, 1988). As Spender and Sarah (1980) argue very forcefully, in education women have learned how to lose even though they may have had the ability to succeed academically. The educational biography of the American Pulitzer prize-winning novelist Carol Shields (born 1935) is revealing. A college graduate and trained teacher, as a young woman her expectations were simple: 'a baby, a TV, a fridge-freezer and a car' (*Guardian*, 23 May 1998).

By the 1960s a radical restructuring of English state education opened up new possibilities for change. This programme of educational reform was informed by human capital theory with its main tenet that the role of education was crucial to the development of economic growth (Schultz, 1970; see Simon, 1991, pp. 222, 229 and 291 for a discussion). Reassessments of the concept of equal access saw the gradual shift to a non-selective system of secondary schooling in England and Wales, a change that accelerated the number of children educated in mixed schools in the state sector. This meant a changing balance of power among women and men staff in senior and managerial positions as schools became mixed, larger and more complex; however, the accepted norm was that mixed-sex schooling was preferable to single-sex schooling on academic as well as social grounds (Deem, 1984). Simply put, it was hoped that the presence of female pupils would have a 'civilizing' influence on their male peers. As Arnot (1984, p. 50) has noted, 'never it would seem has the argument been reversed'. Overall, the removal of barriers to female success in the 11+ examination inevitably benefited some, predominantly middle-class girls; discussion of who benefits academically from mixed or single-sex schooling runs on and will be returned to later.

In theory, Deem (1981) maintains the expansion of the secondary school curriculum should have been 'helpful' to girls. In practice, Benn and Simon (1972) found that very few schools offered a common curriculum to all their pupils in the early days of the comprehensive reform. Divergence in the content of education was clearly seen in the provision of gender-specific courses in such subjects as domestic science, typing and childcare, which were not open to boys; and woodwork, metalwork and technical drawing (TD), which were not open to girls. Links between the distribution of educational knowledge and patterns of women's work remained in evidence despite the rise of a new feminist movement (see Chapter 1) and the greater participation of women in the labour force.

Breaking Boundaries I: Equal Opportunities?

At a policy level the Sex Discrimination Act of 1975 made direct and indirect discrimination on the grounds of gender illegal in a number of spheres of public life, including education. Demands for reform of the law were first expressed formally in 1967, when two women politicians – the Conservative Joan Vickers and Labour's Lena Jeger – sought to include sex within the scope of the Race Relations Act. Seven years later the support of the elected minister, Roy Jenkins, proved crucial to overcome the opposition of some senior staff in the Home Office (Rendel, 1997, pp. 3, 12). Canvassed by feminists as a broad measure to promote women's rights, this legislation was intimately linked with concepts of fair treatment and of equality. Access to education was seen as a basic right and the Act covered admissions, curricular and non-curricular facilities, extra-curricular activities, standards of behaviour, rules regarding pupils' dress and appearance, school discipline and careers guidance. Within this legislative framework the Equal Opportunities Commission (EOC) was empowered to remove discriminatory behaviour through the courts: 'a radical departure in a country with no written constitution or civil rights charter' (Arnot, 1991, p. 452).[1] However, the limitations of the anti-discrimination legislation soon became clear. Not everyone can compete and succeed, and formal equality is not enough to ensure substantive equality; the dilemma is that when considered in the context of school performance, it may legitimate failure.

In the sociology of education literature a wide range of feminist perspectives began to highlight the gendered nature of schooling. There was criticism of gender differentiation across a diversity of areas as studies began to show the ways in which patriarchal relations are deployed and used in schools (Deem, 1978). Teaching styles were challenged to avoid a tendency to encourage competition between the sexes in sports, academic learning and examinations; attention also turned to management hierarchies within schools. Most are dominated by male teachers and the proportion of women holding senior posts in secondary schools was highest in such female 'spaces' as home economics and girls' games. Further, although the 'female' atmosphere of primary schooling was seen to undermine the performance of boys, it seems that even here sexual divisions were constantly reinforced. For instance, research showed that teachers readily clustered behaviour into two categories – one for boys, another for girls (Clarricoates, 1980). Boys were livelier, adventurous, boisterous, self-confident, independent, energetic, couldn't-care-less, loyal and aggressive; girls were obedient, tidy, neat, conscientious, orderly, fussy, catty, bitchy and gossipy. Stanworth (1986) drew a similar picture in her account of the ways in which gender divisions were sustained in a co-educational college of further education. Higher teacher expectations towards boys had implications for the self-image of one young woman:

> I think he thinks I'm pretty mediocre. I think I'm pretty mediocre. He never points me out of the group or talks to me, or looks at me in particular when he's talking about things. I'm just a sort of wallpaper person.
>
> (Stanworth, 1986, p. 37)

Of course, such a description may reflect the use of discipline and control in teaching styles. Early texts dealing with the production of masculinity through resistance to schooling show how anti-school working-class 'lads' block teaching (Willis, 1983). Corrigan (1979) uses the analogy of a 'guerrilla struggle' to represent the ability of working-class male pupils to continue their normal way of life, despite the 'occupying army' of teachers. Within this social arena, transgression involved 'running about in classrooms, underneath chairs and things like that . . . tossing chairs about' (Corrigan, 1979, p. 58). By contrast, the resistance of anti-school girls was individual and personalized or 'invisible' – they 'skived off' school (Llewellyn, 1980).

In relation to fields of study selection, the 1975 report on curricular differentiation highlighted the areas in which sexism flourished (DES, 1975). There were high levels of sex stereotyping in option choices and teachers found themselves being criticized for influencing the preferences of pupils choosing subjects after age fourteen. Beyond that, evidence of illegal segregation of craft subjects was found in 19 per cent of the schools studied by Her Majesty's Inspectorate (HMI) from 1975 to 1978 (cited in Pascall, 1997, p. 119). Research on schoolgirls' option choices shows significant patterns of gender segregation informed by expectations of future employment. As a result it was argued that if any group benefited from moves to promote equal access to curricular options, it was most likely to be the boys:

> Male students who took 'girls' subjects' were assumed to be learning a skill for future use in the labour market. They were taken more seriously than their female peers in the same classes, to whom such skills were supposed to come naturally for use in their future roles as wives and mothers . . . Female students who took 'boys' subjects' were either presumed to be interested solely in flirting with the boys or discounted as unique exceptions.
>
> (Griffin, 1985, pp. 78–9)

Riley (1994) also found the working-class girls attending a co-educational south London comprehensive in the early 1980s experienced a very sex-differentiated curriculum. Institutionalized sexism meant girls were routed into traditional school subjects by the female heads of house. 'The head of design and technology suggested that housemistresses counselled girls against technical drawing as he believed the limited number of places in technical drawing for 4th-year pupils could be best used by boys' (Riley, 1994, p. 60). Clearly school subjects did not become evenly mixed on gender lines in the new climate of change produced by the anti-discrimination legislation. There are pressing implications about divergence in the content of education. Skills and qualifications are not interchangeable and stereotyped views of what is appropriate for each gender have implications for post-school destinations. Measor and Woods (1984) comment that the ambivalence of girls' responses to science was a significant point of contrast between pupils transferring to secondary school. Ten years earlier Kelly (1974) had pointed to the invisibility of girls in school science. In particular, she documented the prevalence of male teachers, male pupils and masculine imagery in the illustrations and examples used in the teaching of chemistry, physics and electronics. Over a decade later Kelly offered a fresh discussion drawing on evidence from the Girls Into Science and Technology Initiative. Her central argument was unchanged (Kelly, 1985).

However, early analysis of the education provisions of the Sex Discrimination Act indicate mild success (Deem, 1981). Using the indicators identified by Stromquist (1990, p. 137) to assess women's progress, the increasing access of women to education must be observed, as must years of education attained. For instance, the ratio of male entry to female entry in the GCE O-level and CSE examinations had changed and fewer of the female candidates failed. At 18+ males left post-compulsory schooling better qualified and cutbacks in teacher training reduced opportunities for some women. Gender patterns in academic subject choice were exacerbated by the class bias of schooling and this had important vocational effects. Thus Arnot (1983, p. 71) argues the development of co-educational state comprehensive schools 'did not represent . . . a challenge to the reproduction of dominant gender relations but rather a modification of the *form* of its transmission'. The ubiquity of those relations is borne out by a homily recorded in a comprehensive school in 1978:

> In assembly the lower school is addressed by the Senior Mistress, Mrs Marks. Pupils are told they will soon be given a form to take home – school wants the phone number of where mother works. Mrs Marks says that if they are ill or have an accident, school tries to get mother. The school try not to bother father, because he is the head of the family, his wage keeps the family while mother's is only for luxuries . . . If there is no-one at home – mum, granny or auntie – they will be put to bed at school.
>
> (Delamont, 1983, p. 93)

By the 1980s, it was observed that the New Right agenda, with its commitment to 'family values' (seen as central to social stability), might conflict with moves that could improve career prospects for girls (David, 1983).

Breaking Boundaries II: Social Justice?

Arguments about social justice were shunned when the then Secretary of State for Education and Science, Kenneth Baker, proposed a radical restructuring of English state education. Introducing the Education Reform Bill at the 1987 Conservative Party Conference he declared 'the pursuit of egalitarianism is over' (cited in Arnot, 1989/90, p. 21). The national goal was quality. The National Curriculum would deliver it 'for all our children, over all our country' (Kenneth Baker, 1987, cited in *From Butler to Baker. The 3Rs*, BBC 2 TV programme, 1993). Effective opposition was contained by the language of access and entitlement (Simon, 1991, p. 531), but the idea of a common 'entitlement' curriculum was not new. HMI had been arguing for it since at least 1977 (Benn and Chitty, 1997, p. 277). Feminist educators also supported the notion of a common curriculum experience, albeit one that encompassed the hidden curriculum of schooling and *not* one posited on a male paradigm (Benn et al., 1982). However, this position is very different from the liberal reformist perspective that is limited by a failure to recognize that educational gender differentiation does not occur in a social and political vacuum. Knowledge is not a neutral commodity, but the emphasis on equal opportunities serves to reinforce the illusion of neutrality (Arnot, 1989/90). Certainly boys and girls now take largely the same courses aged from five to sixteen, but gender hierarchies were reinforced by the privileging of maths, science and technology (Miles and Middleton, 1995). The status accorded male-centred forms of knowledge does little to challenge the values and practices of patriarchy/androcentricity:

> In short, while girls must be educated in the skills and attitudes to achieve an academic equality with boys – and to challenge inequalities within the labour market – the education of boys in the skills and attitudes to address their equal responsibilities within the family are of equal if not greater importance. And this is where the formal equality accorded by the National Curriculum is most lacking, in the 'masculinisation' of the schooling of girls with no corresponding 'feminisation' of the schooling of boys.
>
> (Gomersall, 1994, p. 246)

What this position represents is a concern to restructure boys' education in such a way as to break the circulation of stereotypical sex-role expectations. The views expressed emphasize that the majority of schooling operates for a particular form of hegemonic masculinity. Arnot's (1994) review of gender research in British sociology of education highlights two traditions – the cultural and the political-economy perspectives. Whereas cultural analyses concentrate on different socialization processes, political-economy theories use the method of historical materialism. In this latter tradition the social reproduction theory of Louis Althusser is particularly influential as it points to the school as a social site in which the reproduction of the socio-sexual division of labour occurs. Building on this work, Arnot (1994) uses the concept of 'gender code' to analyse the sets of gender relations made available to men and women through a class-determined educational system. Hegemony is put to the fore to show the possibility of accommodation and resistance.[2] It is accepted that schooling 'can offer routes to change – at an individual or a social level' (Pascall and Cox, 1993, p. 23).

The current situation shows that as girls and women have been granted more equal access to education so the pattern of gender-related performance is changing. The striking change has been at age sixteen. It will be recalled that girls were already improving their results in the early 1980s; more recently gender-related differences within the GCSE (General Certificate of Secondary Education, introduced in 1988) have attracted media headlines. In their longitudinal study of England and Wales from 1985–94, Arnot, David and Weiner (1996) note changing patterns of entry and performance in public examinations. They use the concept of gender gap to show the difference between the sexes in the period under study. Thus, for example, the GCSE entry gender gap is increasing in favour of male students in chemistry and economics, but there has been a change from boys to girls in history and mathematics. Overall, more girls than boys are being entered for GCSE examinations; girls are more successful in terms of the proportion of A–C grades gained (Elwood, 1995, p. 286); but girls in single-sex schools may be at a substantial advantage (Arnot et al., 1996). However, it is important to treat the statistics with care. Teacher perception of girls' maths anxiety means that significantly more girls than boys are entered for the middle tier of mathematics. This acts as a 'safety' option providing 'the key grade C without the possibility of becoming ungraded if performance falls below this grade in the higher tier' (Elwood and Comber, 1996, p. 5). In 1994, 59 per cent of females took this route; in the process they marginalized themselves from participation in higher-level mathematics (Elwood, 1995). Similarly, GCSE combined science has a tiered entry system although there has yet to be an investigation into its implications. However, more boys are entered for the 'élite' single science subjects of physics and chemistry; girls are steered towards biology (Elwood, 1995).

The number of young men and women participating in post-compulsory education and training has changed significantly over the last twenty years. For instance, the proportion of eighteen-year-olds achieving the General Certificate in Education Advanced Level (GCE A Level) has grown from 19 per cent in 1985 to 34 per cent in 1995 (EOC, 1997a). That same year female students made up 53 per cent of the total entry, compared with 38 per cent in 1970 (Murphy and Elwood, 1998). However, the sex segregation of subjects at A level is still marked. Far more men than women take mathematics, physics and technology and the pattern of difference in the performance of the sexes in the various subjects at GCSE is not continued (Arnot et al., 1996, p. 64). The problem of gender stereotyping is also evident among those who take the vocational route. Except for RSAs (largely secretarial and clerical qualifications), it seems that more men than women gain traditional vocational awards and these tend to be at a higher level (EOC, 1997a). Finally, young women have improved their participation rate on the Modern Apprenticeship scheme initiated in 1995, but remain concentrated in traditionally female sectors like the 'caring' occupations, hairdressing and business adminis-tration. Unsurprisingly, the majority of young men can be found in traditionally male occupations such as engineering, manufacturing, construction and the motor industry (EOC, 1997a). Gender patterns in post-compulsory education show the implications of sex-stereotyped decisions. They also suggest that:

> a girl's experience of gender cannot be abstracted so neatly from any other aspects of her life. Girls from different social backgrounds will not experience patriarchal culture in identical ways, and the adult lives they anticipate will promise different kinds of opportunity, responsibility and experience. Their priorities as girls will reflect these disparities.
>
> (Miles and Middleton, 1995, p. 133)

Lees's (1993) research supports this view. She has shown that whereas academic girls expect careers, non-academic girls anticipate the need to combine unskilled and part-time employment with the responsibilities of housework and childcare. Pro-school and academically or work-oriented girls were typically white females from middle-class homes with strong parental support. Mirza (1992) comments that the Irish girls in her study saw their futures as home-makers, childcarers and part-time workers; whereas the black girls she interviewed anticipated a career. Therefore, the way in which women perform relative to men varies according to class and ethnicity, as does the value of having or not having educational qualifications. Significantly, the mature women students interviewed by Pascall and Cox (1993), saw education as an escape route from a lifetime of domesticity and low-paid work but this may change with the introduction of tuition fees. At the time of writing, early indications are that this policy may impact heavily on this group of students.

There is evidence of a backlash against girls' success. Recent years have witnessed a stream of polemic over the prospects and performance of young males. By the spring of 1996 this received official legitimation when Christopher Woodhead, Her Majesty's Chief Inspector and Head of the Government's Office for Standards in Education, wrote a column in *The Times* entitled 'Boys who learn to be losers: on the white male culture of failure'. In it he asserted that the apparent failure of white working-class boys was 'one of the most disturbing problems we face within the whole education system' (quoted in the *TES*, 26 April 1996). Male/female result patterns generated a media debate expressed in terms of threats to male breadwinning, the association of men and crime, the collapse of family life and the crisis of fatherhood (Williams, 1998). Moral imperatives shaping concerns with 'troubled masculinities' have meant 'the story about the extraordinary success of schools and teachers in improving girls' performance at 16 has not been highlighted' (Arnot, 1996, p. 12).

Far from it. In January 1998 the publication of new official statistics showed girls outperforming boys in terms of the proportion of pupils obtaining five A–C grades at GCSE in all but one local authority (Kensington and Chelsea). Schools Minister Stephen Byers responded by calling on schools to 'challenge the laddish, anti-learning culture' (*Guardian*, 6 January 1998). Others added their own recipes for change. Thus Angela Phillips, author of *The Trouble with Boys*, pressed the Education Secretary to allow the London borough of Hackney to change a girls-only school into a co-educational comprehensive. The argument turned on cultural reasons. It is time to 'stand up for boys' who need protection from this 'laddish culture'; girls do not because 'Girl Power . . . really exists' (*Guardian*, 6 January 1998). Commentary in the *Daily Mail* (5 January 1998) suggests boys are losing out because they are being brought up in a woman's world, given the absence of male teachers in most primary schools. Indeed some of the arguments underpinning the drive to recruit more male primary school teachers bear a striking similarity to the NAS backlash in the 1920s and 1930s. It is ironical that Arnot, David and Weiner (1996) identified a persistent 'culture of male management in schools', a finding confirmed by separate research from the University of East London (*TES*, 26 April 1996). Elsewhere, Arnot (1996, p. 13) cites evidence from a 1995 sample of the new generation of teachers that suggests the majority are 'more supportive of class and ethnic equality than of gender equality'. Such attitudes are likely to be reinforced by rhetoric about a generation of male losers and recommendations for future action that focus on traditional concepts of masculinity.

In May 1997 the Professor of Education at Exeter University, Ted Wragg, entered the public debate when he delivered the *Times Educational Supplement*'s Greenwich Lecture. In it he put forward a ten-point plan to help the boys. The plan did not extend to girls; nor did it attend to the implications male conditioning has on behaviour and learning in schools. For instance, the old-fashioned problem of boys behaving badly was resolved by a recommendation that teachers appeal to boys' interests – humour, adventure and sport (*TES*, 23 May 1997). Anti-sexist work might go further. As the British journalist Martin Bright reports in a full-page analysis of 'boys performing badly', macho culture dates from the primary school: 'Reading was regarded as a feminine activity: something children did with their mothers. The essential uncoolness of being studious is introduced at the very earliest age' (*Observer*, 4 January 1998). This is corroborated by Murphy and Elwood (1998) who observe that children's learning out of school has important consequences for what they choose to do within school. It has an effect on performance, views of relevance, expectations, styles of expression and achievement.

But boys are not the only ones to suffer from a lack of insight into the effects of gender. Indeed not all boys are losing. To paraphrase David and Weiner (1997), we need to keep balance on the 'gender agenda'. Several factors have been glossed over amid the hysteria about the current positions of pupils in schools. First, the improvement in female achievement has not occurred for all girls. Interactions based on socio-economic factors and ethnicity are crucial both for girls *and* boys. Current statistics show that 28,500 boys and 21,500 girls finish compulsory schooling without any qualifications each year (*Guardian*, 6 January 1998). Second, the very highest achievers are still in the main male. Boys collect more A grades at A level and more first-class degrees. Even female students who excel at A level see a reversal of fortune. More than 16 per cent of male candidates at Oxford and Cambridge are awarded first-class degrees, compared with about 9 per cent of women (*Guardian*, 13 January 1998). Third, although the emphasis on continual assessment of coursework is generally believed to favour girls, Elwood (1995,

1998) suggests such explanations for why girls have accelerated ahead at GCSE are misplaced. Stereotypical perceptions of female conformity mean female success is often explained in terms of diligence rather than ability (Murphy and Elwood, 1998). Yet Elwood's analysis of the 1997 GCSE data shows coursework does not contribute disproportionately to the final grade. What she found was that 'the more traditionally styled examination papers are more likely to act as powerful discriminators' (Elwood, 1998, p. 17). Key factors in subject performance are pupil motivation and esteem, teacher behaviour and expectations. Schooling does not take place in a vacuum. It is accepted that there are many differences within the broad categories of 'boys' and 'girls'; the origins of underachievement lie outside the school. Changes in male work patterns are important, as is the fact that women's lives continue to be circumscribed by the various assumptions that are made about domestic responsibilities and family life. Gender differentiation has implications for boys and girls, causing each to narrow their expectations accordingly.

Conclusion

To sum up, the debate on male underachievement may be another way of perpetuating the myth of female classlessness in education. The traditional emphasis on the domestic vocation of girls encouraged this, as did the class organization of the state system and the illusion of male meritocracy. Gender patterns in post-compulsory education and different post-school destinations suggest the focus on formal equality ignored the root causes of inequalities in subject choices and careers. Wifehood and motherhood are still frequently upheld as major ideals to which females should aspire, whereas fatherhood has quite different implications. If we adopt a historical perspective it becomes obvious that this is a notion that has shaped the education of girls ever since the development of mass schooling. Lower-attaining girls still face a future of poorly paid 'women's work'. However, there has been something of a shift in attitudes. Rather than marriage and motherhood being seen as an alternative 'career', it is seen as a parallel 'career'. New Labour policies on free childcare for low-paid women and out-of-school clubs for over fives, as well as the New Deal for lone mothers, reflect changing conceptions of femininity and female activities in the labour market.

Not everything is new, despite the backlash against girls' success. Today's 'underachieving' boys are reminiscent of the nonconformist 'lads' described in 1970s sociological research, although the words 'boffin' or 'boff' have replaced 'ear'oles' and 'swot' as the *bêtes noires* of 'new laddism'. For *all* girls, segregated training, career and occupational choices have future consequences for pay and economic independence. Hegemonic masculinities and social class continue to dominate the state education system.

Notes

1   It should be pointed out here that since October 1998, the United Kingdom has a Human Rights Act (for a discussion of this Act, see the Introduction to this volume).

2 The term hegemony was used by the Italian Marxist Antonio Gramsci (1891–1937), founder and briefly leader of the Italian Communist Party. Gramsci was imprisoned by Mussolini and his writings in captivity were later published as *The Prison Notebooks*. The concept of hegemony used here refers to the organizing principle or world view diffused through agencies of ideological control and socialization into every area of social life. In this context the key conceptual tool is what Gramsci calls cultural hegemony. Central to this idea is the notion that the dominant class lays down the terms and parameters of discussion in society; it tries to define and contain all taste, morality, customs, religious and political principles. However, hegemonic control has to be won and maintained. Subordinate classes can always produce a counter hegemony in an attempt to modify, negotiate, resist or even overthrow the dominant culture.

The structuralist Marxism of Louis Althusser takes social structure as its central focus. Here the emphasis is institutional domination through the institutions created by the dominant class to ensure the continuance of their domination. In contrast, humanist Marxism as articulated by Antonio Gramsci takes humankind as its central focus.

References

Arnot, M (1983) 'A cloud over co education: an analysis of the forms of transmission of class and gender relations', in S. Walker and L. Barton (eds), *Gender, Class & Education*, Lewes: Falmer, pp. 69–91

Arnot, M. (1984) 'How shall we educate our sons?', in R. Deem (ed.), *Co-education Reconsidered*, Milton Keynes: Open University Press, pp. 37–56

Arnot, M. (1989/90) 'Consultation or legitimation? Race and gender politics and the making of the national curriculum', *Critical Social Policy*, 29, pp. 20–38

Arnot, M. (1991) 'Equality and Democracy: a decade of struggle over education', *British Journal of Sociology of Education*, 12 (4), pp. 447–66

Arnot, M. (1994) 'Male hegemony, social class and women's education', in L. Stone (ed.), *The Education Feminism Reader*, London: Routledge, pp. 84–104.

Arnot, M. (1996) 'The return of the egalitarian agenda? The paradoxical effects of recent educational reforms', *NUT Education Review*, 10 (1), pp. 9–14

Arnot, M., David, M. and Weiner, G. (1996) *Educational Reforms and Gender Equality*, Manchester: Equal Opportunities Commission.

Attar, D. (1990) *Wasting Girls' Time. The History and Politics of Home Economics*, London: Virago

Benn, C. and Chitty, C. (1997) *Thirty Years on. Is Comprehensive Education Alive and Well or Struggling to Survive?*, 2nd edn, London: Penguin

Benn, C. and Simon, B. (1972) *Half Way There. Report on the British Comprehensive-school Reform*, Harmondsworth: Penguin

Benn, C., Parris, J., Riley, K.A. and Weiner, G. (1982) 'Education and women: the new agenda', *Socialism and Education*, 9 (2), 10–13

Bright, M. (1998) 'Boys performing badly', *Observer*, 4 January 1998

Bryant, M. (1979) *The Unexpected Revolution*, Studies in Education, University of London

Caine, B. (1992) *Victorian Feminists*, Oxford: Oxford University Press

Clarricoates, C. (1980) 'The importance of being Ernest, Emma, Tom, Jane. The perception and categorization of gender conformity and gender deviation in primary schools', in R. Deem (ed.), *Schooling for Women's Work*, London: Routledge and Kegan Paul, pp. 26–41

Corrigan, P. (1979) *Schooling the Smash Street Kids*, London: Macmillan

Daily Mail, commentary, 5 January 1998

David, M. (Winter 1983) 'Thatcherism *is* anti-feminism', *Trouble and Strife*, 1, pp. 44–8

David, M. and Weiner, G. (1997) 'Keeping balance on the gender agenda', *TES*, 23 May 1997

Davin, A. (1979) 'Mind that you do as you are told', *Feminist Review*, 3, 80–98

Davin, A. (1996) *Growing up Poor. Home, School and Street in London 1870–1914*, London: Rivers Oram Press

Dean, D.W. (1991) 'Education for moral improvement, domesticity and social cohesion: the labour government, 1945–1951', *Oxford Review of Education*, 17 (3), pp. 269–86

Deem, R. (1978) *Women and Schooling*, London: Routledge and Kegan Paul

Deem, R. (1981) 'State policy and ideology in the education of women, 1944–1980', *British Journal of Sociology of Education*, 2 (2), pp. 131–43

Deem, R. (ed.) (1984) *Co-education Reconsidered*, Milton Keynes: Open University Press

Delamont, S. (1983) 'The conservative school? Sex roles at home, at work and at school', in S. Walker and L. Barton (eds), *Gender, Class & Education*, Lewes: Falmer, pp. 93–105

Department of Education and Science (1975) *Curricular Differences for Boys and Girls*, Education Survey No. 21, London: HMSO

Digby, A. and Searby, P. (1981) *Children, School and Society in Nineteenth Century England*, London and Basingstoke: Macmillan

Dyhouse, C. (1977) 'Good wives and little mothers: social anxieties and the schoolgirls' curriculum, 1890–1920', *Oxford Review of Education*, 3 (1), pp. 21–35

Dyhouse, C. (1981) *Girls Growing up in Late Victorian and Edwardian England*, London: Routledge and Kegan Paul

Edwards, E. (1990) 'Educational institutions or extended families? The reconstruction of gender in women's colleges in the late nineteenth and early twentieth centuries', *Gender and Education*, 2 (1), pp. 17–35

Elwood, J. (1995) 'Undermining gender stereotypes: examination and coursework performance in the UK at 16', *Assessment in Education*, 2 (3), pp. 283–303

Elwood, J. (1998) 'Equity issues in performance in assessment: the contribution of teacher-assessed coursework to gender-related differences in examination performance', unpublished paper given at 24th Annual IAEA Conference, 10–15 May 1998, Barbados

Elwood, J. and Comber, C. (1996) 'Equity and the "Gold Standard": implications for gender equality in examinations and coursework performance in UK at 18', unpublished paper given at 22nd Annual IAEA Conference, 20–5 September 1996, Beijing, China

Equal Opportunities Commission (1997a) *Briefings on Women and Men in Britain. Education and Vocational Training in England and Wales*, Manchester: Equal Opportunities Commission

Equal Opportunities Commission (1997b) *Facts about Women and Men in Great Britain 1997*, Manchester: Equal Opportunities Commission

Gipps, C. and Murphy, P. (1994) *A Fair Test? Assessment, Achievement and Equity*, Milton Keynes: Open University Press

Gomersall, M. (1988) 'Ideals and realities: the education of working-class girls, 1800–1870, *History of Education*, 17 (1), pp. 37–53

Gomersall, M. (1994) 'Education for domesticity? A nineteenth century perspective on girls' schooling and domesticity', *Gender and Education*, 6 (3), pp. 235–47

Grant, L. (1994) 'First among Equals', *Guardian Weekend*, 22 October, pp. 37–46

Grant, L. (1998) 'Barbarians at the gate?', *Guardian* feature, 25 August, p. 12.

Griffin, C. (1985) *Typical Girls? Young Women from School to the Job Market*, London: Routledge and Kegan Paul

Haywood, C. and Mac an Ghaill, M. (1996) 'Schooling masculinities', in M. Mac an Ghaill, (ed.), *Understanding Masculinities*, Milton Keynes: Open University Press, pp. 51–60

Heward, C. (1993) 'Men and women and the rise of professional society: the intriguing history of teacher education', *History of Education*, 22 (1), pp. 11–32

HMSO (1996) *The Gender Divide: Performance Differences between Boys and Girls at School*, London: HMSO

Hollis, P. (1989) *Ladies Elect. Women in English Local Government, 1865–1914*, Oxford: Clarendon Press

Horn, P. (1988) 'The education and employment of working class girls, 1870–1914', *History of Education*, 17 (1), pp. 71–82

Hunt, F. (1987) (ed.) *Lessons for Life. The Schooling of Girls and Women 1850–1950*, Oxford: Basil Blackwell

Hunt, F. (1991) *Gender & Policy in English Education 1902–1944*, London: Harvester Wheatsheaf

Hurt, J. (1977) 'Drill, discipline and the elementary school ethos', in P. McCann (ed.), *Popular Education and Socialisation in the Nineteenth Century*, London: Methuen and Company, pp. 167–91

Hurt, J. (1979) *Elementary Schooling and the Working Classes 1860–1918*, London: Routledge and Kegan Paul

Kamm, J. (1965) *Hope Deferred. Girls Education in English History*, London: Methuen

Kelly, A. (1974) 'Science for men only?', *New Scientist*, 63 (912), pp. 538–40

Kelly, A. (1985) 'The construction of masculine science', *British Journal of Sociology of Education*, 6 (2), pp. 133–54.

Lawson, D. and Silver, H. (1973) *A Social History of Education in England*, London: Methuen and Company

Le Riche, E. (1988) *Why Do Teenage Girls Truant?*, London: Roehampton Institute of Higher Education, Department of Sociology and Social Administration

Lees, S. (1993) *Sugar and Spice: Sexuality and Adolescent Girls*, London: Penguin.

Littlejohn, M. (1995) 'Makers of Men', in L. Dawtrey, J. Holland and M. Hammer, with S. Sheldon (eds), *Equality and Inequality in Education Policy*, Clevedon: Multilingual Matters in association with the Open University, pp. 46–55

Llewellyn, M. (1980) 'Studying girls at school: the implications of confusion', in R. Deem (ed.), *Schooling for Women's Work*, London: Routledge and Kegan Paul, pp. 42–51

Macleod, D. (1998) 'Confidence trick', *Guardian Higher*, 13 January 1998

Martin, J. (1987) 'The origins and development of gendered schooling', unpublished MA dissertation, University of Warwick

Martin, J. (1999) *Women and the Politics of Schooling in Victorian and Edwardian England*, Leicester: Leicester University Press

McWilliams-Tullberg, R. (1975) *Women at Cambridge*, London: Victor Gollancz

Measor, L. and Woods, P. (1984) *Changing Schools. Pupil Perspectives on Transfer to a Comprehensive*, Milton Keynes: Open University Press

Miles, S. and Middleton, C. (1995) 'Girls' education in the balance: the ERA and inequality', in L. Dawtrey, J. Holland and M. Hammer, with S. Sheldon (eds), *Equality and Inequality in Education Policy*, Clevedon: Multilingual Matters in association with the Open University, pp. 123–39

Mizra, H.S. (1992) *Young, Female and Black*, London: Routledge

Murphy, P. and Elwood, J. (1998) 'Gendered experiences, choices, and achievement – exploring the links', *The International Journal of Inclusive Education*, 2 (2), pp. 95–118

Pankhurst, E. (1979) *My Own Story*, London: Virago

Pascall, G. and Cox, R. (1993) 'Education and domesticity', *Gender and Education*, 5 (1), pp. 17–35

Pascall, G. (1997) *Social Policy. A New Feminist Analysis*, London: Routledge

Phillips, A. (1998) 'Close schools for girls', *Guardian*, 6 January

Purvis, J. (1985) 'Domestic subjects since 1870', in I. Goodson (ed.), *Social Histories of the Secondary Curriculum*, Lewes: Falmer Press, pp. 145–76

Purvis, J. (1995) 'Women and education 1800–1914', in L. Dawtrey, J. Holland and M. Hammer, with S. Sheldon (eds), *Equality and Inequality in Education Policy*, Clevedon: Multilingual Matters in association with the Open University, pp. 3–17

Rendel, M. (1997) *Whose Human Rights?*, London: Trentham

Riley, K.A. (1994) *Quality and Equality. Promoting Opportunities in Schools*, London: Cassell

Schultz, T.W. (1970) 'The reckoning of education as human capital', in W.L. Hansen (ed.), *Education, Income and Human Capital*, New York: National Bureau of Economic Research

Simon, B. (1980) *Education and the Labour Movement 1870–1920*, London: Lawrence and Wishart

Simon, B. (1991) *Education and the Social Order*, London: Lawrence and Wishart

Spender, D and Sarah, E., (eds) (1980) *Learning to Lose*, London: Women's Press

Stanworth, M. (1986) *Gender and Schooling. A Study of Sexual Divisions in the Classroom*, London: Hutchinson

Stromquist, N.P. (1990) 'Gender inequality in education: accounting for women's subordination', *British Journal of Sociology of Education*, 11 (2), pp. 137–53

Thom, D. (1987) 'Better a teacher than a hairdresser? "A mad passion for equality" or, keeping Molly and Betty down', in F. Hunt (ed.), *Lessons for Life. The Schooling of Girls and Women 1850–1950*, Oxford: Basil Blackwell, pp. 124–46

The Times, 5 January 1998

Times Educational Supplement, 'Girls excel despite the male culture', 26 April 1996

Turnbull, A. (1983) '"So extremely like Parliament": the work of the women members of the London School Board, 1870–1904', London Feminist History Group (eds), *The Sexual Dynamics of History*, London: Pluto Press

Turnbull, A. (1987) 'Learning her womanly work: the elementary school curriculum, 1870–1914', in F. Hunt (ed.), *Lessons for Life. The Schooling of Girls and Women 1850–1950*, Oxford: Basil Blackwell

Vicinus, M. (1985) *Independent Women*, London: Virago

Weiner, G. (1994) *Feminisms in Education*, Buckingham: Open University Press

Williams, F. (1998) 'Troubled masculinities in social policy discourses: fatherhood', in J. Popay, J. Hearn and J. Edwards (eds), *Men, Gender Divisions and Welfare*, London: Routledge, pp. 63–97

Willis, P. (1983) *Learning to Labour. How Working Class Kids Get Working Class Jobs*, Aldershot: Gower

Wollstonecraft, M. [1792] (1975) *A Vindication of the Rights of Woman*, Harmondsworth: Penguin

3 'Race', Racism and Resistance

Satnam Virdee and Mike Cole

Introduction

Rather than starting with a search for empirical evidence of discrimination or
the expression of racism, or analysing 'the problems' or 'differentness' of 'black
people', 'Asians' or Jews, our analysis of racism centres on the material processes
themselves, the complex relationship between the state and capital and between
capital and labour and the way in which racism is ideologically constructed.

In this chapter, we begin by considering the origin and validity of the concept
'race'.[1] We then examine the origins of the welfare state, with particular reference
to racism. These origins, we suggest, lay in a political and ideological matrix of
imperialism, nationalism and anti-Semitism. We then go on to trace the continuity
of racism up to the present day and look at forms of resistance to it.

The Pre-World War Two Period[2]

The formalization of the concept 'race' in the English language can be traced back
to 1508 (*Oxford English Dictionary*), when it began to take on a specific economic
connotation with the burgeoning development of the slave trade (Williams, 1964).
For most of that century, however, it was used to refer to a class or category of
persons or things; there was no implication that these classes or categories were
biologically distinct. During the seventeenth century, an historical dimension was
added, and some Englishmen, interested in their historical origins, developed a
view that they were descendants of a German 'race' and that the Norman invasion
of the eleventh century had led to the domination of the Saxons by an 'alien race'.
This interpretation of history gave rise to a conception of 'race' in the sense of
lineage back to the Saxons. Distinction, however, was based on separate history,
rather than biological differences. During the late eighteenth and early nineteenth
centuries, the term finally became associated with physical traits, both within the
boundaries of Europe and beyond (Miles, 1982, pp. 10–11). According to Banton,
by 1850, it is probable that 'a significant section of the English upper class
subscribed to a rudimentary racial philosophy of history' (Banton, 1977, p. 25).

By the end of the nineteenth century, the ideology of the 'inferiority' of Britain's
colonial subjects and the consequent 'superiority' of the British 'race' were

available to all. There were a number of reasons for this. First, important social and economic changes had occurred, especially the transformation of Britain into a predominantly urban, industrial nation (Lorimer, 1978, p. 107). Basic state education, available after the 1870 Act and underpinned by imperial themes (see Chapter 4 of this volume; see also Mangan, 1986) and technical developments (Williams, 1961, pp. 168–72; see also Richards, 1989) facilitated the introduction of a cheap popular imperialist fiction (Miles, 1982, pp. 110 and 119). In addition, missionary work was seen as 'civilizing the natives'. In fact, a plethora of imperial themes permeated popular culture in the late Victorian era (Cole, 1992a, pp. 36–42). As well as in the education system, from the late 1800s to 1914, patriotism, Empire and racism were highly marketable products , in music hall (Summerfield, 1986), in juvenile fiction (Bratton, 1986) and in popular art (Springhall, 1986). Springhall writes of the importance of 'hero-worship and sensational glory, adventure and the sporting spirit: current history falsified in coarse flaring colours, for the direct stimulation of the combative instincts'. 'It was no accident', he goes on:

> that the 'little wars' of Empire, which took place in almost every year of Queen Victoria's reign after 1870, provided the most readily available source for magazine and newspaper editors of romantic adventure and heroism set in an exotic and alien environment.
>
> (Springhall, 1986, p. 49)

Such images, Springhall (1986, p. 50) continues, were also apparent in commercial advertising, school textbook illustrations, postcards, cigarette cards, cheap reproductions and other ephemera which appropriated and mediated the work of popular British artists of the time.

Those at the receiving end of this 'heroism' had to be constructed as biologically inferior.[3] While the 'inferiority' of Britain's imperial subjects was perceived secondhand, the indigenous racism of the period was anti-Irish and anti-Semitic (Kirk, 1985; Miles, 1982). From the 1880s, there was a sizable immigration of destitute Jewish people from the Russian pogroms, and this fuelled the preoccupation of politicians and commentators about the health of the nation, the accompanying fear of the degeneration of the 'race', and the subsequent threat to imperial and economic hegemony (Holmes, 1979; Thane, 1982). 'National efficiency' served as a convenient label under which a complex set of beliefs, assumptions and demands could be grouped – it completed the racist chain of Empire, nation and 'race'.

In 1905, the Liberal government passed the Aliens Act which halted further Jewish immigration. The Act did not exclude 'Jews' by name – just as post-World War Two legislation does not refer specifically to 'Asian', 'black' or other minority ethnic groups.

Anti-Semitism was not merely the province of the ruling élite. Ten years earlier (1895), the Trades Union Congress (TUC) had convened a special conference at which it compiled a list of questions to be asked of all members of Parliament. These questions were described as a 'labour programme' and included a number of progressive demands: for the nationalization of land, minerals and the means of production; old age pensions; adequate health and safety facilities; the abolition of the House of Lords; workers' industrial injury compensation; the eight-hour day and the reform of the Poor Law system. They also demanded the restriction of Jewish immigration (Cohen, 1985, pp. 75–6). Robert Blatchford, a founding member and representative of the Manchester and Salford Independent Labour Party (ILP) and one of the leading socialist journalists of his generation, queried the 'racial results likely to follow on the infusion of so much alien blood into the British stock' (Howell, 1983, p. 292). As Cohen argues, 'it was a common theme amongst many socialists that England was eugenically doomed if it carried on sending its own citizens to the colonies while receiving Jews from Europe' (Cohen, 1985, p. 80).

Such racist thinking went largely unchallenged apart from during those short periods of intense class conflict like that witnessed during the New Unionism in the late 1880s and early 1890s, when Jewish and English workers united in pursuit of common economic goals (Buckman, 1980; Williams, 1980).

It is important to note that anti-Semitism was not solely based on the stereotype of the poor Jew – a member of the lower social orders – threatening to pollute the racial purity of the British 'race', but on the ideology of the 'Jewish-capitalist conspiracy' and perceived attempts at world domination. In 1904, the ILP issued a pamphlet entitled *The Problem of Alien Immigration*, the first page of which mounted an attack on 'the rich Jew who has done his best to besmirch the fair name of England and to corrupt the sweetness of our national life and character' (Cohen, 1985, p. 76; for a discussion of this dual form of racism, see Cole, 1998a, p. 41).[4]

Following World War One, it was emigration rather than immigration which dominated the agenda (Branson, 1975; Mowat, 1968; Stevenson, 1984). However, this did not prevent the state from renewing anti-alien legislation throughout the 1920s. By the 1930s, the focus had shifted to a concern about falling birth rates, in the light of worries about both 'race' preservation and the efforts of dictators in Italy and Germany to increase birth rates in those countries (Mowat, 1968, pp. 517–18).

It is within the context of these historical antecedents that the Beveridge Report of 1942, one of the key documents informing the founding of the welfare state, was written. Here, the links between welfare and 'race', and indeed gender and nation, were made explicit. For example, the argument deployed in favour of introducing child allowances was that: 'with its present rate of reproduction the British race cannot continue, means of reversing the recent course of the birth rate must be found' (paragraph 413). Women were assigned the role of baby-machines in the service of capitalism and British culture and were told: 'In the next thirty years housewives as Mothers have vital work to do in ensuring the adequate continuance of the British Race and British Ideals in the world' (paragraph 117).

The clearest example of Beveridge's own patriotism can be seen in his essay, *Children's Allowances and the Race*. In it he stated:

Pride of race is a reality for the British as for other peoples . . . as in Britain today we look back with pride and gratitude to our ancestors, look back as a nation or as individuals two hundred years and more to the generations illuminated by Marlborough or Cromwell or Drake, are we not bound also to look forward, to plan society now so that there may be no lack of men or women of the quality of those earlier days, of the best of our breed, two hundred and three hundred years hence?

(cited in Cohen, 1985, pp. 88–9)[5]

The Post-World War Two Period[6]

In this section we limit our discussion of migrant labour to the postwar experience of South Asians and Caribbeans and their English-born children. This is not to deny that 'white' groups have been subject to a process of racialization: they clearly have (see preceding discussion of Jewish experiences in the nineteenth century, also Grosvenor's reference (1998) to the Cypriot experience in twentieth-century England; see also Kirk, 1986 and Miles, 1982 for a discussion of anti-Irish racism). Additionally, we restrict our analysis to England. The small literature that exists on racism in Scotland (see, for example, Miles, 1982, pp. 121–50; Miles and Dunlop, 1986) suggests that it has taken a rather different form and trajectory to that in England and cannot be adequately assessed within the limited confines of this chapter.

The demands of an expanding postwar economy meant that Britain, like most other European countries, was faced with a major shortage of labour (Castles and Kosack, 1985). The demand for labour was met by a variety of sources, including 500,000 refugees, displaced persons and ex-prisoners of war from Europe between 1946 and 1951, and a further 350,000 European nationals between 1945 and 1957 (Sivanandan, 1976, p. 348). However, the overwhelming majority of migrants who came to Britain were from the Republic of Ireland, the Indian subcontinent and the Caribbean (Miles, 1989).

On the whole, the labour migration from the Indian subcontinent and the Caribbean proceeded by informal means with little effort made to relate employment to vacancies. Instead, it was left to free market forces to determine the size of immigration (Sivanandan, 1976, p. 348). However, those industries where the demand for labour was greatest actively recruited Asian, black and other minority ethnic workers in their home countries (Fryer, 1984; Ramdin, 1987). Employers such as the British Transport Commission, the London Transport Executive, the British Hotels and Restaurants Association and the Regional Hospitals Board all established arrangements with Caribbean governments to ensure a regular supply of labour (Ramdin, 1987, p. 197). By 1958, and a decade of 'black' labour migration, there were 125,000 Caribbean and 55,000 Indian and Pakistani workers in England (Fryer, 1984, p. 373).

Despite the heterogeneous class structure of the migrating populations (see Heath and Ridge, 1983), they came to occupy, overwhelmingly, the semi-skilled and unskilled positions in the English labour market (Daniel, 1968; Smith, 1977).

Furthermore, they found themselves disproportionately concentrated in certain types of manual work characterized by a shortage of labour, shift working, unsocial hours, low pay and an unpleasant working environment (Smith, 1977).

Importantly, research suggests that elements of organized labour colluded with employers to exclude South Asian and Caribbean workers from key forms of employment, especially skilled work (Fryer, 1984; Wrench, 1987). With little evidence of a class consciousness constructed around an identity of working-class solidarity but rather a sectionalist class consciousness characterized by the primary concern of protecting the terms and conditions of their immediate work colleagues (Kelly, 1988; Hyman, 1972; Beynon, 1984) elements of skilled organized labour, fearful of the perceived threat posed by migrant labour, colluded with employers to ensure that the trade union strategy of restrictive practices took on an added racist dimension by excluding migrant labour from skilled jobs (Virdee, 1999b).

It was not only in the economic sphere that Asian, black and other minority ethnic workers found themselves discriminated against during this period. It is important to emphasize that the state played a critical and formative role in restricting the immigration of non-whites. In the late 1950s, there was growing concern within Parliament, the media and the major political parties of the 'dangers of unrestricted immigration'. This contributed to an important shift in public policy towards migrant labour from one of support for unrestricted immigration to one that stressed that the immigration of 'non-whites' had to be curbed if the social fabric and cohesion of the country was not to be irreparably undermined. As a result, in 1962, an Immigration Act was introduced which had as its primary objective the curbing of 'non-white' labour from the Indian subcontinent and the Caribbean only, with immigration from the Republic of Ireland remaining unaffected (see Miles and Phizacklea, 1984).

The consequences of this process of racialization, whereby relations between people are determined by perceived differences in 'race', were clear, as we have already demonstrated. According to Miles (1982, p. 165), these different racialized groups came to

> occupy a structurally distinct position in the economic, political and ideological relations of British capitalism, but within the boundary of the working class. They therefore constitute a fraction of the working class, one that can be identified as a racialised fraction.[7]

'Black' Self-organization: A Strategy of Collective Anti-racist Action

Apart from a few exceptions (see, for example, Virdee and Grint, 1994; Virdee, 1999b), an often neglected aspect of the racialization process has been any critical investigation of the forms of resistance to it (see Solomos, 1993). If we undertake an assessment of the 1950s and 1960s, it is clear that apart from isolated cases such as the campaign mounted by 'black' community organizations and individual 'whites' against the operation of a 'colour bar' introduced by 'white' bus workers in Bristol in 1955 (see Dresser, 1986 for a detailed discussion) there is little evidence of collective resistance to such racist exclusionary practices from either racialized or 'white' workers until the mid-1960s. As Sivanandan (1982, p. 5) argues, 'resistance to racial abuse and discrimination on the shopfloor was more spontaneous than organised'.

However, by the mid-1960s, the discriminatory practices enforced by employers and trade unions alike came under growing pressure from a series of strikes by racialized workers in the textile and foundry industries (Moore, 1975; Duffield, 1988; Wrench, 1987). Importantly, nearly all of these disputes were characterized by a substantial level of support from the different racialized communities and an almost complete lack of support from the 'white' working class (Sivanandan, 1982; Wrench, 1987).

Drawing inspiration from the civil rights struggles in the USA and the visits to Britain of the two main leaders of the American anti-racist movement – Martin Luther King in December 1964 and Malcolm X in January 1965 (Sivanandan, 1982) – this period witnessed the racialized community establishing numerous organizations committed to challenging racism through self-organization constructed around the identity 'black'. Importantly, and unlike the USA, 'black' became an identity that was inclusive of all the main 'non-white' social groups that were subject to racialization during this period. Shukra (1996, pp. 30–1) describes how activists within these communities set about attempting to establish a South Asian–Caribbean alliance against racism:

> The 'black' radical activist was usually an unpaid campaigner who operated intensively with a small group of like-minded people, went from meeting to meeting, distributed pamphlets, spoke at rallies, carried banners and organised demonstrations to convince what was termed 'West Indian', 'Indian' and 'Pakistani' people that their experience of inferior treatment at the hands of employers, schools, local authorities, government officials, politicians and the police was unacceptable. Crucially, they also argued that this situation could be changed through militant political activity, primarily against employers and the state . . . the black activists used the term 'black' to build a movement to mobilise and cohere self-reliant communities of resistance to racism.

Among some of the more prominent organizations that South Asians and Caribbeans joined to combat racism and exclusionary practices were the Racial Action Adjustment Society (RAAS), a 'black' radical organization whose slogan was 'Black men, unite . . . we have nothing to lose but our fears' (cited in Sivanandan, 1982, p. 16) and the Black People's Alliance (BPA; see Josephides, 1990). The outcome was that an identity previously employed to disparage particular racialized social groups was appropriated by the racialized communities themselves and infused with new meaning and an ideology of resistance – a process which Gilroy (1987) in Britain and Omi and Winant (1986) in the USA have come to define as 'race' and 'racial' formation, respectively.

The impact of such 'racial' formation coupled with growing academic evidence which demonstrated that 'racial' discrimination in the labour market ranged from the 'massive to the substantial' (Daniel, 1968) forced the state into introducing reforms to curb the worst excesses of racist exclusionary practices. One of the most important measures was the introduction of a Race Relations Act in 1968 which outlawed discrimination in the areas of employment, housing and the provision of goods, facilities, services and planning. Additionally, the Race Relations Board, established in 1965 by the first Race Relations Act, was given stronger enforcement powers, and a new body – the Community Relations Council (CRC) – was created to promote 'harmonious community relations' (Wrench, 1996, p. 24).

Consequently, by 1968, accompanying the legislation designed to curb 'non-white' immigration was the recognition by the state of the need for anti-discrimination legislation for those racialized migrants and their children already resident in Britain. These two aspects of state policy were neatly encapsulated by Roy Hattersley (a former Home Office minister) in his formulation: 'Integration without control is impossible, but control without integration is indefensible' (cited in Solomos, 1993, p. 84).

However, for some elements of the British élite and 'white' working class, the introduction of reforms, even while conceding the need for racist immigration controls, was tantamount to undermining the social basis of a much revered imagined community (Anderson, 1983) – the British (i.e. 'white') 'race' and its 'traditional' way of life. This current of opinion was most significantly reflected in the speeches of Enoch Powell, who, ironically, in a previous guise as Minister of Health had been responsible for the recruitment of Caribbean nurses during the postwar era of capitalist expansion (Fryer, 1984). In April 1968 Powell set out his opposition to attempts by the state to curb racist discriminatory practices when he claimed that racialized migrant labour and their children should not be 'elevated into a privileged or special class . . . The discrimination and the deprivation, the sense of alarm and of resentment, lies not with the immigrant population but with those among whom they have come and are still coming' (cited in Miles and Phizacklea, 1984, p. 3). The ideological hold of such racist thought over parts of the 'white' working class was forcefully demonstrated by the marches in support of Powell by the Smithfield meat porters and the dockers of east London (Sivanandan, 1982; Miles and Phizacklea, 1984) who chanted 'Back Britain, not Black Britain' (*The Trial of Enoch Powell*, Channel 4, 20 April 1998).

Racialized workers responded to this racist threat by establishing the Black People's Alliance (BPA), an organization which marked the high-point of the anti-racist 'racial' formation project in Britain, including both South Asian and Caribbean activists, with Jagmohan Joshi, the leader of the Indian Workers Association (IWA-GB), becoming its general secretary (Josephides, 1990). Despite such collective resistance, persistent pressure from the racist right served to forge the necessary political climate for the Labour government to introduce the Commonwealth Immigrants Act in 1968. This piece of legislation removed the right of entry into Britain from all British passport holders who did not have a parent or grandparent born in Britain (Miles and Phizacklea, 1984, p. 60). Such racist immigration controls were further strengthened with the election of a Conservative administration in 1970, which, within a year, had introduced an Immigration Act that effectively marked the end of Asian and black immigration for settlement (Gordon and Klug, 1985, p. 7).

By the early 1970s, research conclusively demonstrated that after having been resident in Britain for over a quarter of a century and despite almost a decade of collective resistance by the racialized communities themselves, racialized workers from the Indian subcontinent and the Caribbean continued to be substantially disadvantaged in the British labour market, as well as in other areas of resource allocation (Smith, 1977). A national survey carried out during this period showed the continuing importance of colour racism in defining the life chances of these social groups who were all lumped together as 'coloured people' (*ibid.*, p. 111).

However, at the same time, wider events, in particular the growing class conflict between organized labour and the state and employers (Hyman, 1972; Crouch, 1977) was increasingly undermining the highly sectionalist working-class consciousness that had hindered the formation of a current of 'white' anti-racism during the 1950s and 1960s.

Growing Class Conflict in the 1970s and the Formation of a Current of 'White' Anti-racism

The attempts to curb unofficial trade union activity by the state during the late 1960s and early 1970s served to politicize key elements of organized labour and contributed significantly to the formation of an oppositional class identity (Hyman, 1972; Kelly, 1988). In particular, there began to take place a significant shift beyond the narrow, sectionalist class consciousness of the 1950s and 1960s to a more politicized form of class consciousness which recognized the value of working-class solidarity and collective action to defend working-class interests.

This important development coupled with almost a decade of industrial struggles against racism and exclusionary practices by racialized workers and the growing fear of far-right influence in trade unions (see Miles and Phizacklea, 1978) created the necessary conditions for anti-racist ideas and the need for solidarity between 'black' and 'white' labour to gain a wider audience within many trade unions. By the mid-1970s, the TUC (see Miles and Phizacklea, 1978) and major trade unions, including the TGWU, GMBWU, NALGO, CPSA and the SCPS, recognized that working-class solidarity, necessary to combat growing employer and state encroachment of trade union rights, could only be achieved by explicitly challenging racism both within the workplace and outside. It was during this period that most large trade unions introduced anti-discriminatory measures (see, for example, the annual reports of NALGO 1977; 1979; 1981) which marked the beginnings of a decisive shift in policy within British trade unions from the 'problem of integration' to the 'problem of racism' (Miles and Phizacklea, 1978).

Importantly, it was amid this growing industrial unrest and the shift to the left among key sections of organized labour (Hyman, 1972; Crouch, 1977; Marsh, 1992; Kelly, 1988), that the incoming Labour government introduced several important pieces of legislation, including the Sex Discrimination Act in 1975 and the Race Relations Act in 1976 (Marsh, 1992). While the latter piece of legislation was subsequently shown to have been largely ineffective in challenging the prevalence of racism and exclusionary practices because of the sheer magnitude of the problem (see McCrudden et al., 1991), its introduction nevertheless represented a highly symbolic indication of the commitment to combat racism and exclusionary practices by the state under pressure from the organized labour movement and the racialized communities.

However, the most visible manifestation of the solidarity between 'black' and 'white' labour came during the course of the Grunwick dispute when thousands of 'white' (and non-white) workers, including miners, dockers (some of whom had demonstrated in favour of immigration controls in 1968), transport workers and post office workers, undertook secondary picketing to support South Asian women on strike (Rogaly, 1977; Ramdin, 1987). While the dispute ended in defeat for the strikers in 1978, it nevertheless demonstrated that amid the growing radicalization of parts of the organized labour movement, many 'white' workers overcame the ideology of racism and acted along the fault line of class in solidarity with racialized workers.

There is some evidence to suggest that this current of 'white' anti-racism at work was also influential in building resistance to racism outside of the workplace. In particular, primary research evidence suggests that parts of the organized labour movement played a decisive role in the formation of such anti-racist and anti-fascist organizations as the Anti-Nazi League (ANL) (see, for example, the annual reports of Civil and Public Servants Association (CPSA), 1980, p. 13; 1981, p. 11; Society of Civil and Public Servants (SCPS), 1983, p. 26; 1984, p. 54; and National and Local Government Officers (NALGO), 1981, p. 15). In addition to the longer-established 'black' anti-racist groups, by 1973–4, many 'whites' had also begun to establish anti-racist committees supported by local trades councils. The racist pronouncements of some rock stars led to the formation of a national organization called Rock Against Racism in August 1976 (Gilroy, 1987, pp. 120–1). The years 1976 and 1977 were important because they saw growing confrontation between racists and anti-racists which culminated in anti-racists preventing the far-right National Front from marching through Lewisham in south London – an area of relatively high 'black' concentration. In 1977 the National Front polled 119,000 votes in the Greater London local council elections and threatened to become the third party in British politics. The Anti-Nazi League (ANL) was established in 1977 to counter the threat from the National Front (Gilroy, 1987), and, in alliance with more locally based anti-racist organizations such as the Campaign Against Racism and Fascism (CARF) (CARF, 1992, p. 2), they successfully exposed the National Front as 'Nazis', contributing greatly to driving a wedge between them and a potentially sympathetic 'white' British public, and ultimately leading to their electoral demise (Messina, 1989).

Of course, such evidence by no means suggests that the 'white' working class moved *en bloc* towards an anti-racist position; otherwise, there would have been little need for the establishment of a national anti-racist organization in the first instance. Rather, this chapter has highlighted an important yet greatly neglected aspect of anti-racist politics during this period – the formation of a current of 'white' anti-racism. The consequences of such political developments were that by the late 1970s Britain had a significant anti-racist movement built around the dual ideological currents of 'racial' formation and working-class solidarity.

Anti-racism in an Era of Neo-liberalism: The 1980s

The economic and political forces that had helped to shape the formation of an activist 'inter-racial' unity within parts of the organized labour movement was not to last long, however. The failure of the 1974–9 Labour government and 'left' trade union leaders to arrest the rising levels of unemployment and the decline in real wages of many sectors of organized labour contributed greatly to a sense of disillusionment with such politics which ultimately manifested itself in the return of the Conservative Party to office in May 1979 with a substantial working-class vote (Marsh, 1992).

However, the introduction of neo-liberal economic policies designed with the primary purpose of curbing public spending through the stringent use of monetarist procedures served merely to accelerate the de-industrialization of Britain that had been under way since the mid-1970s (Eldridge et al., 1991). The recession was particularly marked in parts of the north and north-west of England, Scotland and many of the inner-city areas of the major conurbations (including Greater London) where both 'black' and 'white' workers were laid off in large numbers (Brown, 1982). Due to a complex interaction of the occupational and regional distribution of different racialized social groups, some were worse affected than others by the decline in manufacturing employment. Specifically, workers of Pakistani origin who found themselves disproportionately concentrated within the collapsing textile industry and residentially concentrated in the north and north-west were more adversely affected than workers of Indian and African-Asian origin (or, for that matter, 'whites') who were relatively more evenly distributed across several major manufacturing industries and were also more residentially dispersed (see Modood, 1997).

It was this economic decay coupled with the exacerbation of more specific problems, such as the growing deterioration in the relationship between the police and inner-city youth, that contributed greatly to the urban unrest in many of the English conurbations during the early 1980s (Benyon, 1984; Solomos, 1988). Although the research evidence strongly suggests that the participants of the urban unrest comprised 'white' youths as well as 'Asian' and 'black' youths (see Benyon 1984; Gilroy, 1987; Solomos, 1988), two mutually antagonistic sets of social forces ensured that racism, or, more precisely, the social construction of 'race', came to dominate public policy debate about the main causes of the unrest.

On the one hand, the anti-racist movement insisted that the root causes of the unrest lay in the systematic destruction of the lives of racialized communities through the operation of racism and exclusionary practices and state (mainly police) harassment which had served to create a 'racially defined' sub-proletariat (see

Sivanandan, 1993). On the other hand, the tabloid press forcefully denied that the unrest was the result of racism and instead attempted to criminalize the unrest by claiming it was the product of a 'black' criminal underbelly within society (see Solomos, 1988; Gilroy, 1987). In both sets of analyses far less attention was paid to explaining the plight of 'white' working-class youth who had also been active participants of the unrest (Benyon, 1984).

It was amid this highly charged political atmosphere that the Scarman Inquiry into the urban unrest was published in November 1981 (Scarman, 1981). The report advanced a series of recommendations: including calling for a more effective co-ordinated approach to tackling the problem of the inner cities; adopting a policy of positive discrimination to combat 'racial' discrimination among racialized social groups; reforming the police force and introducing new methods of policing (Taylor, 1984, p. 29). However, apart from giving qualified support to the findings contained in the Scarman Report (see Raison, 1984, pp. 244–57), the right-wing Conservative administration proved to be highly averse to introducing even minor reforms necessary to tackle racism and exclusionary practices because of its disagreement with the material explanations of the unrest advanced by the Scarman Inquiry (Ball and Solomos, 1990).

At this juncture, the trade unions could have colluded with employers to exclude racialized workers from the remaining areas of employment growth and stability (such as the service sector) within the British social formation. However, they did not: the political relations in 1980s England were rather different to those during the 1950s and 1960s when the prevalence of a highly sectionalist class consciousness had greatly hindered the formation of an indigenous current of 'white' anti-racism.

While the mass 'inter-racial' rank-and-file solidarity evident at Grunwick had subsided, the trade union activists who had come to prominence during the 1970s on a platform that articulated the defence of general working-class interests remained in positions of responsibility. As a result, by the early 1980s, activists in the trade union movement were, in political terms at least, far to the left of their membership over a range of important issues (Marsh, 1992), including the need to combat racism.

An anti-racist coalition comprising 'black' activists, trade union activists and the left of the Labour Party ensured that the recommendations of the Scarman Report, and in particular the need to tackle 'racial' disadvantage, was forced on to the social policy formation agendas of the local state. Under such pressure, the recommendations acted as a catalyst, particularly in those local authority areas that were politically controlled by left-wing Labour parties in the Greater London area where nearly half of the racialised population resided (Owen, 1993), to undertake anti-racist action (Ball and Solomos, 1990).

One practical example of the kind of anti-racist initiative launched during this period was collection by employers of systematic data on the ethnic origin of their applicants and employees so that the extent of disadvantage could be effectively assessed and thereby more systematically remedied through the adoption of positive action programmes. Pressured by developments in parts of local government, other large public sector employers such as the British Civil Service and the National Health Service were forced to follow suit and introduced equal opportunity policies (see OMCS, 1990; Beishon et al., 1995), quickly followed by large private sector organizations, especially in the retail sector (Wrench, 1996).

Subsequent research that has undertaken a critical assessment of the relative success of such equal opportunity policies in reducing the impact of racist exclusionary practices has shown that while such policies were successful in facilitating the entry of racialized social groups into non-manual forms of employment (see Jenkins and Solomos, 1986; Ball and Solomos, 1990), these racialized social groups remained disproportionately concentrated within the lower grades of these forms of employment (see Ouseley, 1990), particularly working within those jobs that some authors have referred to as new working class (Hyman and Price, 1980).

Despite such qualifications of anti-racist initiatives, by the late 1980s research evidence conclusively demonstrated that an important reconfiguration in the position of racialized social groups in economic relations in England had taken place (see Jones, 1993; Modood, 1997). This can be empirically substantiated with reference to Table 3.1. Specifically, it shows that similar proportions of 'white' men and men of Indian origin are now represented in non-manual work while a slightly higher proportion of men of African-Asian origin are in such work. Although men of Caribbean, Pakistani and Bangladeshi origin continue to be significantly under-represented in non-manual work compared to 'white' men, this differential has closed over recent years (Iganski and Payne, 1996). On the other hand, men of Caribbean, Pakistani and Bangladeshi origin continue to be over-represented in manual jobs compared to men of 'white', African-Asian and Indian origin.

Detailed analysis by individual job categories reveals further important insights. Table 3.1 shows that the same proportion of men of African-Asian origin in paid work were in professional and managerial jobs as 'white' men with only a slightly smaller proportion of men of Indian origin working in these jobs. Although men of Caribbean, Pakistani and Bangladeshi origin were significantly under-represented in this socio-economic group compared to men of 'white', African-Asian and Indian origin, about one in six were professional workers and managers.

Analysis of the intermediate and junior non-manual jobs demonstrates further the growing representation of Britain's racialized groups at all levels of the class structure. Apart from men of Pakistani origin, all the men from the different racialized groups had almost identical levels of representation in these jobs as 'white' men. The lower level of representation of men of Pakistani origin in junior non-manual jobs was almost entirely attributable to their greater representation in skilled manual jobs compared to men from the other 'South Asian' groups and 'white' men. Importantly, men of Bangladeshi origin were significantly less likely to be represented in skilled manual work than men from any other racialized social group, as well as 'white' men. This brings us to the position in the class structure that migrants from all the different groups used to occupy overwhelmingly: semi- and unskilled work (Miles, 1982). Table 3.1 shows that while men of Caribbean,

Table 3.1 Jobs levels of men by ethnic group

Category	White %	Caribbean %	Indian %	African-Asian %	Pakistani %	Bangladeshi %	Chinese %
Professional/Manager/Employers	30	14	25	30	19	18	46
Intermediate/junior non-manual	18	19	20	24	13	19	17
Skilled manual and foremen	36	39	31	30	46	7	14
Semi-skilled manual	11	22	16	12	18	53	12
Unskilled manual	3	6	5	2	3	3	5
Non-manual	48	33	45	54	31	37	63
Manual	50	67	52	44	67	63	32
Weighted base	789	365	349	296	182	61	127
Unweighted base	713	258	356	264	258	112	71

Note: Base: men in paid work

Source: adapted from Modood and Berthoud, 1997

Indian and Pakistani origin continue to be slightly over-represented in these jobs than 'white' men, it is men of Bangladeshi origin who comprise the one remaining group of migrant labour that finds itself overwhelmingly located in this type of work: specifically, they were four times as likely as 'white' men to be in such work. Apart from some important differences in the economic activity rates of Muslim women (that is, women of Bangladeshi and Pakistani origin), the overall trends for women were broadly similar (see Modood, 1997 for a descriptive analysis of such trends).[8]

Overall, national survey evidence since the 1980s has consistently demonstrated that significant proportions of migrant labour and their children have managed to extricate themselves from semi-skilled and unskilled work and move into skilled manual and junior non-manual work (and, increasingly, the petty bourgeoisie (see Metcalf et al., 1996)). As a result, the racialized social groups no longer occupy a largely homogeneous class position in the semi-skilled and unskilled site of the working class. However, as Table 3.1 clearly indicates, this process of social change has taken place at a different rate for different racialized social groups. Briefly, this has been the result of a highly complex and often contradictory interaction of several factors, including the initial class origin of migrants, the restructuring of the British social formation, the political changes introduced at both national and local government level to address the worst excesses of racist exclusionary practices and the differential operationalization of racism on different racialized social groups both in the labour market and in the wider society. These developments have served to produce a racialized population that has strikingly similar class cleavages to those of the 'white' population in England (Virdee, 1999b).

Of course, by advancing such propositions, we are by no means suggesting that racism and exclusionary practices play no part in defining the economic position of racialized social groups in the contemporary social formation; they clearly do (see Esmail and Everington, 1993). An additional and often neglected aspect of racism at work is racist violence and harassment (see, for example, Virdee, 1995). A nationally representative sample survey of racialized social groups carried out in 1994 found that over a quarter of a million people, that is, one in eight of the total adult racialized population in England and Wales, were subject to some form of racist harassment in one year (Virdee, 1997). The second most likely location of such harassment was at work. More detailed evidence of the problem was gathered with respect to the nursing profession – an occupation employing substantial numbers of black and Asian nurses (Beishon et al., 1995). Specifically, these nurses reported extensive racist harassment in their workplaces – sometimes from colleagues, frequently from patients. Few reported such harassment to the authorities and most felt that they had to accept it as 'part of the job'.

Conclusions

In this chapter we began by considering the origins of 'race' and racism. We then briefly considered the racist origins of the welfare state and traced the racist practices of the state, capital and sections of organized labour in the post-World War Two period. It was not until the mid-1960s that collective action against such racist practices emerged. Due to the continued prevalence of a sectionalist class consciousness among elements of 'white' labour and the dominance of racist sentiment, it was racialized workers organizing independently who first began to challenge such practices. However, attempts to curb unofficial trade union activity in the late 1960s and early 1970s served to politicize key elements of organized labour and resulted in the formation of an oppositional working-class identity. This major development, coupled with almost a decade of industrial struggles against racism by racialized workers and growing fear of far-right influence in trade unions created the necessary preconditions for the ideas of anti-racism and solidarity between racialized and 'white' labour to gain a wider audience in the trade unions. By the mid-1970s, the TUC and some of the larger affiliated trade unions explicitly recognized that working-class solidarity could only be achieved through combating racism.

However, it required the urban unrest and the political pressure that followed from organized labour and the racialized communities themselves finally to force the state to introduce reforms to curb the worst excesses of racist discriminatory practices. Specifically, non-manual forms of employment, albeit at the lower grades, were opened up to large numbers of racialized workers for the first time. This process acted as a catalyst and other large employers were forced to consider the employment and promotion of racialized workers. Despite continuing evidence of the prevalence of racism and exclusionary practices in the contemporary social formation, these developments have led to an important reconfiguration in the position of racialized social groups in economic relations: they no longer occupy a position in the semi-skilled and unskilled sites of the manual working class but instead display strikingly similar class cleavages to those of the 'white' population.

Endnote

Throughout this chapter, we employ the terms 'black' and 'white' to distinguish different elements of the English working class. Where necessary, we also distinguish between different 'non-white' groups by using the terms 'South Asian' and 'Caribbean'. While the purpose of enclosing these terms in quotation marks is to highlight their problematic scientific status (Miles, 1982, 1989), it is not our intention to render illegitimate the anti-racist action that has been undertaken employing such nomenclature.

Notes

1   We put 'race' in inverted commas because we question its validity as a scientific concept. Robert Miles has argued cogently against the notion that there exist distinct 'races' (1982, pp. 9–16). After a review of the literature, he gives three reasons for this. First, the extent of genetic variation within any population is usually greater than the average difference between populations. Second, while the frequency of occurrence of possible forms taken by genes does vary from one so-called 'race' to another, any particular genetic combination can be found in almost any 'race'. Third, owing to

interbreeding and large-scale migrations, the distinctions between 'races', identified as dominant gene frequencies, are often blurred (*ibid.*, p. 16).
2 This section draws on Cole, 1997, pp. 451–2 and Cole 1992a.
3 For a discussion of biological (and cultural) racism, see, for example, Cole, 1997. For the role of education in the construction of colonial citizens as biologically inferior, see Chapter 4.
4 Not all leaders of the Labour movement at the time were pro-imperialist and anti-Semitic. William Morris, Sylvia Pankhurst, Annie Besant, Fenner Brockway and George Lansbury are notable exceptions.
5 Our historical contextualizing of the foundation of the welfare state should not be seen as a critique of the notion of a welfare state *per se*. As socialists, we would see it as something we must defend. It is the most equitable institution possible under capitalism. We would particularly wish to rise to its defence, in the present historical conjuncture, when its very existence is under threat (Cole, 1998b; Hatcher 1998).
6 The following analysis draws heavily on Virdee, 1999a.
7 From the 1980s these racialized (non-white) groups occupied different positions according to whether they were male or female. They were a racialised fraction, differentiated by gender (Cole, 1989).
8 Only 15 per cent of Pakistani women and 6 per cent of Bangladeshi women are in full-time work compared with half of Caribbean, Chinese and African-Asian women (Modood 1997).

References

Anderson, B. (1983) *Imagined Communities*, London: Verso
Ball, W. and Solomos, J. (eds) (1990) *Race and Local Politics*, Basingstoke: Macmillan Education Limited
Banton, M. (1977) *The Idea of Race*, London: Tavistock
Banton, M. (1983) *Racial and Ethnic Competition*, Cambridge: Cambridge University Press
Beishon, S., Virdee, S. and Hagell, A. (1995) *Nursing in a Multi-ethnic NHS*, London: Policy Studies Institute
Benyon, J. (ed.) (1984) *Scarman and after*, Oxford: Pergamon Press Limited
Beynon, H. (1984) *Working for Ford*, London: Penguin
Branson, N. (1975) *Britain in the 1920s*, London: Weidenfeld & Nicolson
Bratton, J.S. (1986) 'Of England, Home and Duty: The Image of England in Victorian and Edwardian Juvenile Fiction', in Mackenzie, J.M. (ed.), *Propaganda and Empire: The Manipulation of British Public Opinion 1880–1960*, Manchester: Manchester University Press
Brown, C. (1982) *Black and White Britain*, London: Heinemann Educational Books
Buckman, J. (1980) 'Alien Working Class Responses', in Lunn, K. (ed.), *Hosts, Immigrants and Minorities*, Folkestone: Dawson
Campaign Against Racism and Fascism (CARF) (1992) 'Where CARF Stands', *Campaign Against Racism and Fascism (CARF)*, 6, January/February, p. 2
Carter, B., Harris, C. and Joshi, S. (1987) 'The 1951–55 Conservative Government and the Racialisation of Black Immigration', *Policy Papers in Ethnic Relations*, 11, Coventry: University of Warwick, Centre for Research in Ethnic Relations
Castles, S. and Kosack, G. (1985) *Immigrant Workers and Class Structure in Western Europe*, Oxford: Oxford University Press
Centre for Contemporary Cultural Studies (1982) London: Hutchinson
Civil and Public Servants Association (1980) *1979 Annual Report*, London: CPSA
Civil and Public Servants Association (1981) *1980 Annual Report*, London: CPSA

Cohen, S. (1985) 'Anti-Semitism, Immigration Controls and the Welfare State', *Critical Social Policy*, 13, Summer

Cole, M. (1989) '"Race" and Class or "Race", Class, Gender and Community?: A Critical Appraisal of the Racialised Fraction of the Working-class Thesis', *British Journal of Sociology*, 40 (1), pp. 118–29

Cole, M. (1992a) *Racism, History and Educational Policy: From the Origins of the Welfare State to the Rise of the Radical Right*, unpublished PhD thesis, Department of Sociology, University of Essex

Cole, M. (1992b) 'British Values, Liberal Values or Values of Justice and Equality: Three Approaches to Education in Multicultural Britain', in Lynch, J., Modgil, C. and Modgil, S. (eds), *Cultural Diversity and the Schools. Volume Three. Equity or Excellence? Education and Cultural Reproduction*, London: The Falmer Press

Cole, M. (1993) '"Black and Ethnic Minority" or "Asian, Black and Other Minority Ethnic": A Further Note on Nomenclature', *Sociology*, 27, pp. 671–3.

Cole, M. (1997) '"Race" and Racism', in Payne, M. (ed.), *A Dictionary of Cultural and Critical Theory*, Oxford: Blackwell Publishers

Cole, M. (1998a) 'Racism, Reconstructed Multiculturalism and Antiracist Education', *Cambridge Journal of Education*, 28 (1), pp. 37–48

Cole, M. (1998b) 'Globalization, Modernization and Competitiveness: A Critique of the New Labour Project in Education', *International Studies in Sociology of Education*, 8 (3), pp. 315–32

Crouch, C. (1977) *Class Conflict and the Industrial Relations Crises*, London: Heinemann

Daniel, W.W. (1968) *Racial Discrimination in England*, London: Penguin

Dresser, M. (1986) *Black and White on the Buses: The 1963 Colour Bar Dispute in Bristol*, Bristol: Bristol Broadsides

Duffield, M. (1988) *Black Radicalism and the Politics of De-industrialisation: The Hidden History of Indian Foundry Workers*, Aldershot: Avebury

Eldridge, J., Cressey, P. and MacInnes, J. (1991) *Industrial Sociology and Economic Crisis*, Hemel Hempstead: Harvester Wheatsheaf

Esmail, A. and Everington, S. (1993), 'Racial Discrimination against Doctors from Ethnic Minorities', *British Medical Journal*, 306, March, pp. 691–2

Fryer, P. (1984) *Staying Power: The History of Black People in Britain*, London: Pluto Press

Gilroy, P. (1987) *There Ain't No Black in the Union Jack*, London: Hutchinson

Gordon, P. and Klug, F. (1985) *British Immigration Control*, London: Runnymede Trust

Grosvenor, I. (1998) *Assimilating Identities*, London: Lawrence & Wishart

Hatcher, R. (1998) 'Labour, Official School Improvement and Equality', *Journal of Education Policies*, 13, pp. 485–99

Heath, A. and Ridge, J. (1983) 'Social Mobility of Ethnic Minorities', *Journal of Biosocial Science*, Supplement 8, pp. 169–84

Holmes, C. (1979) *Anti-Semitism in British Society 1876–1939*, London: Edward Arnold

Howell, D. (1983) *British Workers and the Independent Labour Party, 1888–1906*, Manchester: Manchester University Press

Hyman, R. (1972) *Marxism and the Sociology of Trade Unionism*, London: Pluto Press

Hyman, R. and Price, R. (1980) *The New Working Class? White-collar Workers and Their Organisations*, London: Macmillan

Iganski, P. and Payne, G. (1996) 'Declining Racial Disadvantage in the British Labour Market', *Ethnic and Racial Studies*, 19 (1), pp. 113–33

Jenkins, R. and Solomos, J. (eds) (1986) *Racism and Equal Opportunity Policies in the 1980s*, Cambridge: Cambridge University Press

Jones, T. (1993) *Britain's Ethnic Minorities*, London: Policy Studies Institute

Josephides, S. (1990) 'Principles, Strategies and Anti-racist Campaigns: The Case of the Indian Workers' Association', in Goulbourne, H. (ed.), *Black Politics in Britain*, London: Avebury, pp. 115–29

Kelly, J. (1988) *Trade Unions and Socialist Politics*, London: Verso

Kirk, N. (1985) *The Growth of Working Class Reformism in Mid-Victorian England*, London: Croom Helm

Lorimer, D.A. (1978) *Colour, Class and the Victorians: English Attitudes to the Negro in the Mid-nineteenth Century*, Leicester: Leicester University Press

McCrudden, C., Smith, D.J. and Brown, C. (1991) *Racial Justice at Work*, London: Policy Studies Institute

Mangan, J.A. (1986) '"The Grit of our Forefathers": Invented Traditions, Propaganda and Imperialism', in Mackenzie, J.M. (ed.), op. cit.

Marsh, D. (1992) *The New Politics of British Trade Unionism: Union Power and the Thatcher Legacy*, London: The Macmillan Press Limited

Messina, A. (1989) *Race and Party Competition in Britain*, Oxford: Clarendon Press

Metcalf, H., Modood, T. and Virdee, S. (1996) *Asian Self-employment in England: The Interaction of Culture and Economics*, London: Policy Studies Institute

Miles, R. (1982) *Racism and Migrant Labour*, London: Routledge and Kegan Paul

Miles, R. (1989) *Racism*, London: Routledge

Miles, R. (1993) *Racism after 'Race Relations'*, London: Routledge

Miles, R. and Dunlop, A. (1986) 'The Racialisation of Politics in Britain: Why Scotland Is Different', *Patterns of Prejudice*, 20 (1), pp. 23–32

Miles, R. and Phizacklea, A. (1978) 'The TUC and Black Workers: 1974–1976', *British Journal of Industrial Relations*, 16 (2), pp. 244–58

Miles, R. and Phizacklea, A. (1984) *White Man's Country*, London: Pluto Press

Modood, T. (1997) 'Employment', in Modood, T., Berthoud, R., Lakey, J., Nazroo, J., Smith, P., Virdee, S. and Beishon, S., *Ethnic Minorities in Britain*, London: Policy Studies Institute

Moore, R. (1975) *Racism and Black Resistance in Britain*, London: Pluto Press

Mowat, C.L. (1968) *Britain between the Wars*, London: Methuen

National and Local Government Officers (1977) *1976 Annual Report*, London: NALGO

National and Local Government Officers (1979) *1978 Annual Report*, London: NALGO

National and Local Government Officers (1981) *1980 Annual Report*, London: NALGO

OMCS (1990) *Programme for Action on Race*, London: OMCS

Omi, M. and Winant, H. (1986) *Racial Formation in the United States of America*, New York: Routledge

Ouseley, H. (1990) 'Resisting Institutional Change', in Ball, W. and Solomos, J. (eds), *Race and Local Politics*, London: Macmillan

Owen, D. (1993) *Ethnic Minorities in Great Britain: Settlement Patterns*, Census Paper 1, Coventry: Commission for Racial Equality, University of Warwick

Phizacklea, A. and Miles, R. (1980) *Labour and Racism*, London: Routledge and Kegan Paul

Raison, T. (1984) 'The View from the Government', in Benyon, J. (ed.), op. cit., pp. 244–58

Ramdin, R. (1987) *The Making of the Black Working Class in Britain*, London: Gower

Rex, J. (1970) *Race Relations in Sociological Theory*, London: Routledge and Kegan Paul

Rex, J. and Tomlinson, S. (1979) *Colonial Immigrants in a British City*, London: Routledge and Kegan Paul

Richards, J. (1989) *Imperialism and Juvenile Literature*, Manchester: Manchester University Press

Roediger, D.R. (1994) *Towards the Abolition of Whiteness*, London: Verso

Rogaly, J. (1977) *Grunwick*, London: Penguin

Scarman, Lord (1981) *The Brixton Disorders 10–12 April 1981*, London: HMSO

Shukra, K. (1996) 'A Scramble for the British Pie', *Patterns of Prejudice*, 30 (1), January, pp. 28–36

Sivanandan, A. (1976) 'Race, Class and the State: The Black Experience in Britain', *Race and Class*, 17 (4), p. 348

Sivanandan, A. (1982) *A Different Hunger: Writings on Black Resistance*, London: Pluto Press

Sivanandan, A. (1993) *Writings on Black Resistance*, London: Verso

Smith, D.J. (1977) *Racial Disadvantage in Britain*, London: Penguin

Society of Civil and Public Servants (1978) *1977 Annual Report*, London: SCPS

Society of Civil and Public Servants (1983) *1982 Annual Report*, London: SCPS

Society of Civil and Public Servants (1984) *1983 Annual Report*, London: SCPS

Solomos, J. (1988) *Black Youth, Racism and the State*, Cambridge: Cambridge University Press

Solomos, J. (1993) *Race and Racism in Britain*, London: Macmillan

Springhall, J.O. (1986) '"Up Guards and at Them!": British Imperialism and Popular Art, 1880–1914', in Mackenzie, J.M. (ed.), op. cit.

Stevenson, J. (1984) *British Society 1914–1945*, London: Lane

Summerfield, P. (1986) 'Patriotism and Empire: Music Hall Entertainment 1870–1914', in Mackenzie, J.M. (ed.) op. cit.

Taylor, S. (1984) 'The Scarman Report and an explanation of the riots', in Benyon, J. (ed.), op. cit.

Thane, P. (1982) *Foundations of the Welfare State*, London: Longman

Virdee, S. (1992) *Part of the Union? Trade Union Participation by Ethnic Minority Workers*, London: Commission for Racial Equality

Virdee, S. (1995) *Racial Violence and Harassment*, London: Policy Studies Institute

Virdee, S. (1997) 'Racial Harassment', in Modood, T., Berthoud, R., Lakey, J., Nazroo, J., Smith, P., Virdee, S. and Beishon, S., op. cit.

Virdee, S. (1999a) 'England: Racism, Anti-racism and the Changing Position of Racialised Groups in Economic Relations', in Dale, G. and Cole, M. (eds), *The European Union and Migrant Labour*, Oxford: Berg

Virdee, S. (1999b) 'Racism and Resistance in British Trade Unions: 1948–79', in Alexander, P. and Halpern, R. (eds), *Labour and Difference in the USA, Africa and Britain*, London: Macmillan

Virdee, S. and Grant, K. (1994) 'Black self-organisation in Trade Unions', *Sociological Review*, 42 (2) pp. 202–26

Williams, B. (1980) 'The beginnings of Jewish Trade Unionism in Manchester 1889–1891', in Lunn, K. (ed.), *Hosts, Immigrants and Minorities*, Folkestone: Dawson

Williams, E. (1964) *Capitalism and Slavery*, London: André Deutsch

Williams, R. (1961/1965) *The Long Revolution*, London: Chatto & Windus, Harmondsworth: Penguin

Wrench, J. (1987) 'Unequal Comrades: Trade Unions, Equal Opportunity and Racism', in Jenkins, R. and Solomos, J. (eds), *Racism and Equal Opportunity Policies in the 1980s*, Cambridge: Cambridge University Press

Wrench, J. (1996) *Preventing Racism at the Workplace*, Dublin: European Foundation for the Improvement of Living and Working Conditions

4   Racism and Education

The imperial legacy

Maud Blair and Mike Cole

Introduction

In this chapter we begin by examining Britain's historical legacy of 'race', class and Empire, and look at the way this was represented in the school curriculum of the early twentieth century. We argue that the attitudes and images projected by school texts at this time and reinforced in government statements and policies served in part to construct the children of colonial and post-colonial immigrants as 'a problem', after mass immigration in the post-World War Two period. We then look at the educational experiences of minority ethnic group pupils/students, before looking at some ways that were adopted to address the problems, which we argue lay in the education system itself and *not* in the pupils/students. We conclude with some suggestions of how we might proceed in the new millennium.

'Race', Class and Empire[1]

At the outset, we would stress that the social, cultural and religious diversity of British society is not a new phenomenon. Britain is a multicultural society and always has been. This is exemplified by the separate existences of England, Scotland and Wales. It is also evidenced by settlement from Ireland and elsewhere in Europe, both far in the past and more recently.

Britain's links with Africa and Asia are particularly longstanding. For example, there were Africans in Britain – slaves and 'soldiers in the Roman imperial army that occupied the southern part of our island for three and a half centuries' (Fryer, 1984, p. 1) – before the Anglo-Saxons ('the English') arrived.[2] There has been a long history of contact between Britain and India, with Indian links with Europe going back 10,000 years (Visram, 1986). Africans and Asians have been born in Britain from about the year 1505 (Fryer, 1984),[3] and their presence has been notable from this time on.

Our concern in this chapter, however, is with the era of imperialism and its immediate and longer-term aftermath.[4] In Chapter 3, Virdee and Cole argued that the origins of the welfare state cannot be understood without reference to imperialism and nationalism. The role assigned to mass schooling in maintaining the Empire was well expressed by Lord Rosebury, leader of the Liberal Imperialists: 'An Empire such as ours requires as its first condition an imperial race, a race vigorous and industrious and intrepid, in the rookeries and slums which still survive, an imperial race cannot be reared' (cited in Simon, 1974, p. 169). Here we see the links between the British 'race' and social class. Schooling was seen as a way of creating workers who could compete efficiently with other capitalist nations (epitomized in the slogan 'national efficiency'). In the 1860s, British capitalists were particularly worried about competition with Germany and the poor British showing at the Paris Exposition in 1867 was seen as exemplifying British backwardness in technological education (Shannon, 1976, p. 86). The dual themes of nationalism and imperialism can be gleaned in the major landmark in mass schooling in the Victorian age:

> Upon this speedy provision of education depends . . . our national power. Civilized communities throughout the world are massing themselves together . . . and if we are to hold our position among men of our own race or among the nations of the world we must make up the smallness of our numbers by increasing the intellectual force of the individual.
>
> (Forster, 1870, cited in Maclure, 1979, p. 105)

This is how W.E. Forster, Vice-President in charge of the Education Department in Prime Minister Gladstone's first administration, introduced the Elementary Education Bill in the House of Commons in February 1870. Although the 1870 Education Act, passed three years after the humiliation in Paris, made education neither compulsory nor free, it laid the foundations for a system which was soon to begin to abolish fees and make attendance compulsory.

The quest for 'national efficiency' continued in the Samuelson Report of 1882–4, whose terms of reference were:

> to inquire into the instruction of the industrial classes of certain foreign countries in technical and other subjects for the purpose of comparison with that of the corresponding classes in this country; and into the influence of such instruction on manufacturing and other industries at home and abroad.
>
> (Cited in Maclure, 1979, p. 122)

'National efficiency' served as a convenient label under which a complex set of beliefs, assumptions and demands could be grouped – it completed the imperial chain of social class, nation and 'race'. The survival and hegemony of the imperial 'race' were of course mutually reinforcing, as evidenced in the lead up to the 1902 (Balfour) Education Act, which established an integrated system of elementary, secondary and technical education under the general direction of the Education Department (Shannon, 1976, p. 303). There was a fear that the 'race' might be dying. For example, the Reverend Usher (quoting Darwin's forecast that, if artificial limitation of families came into general use, Britain would degenerate into one of 'those arreous societies in the Pacific') in his book *New Malthusianism* was sure about this: 'yes we cannot deny it, we are a decaying race' (cited in Armytage, 1981, p. 183). Gladstone held similar views.

It was not just the ruling class which held such opinions. The Webbs, Sydney and Beatrice, were most interested in education. Somewhat confusedly, the former once remarked that the role of London University in the new (twentieth) century should be to combine 'a sane and patriotic imperialism with the largest minded internationalism' (cited in *ibid.*, p. 190). Elsewhere, Sydney was less ambiguous. He once declared that he felt that at every moment he was 'acting as a Member of a Committee . . . in some affairs a committee of my own family members, in others a committee *as wide as the Ayrian race*' (Webb, 1896, p. 6; my emphasis). Like most Fabians, Webb was an avid supporter of imperialism (Hobbsbawm, 1964), and, with Liberal front-bencher Richard Haldane, set up Imperial College in 1903. At one stage, Sydney, like Lord Rosebury, called for the formation of a new party to plan the aims and methods of Imperial Policy (Simon, 1974, p. 174), a party of 'national efficiency' – a party that would advocate sanitary reform, at least 'the minimum necessary for breeding an even moderately Imperial race' (Semmel, 1960, p. 73). Since it was 'in the classrooms . . . that the future battles for the Empire for commercial prosperity are being lost', the working class wanted to know, argued Webb, 'what steps' the followers of Rosebury would 'take to insure the rearing of an Imperial race' (*ibid.*). The general mood of the times was that the 'inferior races' of the colonies were a direct threat to the 'superior white races' (Armytage, cited in Maclure, 1979, p. 171).

Particularly influential in schools were the Empire Day Movement, the Lads' Drills Association and the Duty of Discipline Movement, all especially associated with the Earl of Meath, who particularly relished the idea of 'hardness' and believed that the 'British race . . . have ruled in the past because they were a virile race' (Lord Meath, 1910, cited in Mangan, 1986, p. 129). Meath was greatly concerned with the moral deterioration of the 'Anglo-Saxon' woman who should be prepared to face the obligations of the marriage tie (subordination to husband and state) and the sufferings and dangers of childbirth 'with as much coolness and courage as was expected of the man on the field of battle' (Lord Meath, 1910, cited in *ibid.*). He was also concerned with the 'Anglo-Saxon' man's increasing tendency to watch sport, rather than take part in it (*ibid.*). His solution was thus to train youth, via his various organizations, to build an imperial 'race', 'worthy of responsibility, alive to duty, filled with sympathy towards mankind and not afraid of self-sacrifice in the promotion of lofty ideals' (Lord Meath, 1910, cited in *ibid.* p. 130). Empire Day was said to have been celebrated in 1905 in 6,000 schools throughout the Empire and, by 1922, in 80,000 (*ibid.*, p. 132).

By 1922, another Education Act, that of 1918, had been passed. Its background was, of course, World War One. The higher level of German education was seen as a threat, and the Act's most important clauses concerned continuation schools, and followed the German example (Simon, 1974, p. 343). What this meant was that, with certain exceptions, every young person not undergoing full-time instruction was to be liberated from industrial toil for the equivalent of three half-days a week during forty weeks of the year – two half-days to be spent in school, and one half-day holiday (H.A.L. Fisher, MP, President of the Board of Education and architect of the 1918 Act, introducing the Bill, cited in Maclure, 1979, p. 174).

However, the Act was also directly related to social control. As Fisher put it, 'Education dispels the hideous clouds of class suspicion and softens the asperities of faction' (cited in Simon, 1974, p. 344). It is encouraging to observe, he went on, that 'the sense of the value in education as an end in itself, as one of the constituent elements in human happiness, is now widely spread among the manual workers of the country' (*ibid.*). Note that he stresses 'end in itself'. Fisher is most definitely not advocating a meritocracy or social class mobility. He registered his disgust at any such notions when introducing the Bill:

> I notice . . . that a new way of thinking about education has sprung up among many of the more reflecting members of our industrial army. They do not want education only in order that they may become better technical workmen [*sic*] and earn higher wages. *They do not want it in order that they may rise out of their own class, always a vulgar ambition*, they want it because they know that in the treasures of the mind they can find an aid to good citizenship, a source of pure enjoyment and a refuge from the necessary hardships of a life spent in the midst of clanging machinery in our hideous cities of toil.
>
> (Cited in Maclure, 1979, pp. 173–4; my emphasis)

The 1918 Act, then, was intended to increase 'national efficiency' by promoting education. It was also intended as a means of social control, which of course also related to improved efficiency. As it turned out, by 1921, the continuation school sections of the Act had been abandoned for financial reasons (Simon, 1974, p. 30).

The Curriculum

The curriculum of the early twentieth century was overtly racist. The primacy of the Bible and religion was replaced by the growing influence of imperialism which was very central in shaping the changing school syllabus, especially from the 1900s onwards. The addition of subjects like history, domestic science and games to the elementary school curriculum was conceived and justified by reference to their contribution to national strength, efficiency and, of course, the Empire. Thus, history texts, for example, told its readers that the British Empire was 'gained by the valour of our soldiers, or by the patient toil and steady enterprise of colonists from the mother country', and that Britain's imperial subjects in the colonies, 'of almost every race, colour and religion', were 'all living peacefully and prospering under the British flag, and content with the knowledge that the strong arm and brave spirit that gained freedom for them will always be ready to defend the precious gift' (Pitman's *King Edward History Readers – for Juniors* (1901) cited in Chancellor, 1970, pp. 127–8). The propagation of the British 'race' depended on the continued subordination of women in the home. Thus while boys were encouraged to think that 'the only safe thing for all of us who love our country is to learn soldiering at once and be prepared to fight at any moment' (Fletcher and Kipling's *A School History of England – for Juniors* (1911) cited in *ibid.*, p. 130) and were told not to 'forget the man in the labourer . . . he is the autocrat of the home, the father of the family, and as a voter, one of the rulers of the Empire' (Bray's *Boy Labour and Apprenticeship* (1911) cited in Hendrick, 1980, p. 166), working-class girls were being taught how to manage their homes efficiently. As Humphries (1981, p. 40) explains, the introduction of domestic science subjects was directly related to the fear of 'race' degeneracy. As he puts it, following Dyhouse and Davin:

> Subjects such as home economics, laundrywork, cookery and needle-work aimed to instruct working-class girls in the correct performance of their future duties of motherhood, housework and domestic service, thereby promoting the reinvigoration of the nation and Empire through a sexist division of labour.

Geography texts were the prime conveyors of racial ideas. Each text laid out the conventional progression from hunting to pastoral to agricultural and finally to industrial societies (MacKenzie, 1984, p. 184). Thus, in Nelson's *The World and its Peoples* (*c*. 1907), the African was described as 'an overgrown child, vain, self-indulgent, and fond of idleness', while the 'wretched bushmen [were] the lowest and most debased human beings on the face of the globe' (*ibid.*). Asia was similarly demeaned by Nelson as a continent of dying nations rapidly falling back in civilization (*ibid.*) and Australian Aboriginals were 'among the most miserable of men' whose 'great poverty led them to practise vices like cannibalism and the murder of the sick and helpless' (A.J. Herbertson, *Man and his Work* (1902) cited in MacKenzie, 1984, p. 185). The 'English', by way of contrast, were portrayed as morally irreproachable. As one history text put it, '[t]hey all show the bold, frank, sturdy character which so strongly marks out the Anglo-Saxon race' (T.J. Livesey, *Granville History Reader* (1902) cited in Chancellor, 1970, p. 118).

Drawing on Edward Said's influential book *Orientalism*, (1979), Gauri Viswanathan (1992) discusses how literature was used as one of the strategies for producing an image and then regulating the lives of colonial peoples in India (see also Fanon, 1970). This cultural imaging of ex-colonial and other 'non-white' peoples as 'Other' and inferior was a necessary strategy, but one which did not end once former colonial countries gained their independence. Instead the context shifted from the colonies to a need to regulate and police the lives of those 'subjects' who came to settle in the 'mother country'. That (white) teachers and students would be influenced by this collective cultural history and social practice goes without saying, as must the consequences of this cultural outlook on relationships in schools. These have been well documented over the years (Driver, 1979; Fuller, 1984; Rampton, 1981; Swann et al., 1985; Eggleston et al., 1986; Mac an Ghaill, 1988; Brandt, 1990; Gillborn, 1990; Wright 1992a and 1992b; Troyna, 1993; see also the various Commission for Racial Equality and Runnymede Trust publications). This is not to suggest that racism was experienced as one continuous narrative of oppression. We would nevertheless argue that contra-dictions and the ambivalent experience of individuals notwithstanding, these textual representations of 'Others' worked alongside a range of other mechanisms of control to produce a 'normative' image of black[5] and South Asian children and their families in British schools. Such negative and demeaning texts, moreover, could still be found in school libraries well into the 1980s.[6]

The Post-World War Two Period

The attitudes and images projected by texts were, as we have shown above, reinforced in government statements and policies, and this continued to occur after the mass migrations of former colonial citizens to Britain.

For example, in the 1960s Sir Edward Boyle, the Minister for Education, heard complaints from white parents, in Southall in London, that there were too many immigrant children in the schools. These parents demanded separate classes for fear that their children would be retarded by the newcomers. The policy that ensued was to disperse minority children to different schools in order to ensure that there were no more than 30 per cent in any one school (Hiro, 1971). The idea was both to prevent 'a lowering of standards in the schools' and to ensure rapid assimilation of the children into the 'British culture'.

In the following years it became clear from investigations carried out in London schools that another image – that of black people as threatening and needing to be firmly controlled – was also being transferred from the colonies to the 'mother country'. In 1971 Bernard Coard exposed the iniquitous system of placing children into disciplinary units or 'sin-bins'. The majority of these children, as he discovered, were black (Coard, 1971). What these actions against black children underscored was the deep-rooted nature of the assumptions and stereotypes held of black and minority peoples and which formed part of the 'common-sense' and 'taken-for-granted' ways in which white British made sense of 'non-white' British (Lawrence, 1982). Examples of the kinds of assumptions which underpinned suspensions of black children in British schools can be found in community and local authority journals and newsletters. A copy of *Issues* (1981, p. 11) states,

> A study of disruptive units in a West Midlands local authority included a range of explanations from teachers for the disproportionate numbers of ethnic minority children in the units. One teacher referred to the children of West Indian origin as being physically larger than their white counterparts, and therefore 'more difficult to handle'; another that, 'West Indian children are lively and their liveliness gets them into trouble because teachers fear liveliness and schools like silence'.

Constructing an Educational Problem

The construction of black children as a problem for the education system thus had an early history. The consequences of this for the education of black and minority ethnic group children have been profound and far-reaching. In the following sections we explore, first, some of the ways in which minority ethnic group children have been represented in educational discourses; second, the educational experiences of minority group children; and finally some of the attempts that have been made to address these experiences.

We discussed above the deep roots of the British colonial mentality towards colonized peoples and towards diasporic peoples in post-colonial times. The British views both of themselves and the colonial 'Other' coalesced to create an image of an 'alien threat' facing British schools and British society in general. While the belief that black children were disruptive was having an effect during the 1970s (via their mass allocation to 'sin-bins') this image was particularly strong during the 1980s when, through a series of urban disturbances, the first substantial number of black young people born in Britain began to assert their rights and rejected the assimilationist tendencies of their parents. The manner in which these disturbances were projected via media and official sources such as the Scarman Report seemed to fix in the minds of white society the image of young black people (especially males) as representing trouble. One of the effects of presenting this kind of 'knowledge' about black children and young people was the disproportionate number of black (male) students being placed into alternative educational centres and schools for children with 'educational and behavioural difficulties' (EBD; Cooper et al., 1991). The view which carried into the classroom was that black children were not only disruptive (Wright, 1992a; Connolly, 1995, but violent (Gillborn, 1990; Sewell 1997).

In addition to this physical pathology of black children, there developed alongside it another ancient and pernicious form of representation – that of the educationally inferior black child. This image was no longer reproduced through the crude forms of representation which had led to the dispersal of minority ethnic group children, but through the educational discourses of 'underachievement'. As Troyna (1984) argued, 'underachievement' became part of the received wisdom about black students rather than the essential question which needed to be asked. According to Blythe and Milner (1994), such categorization provides a wider social function in that it legitimates and produces a troublesome group in the population which is then stigmatized as an inferior group. 'Underachievement', according to Ladson-Billings (1990), may well be the logical outcome of this kind of racialized thinking because of the 'psychic cost' borne by black children in their attempts to acquire success. She warns against a new form of pathology which has replaced 'underachievement': that of the students who are said to be 'at-risk'. This, she warns, can become but another way to blame students for both systemic neglect and the failure of schools to provide a decent education for minority ethnic group students (see also, Fine, 1991).

There were different kinds of representation for different minority ethnic group students. Students of South Asian background (namely Indian, Pakistani and Bangladeshi) were generally defined by the languages they spoke, and therefore were seen as an academic (and social) threat to white children (see Hiro, 1971), or as religious 'aliens' whose 'specific needs' posed a threat to the autonomy of schools (Blair, 1994). The notion that the bilingualism of 'Asian'[7] students was a problem for both the students themselves and for their teachers and fellow students remained an underlying theme in the government policies of both the Conservatives and the Labour Party (Gillborn, 1998a). Indeed, this has been demonstrated by the low level of priority accorded to the allocation of Section 11 funding,[8] and the problems created in the administration of staff and money for the benefit of bilingual students (Blair et al., 1998). Not only did this budget face successive cuts under Conservative administrations, but Section 11 staff have continued to live with the insecurity of not knowing how long this funding will last (Richardson, 1993; Gillborn, 1998a).[9]

South Asian students were also presented in seemingly benign terms as passive and studious and not presenting a disciplinary problem for teachers. This notion of the 'passive' 'Asian' student was juxtaposed against the 'aggressive' student of Caribbean origin and became, as Sally Tomlinson (1984) declared, 'a stick to beat the West Indian pupil with'. This image of passivity applied in particular to 'Asian' girls, but while, on the one hand, it presented 'Asian' girls as 'ideal' students, on the other hand, this same 'passivity' was said to reflect their supposed cultural subordination (Brah and Minhas, 1985) and so was itself a 'stick to beat the Asian man with', as well as 'proof' of the 'cultural inferiority' of these groups. Despite this image of the 'ideal Asian pupil', this has not prevented widespread low expectations of the abilities of these students, or of the inherent contradiction in the class-based view that 'Asian' students are studious yet have no ambitions other than to be taxi drivers, as one teacher stated of the students in his school, which was located in an area where taxi drivers were predominantly of South Asian origin (see Blair et al. 1998).

By the early 1970s, it had become clear that minority ethnic group children were not gaining the opportunities and advantages from the British education system that their parents had hoped for (Bryan et al., 1985). Black students in particular were over-represented in suspensions and expulsions from school, and in units for students with emotional and behavioural difficulties, and were clearly not performing to the same level as their white peers in public examinations. Theories about the assumed disruptive, aggressive and violent natures of black children informed a number of strategies intended to contain such behaviour. Writers have pointed, for example, to the disproportionate levels of reprimands and criticisms of black students by teachers (Tizzard et al., 1988; Mortimore et al., 1988; Gillborn, 1990; Connolly, 1995). Besides removing black students from conventional education and placing them in EBD units, or suspending and expelling them, more 'liberal' strategies of control were used. There were attempts, for example, to channel the supposed excess energy of black students into more physical activities such as sport. The notion that black children were 'naturally' physically well co-ordinated worked hand in hand with the idea that academically they were not able. This linked with another theory about black students: that they suffered from low self-esteem, a consequence of being members of a disadvantaged minority group. In order to build their self-esteem it was also suggested that they needed to be encouraged in those areas in which they were able to excel, such as sport. A consequence of this was that in order to ensure their peaceful compliance, black students were more likely to be encouraged to achieve in the physical subjects than they were in the academic.

The Educational Experiences of Minority Ethnic Group Students

It was in the academic area that the experiences of black and South Asian students raised most concern. A number of studies have attempted over the years to explain the level of under-performance of black students. Two types of theory have been put forward to explain the cause: those that look towards the children themselves and their families, and those that point to schools and society. Among those that find explanations in students and their families is the theory that black students (and black people in general) have lower IQs than white people (Jensen, 1969; Eysenck, 1971). This theory seems to have had some effect on the thinking of teachers. For example, in a study conducted by Cecile Wright, she found that black students were automatically placed into lower sets and streams than their white counterparts. She also discovered that black students were entered for the lower CSE examination and not for the higher O-level qualification,[10] regardless of their abilities in particular subjects (Wright, 1987). The debate about lower IQ of black people has since been revived in America by Herrnstein and Murray (1994), but though such theories have been largely discredited, the influence they might yield on systemic practices has yet to be seen.

One writer who has tried to explain the tendency for black students to be placed in lower bands and sets argued that in his study such action was justified because the black students behaved worse than other students and therefore were undeserving of places in higher academic sets (Foster, 1990). Foster's inability to engage with, the historical relationship between minority ethnic groups (in particular African-Caribbean people) and the education system exposes a fundamental weaknesses in his analysis (Gillborn, 1998b; Blair, 1998). It is worth noting too that studies carried out in the United States revealed a clear pattern in the class and ethnic distribution of students in low academic sets and streams (Oakes, 1985; Goodlad, 1984). Goodlad reported that these students in the lower academic 'tracks' were treated differently, received inferior materials and inferior instruction compared to those in higher 'tracks' and fell so far behind their peers that all hope of moving up to a more academic class was lost. Foster's lack of critique of the role of schooling in determining and influencing life chances of students, and his uncritical support of the status quo is therefore regrettable. Also writing in the American context, Haberman (1995, p. 50) attributes the unfair treatment of students to a teacher education system which does not prepare teachers to accept and understand diversity, so that teachers define children who are different from themselves as 'people who should not be there, or people they are unable to teach'. He adds that 'Many teachers have so completely internalized the process of blaming the victim and not holding schools themselves even partly responsible for children's failure that they are not even aware that they are doing so' (*ibid.*, p. 53).

This links with the second type of explanation for the experiences of minority group students: that racism – structural, institutional and individual – has been the main cause of the negative experiences of schooling of black and minority ethnic group students. Researchers have obtained evidence of some of the unfair ways in which black students have been treated. From his observations, Gillborn (1990, p. 30), for example, reported that

> Perhaps even more significant than the frequency of criticism and controlling statements which Afro-Caribbean students received was the fact that they were often singled out for criticism even though several students of different ethnic origins were engaged in the same behaviour . . . In sum, Afro-Caribbean students were not only criticised more often than their white peers, but the same behaviour in a white pupil might not bring about criticism at all.
>
> (Gillborn, 1990, p. 30)

The result of these kinds of interactions has been widespread antagonism between white teachers and black students because, as Wright (1987, p. 111) reported,

> students were inevitably forced into highly significant face-winning, face-retaining and face-losing contests between themselves and the teachers.

This tendency to over-discipline black students has resulted over the years in high percentages of black students facing suspension and expulsion. More recently, surveys carried out by the DfE, later known as the DfEE (Department for Education and Employment) as well as by a number of official bodies (ACE, 1993; NUT, 1992; OFSTED, CRE, 1996; SEU, 1998), have revealed the extent to which black students, and in particular boys, are over-represented amongst those who are excluded[11] from school. The long-term effects of this can at present only be a matter of speculation. However, it does not require empirical research to conclude that the disruption or curtailment of a child's education is likely to have a negative effect on their chances in life.

The issues for students of South Asian origin have differed in some ways to those of black students. The 'positive' stereotype as 'ideal students' which they have acquired masks some of the negative experiences which they have. Researchers have documented some of the overt as well as unintentional racisms of teachers against students of South Asian origin (Bagley, 1992; Wright, 1992a; Blair et al., 1998), while others have revealed the extent of racial harassment to which they are often subjected by their peers (Kelly and Cohn, 1988).

The definition of South Asian students as 'language problems' has had a deleterious effect on their academic progress. In 1996 Gillborn and Gipps carried out an overview of the literature on the academic achievement of minority ethnic group students and reported that students of Pakistani and Bangladeshi, as well as of African-Caribbean, origin were under-performing in relation to their white peers. Indian students, on the other hand, appear to perform well in relation to all their peers, pointing to the interactions of class and ethnicity in the academic performance of South Asian students. Although most schools now adopt bilingual policies which ensure that the child uses his or her first language in the acquisition of English[12] Blair et al. (1998) found that teachers were largely ill-equipped to incorporate bilingual issues in their everyday classroom practice. A major underlying problem has been different government policies towards minority ethnic group languages, as already discussed above.

There has been general criticism of studies which present minorities as single, undifferentiated groups. Mirza (1992), for example, criticized the tendency of researchers to subsume girls' experience within boys' experience, or else to present boys' experience as representative of all pupil experience. Research has shown that black girls face different forms of exclusion and marginalization in schools and also that they respond differently from boys to these experiences (Fuller, 1984; Mac an Ghaill, 1994; Mirza, 1992). For example, in interactions with male teachers girls are more likely to face stereotypes about their sexuality, and while girls of Caribbean origin are more likely to be seen as 'bossy' and 'loud' – a supposed indicator of the matriarchal tendencies in black families – 'South Asian' girls are likely to be seen as destined for early (forced) marriage upon whom education is somewhat wasted (Brah and Minhas, 1985). This highlights that racism is not the only factor in the experience of black students and that schools are equally implicated in those institutionalized modes of social production which reproduce the subordination of women (Mac an Ghaill, 1994). Researchers have also reported the different responses of black girls to discriminatory and unfair practices. Fuller (1984), Mac an Ghaill (1988) and Mirza (1992) found that black girls present an image of co-operation but resist internally teacher assumptions and attitudes, and will attempt to succeed academically despite their negative experiences. However, Mac an Ghaill (1994) also documented that not all girls are 'pro-school' but they are largely 'invisible' as disciplinary problems, resulting in more resources being allocated to male students who are perceived as a threat to the institution. Mirza also concluded that black girls in her study, if given support, would have achieved their high ambitions but were often held back by the lack of, or the inadequate or inappropriate, career advice which they received, advice based on assumptions about their gender, class and 'race'. Writers have also pointed to the complexities of ethnic identification (Blair et al., 1998; Gillborn and Gipps, 1996) and the importance of breaking down labels such as 'Asian' in order to make obvious the differences in academic performance between the different 'Asian' groups. The tendency to view Indians, Pakistanis and Bangladeshis as one homogeneous group had disguised the different experiences of these groups within the education system.

Addressing the Problems

The momentum for changing the situation of minority ethnic group students came from minority groups themselves. Parents, sometimes with the help and support of Section 11 teachers, organized 'mother-tongue' teaching for children in addition to instruction in the faith which they received at Mosque. Black parents started their own supplementary or Saturday schools. This reflected a growing frustration in black communities over the failure of the education system to produce positive results for their children. Supplementary schools were intended to counteract some of the distortions of history, the misinformation and the inadequate academic instruction which parents believed their children were receiving (Chevannes and Reeves, 1987). Through black parent and teacher associations and community action, the disadvantaged position of black students in schools was placed on the public and educational agenda. In 1979 the government commissioned an inquiry into 'the education of West Indian children'. The Rampton Report was made available in 1981 and confirmed what black parents had been saying all along – that racism against black children was indeed a major factor in their experience of school. However, the report was not received wholeheartedly by the government, which commissioned another study, whose brief this time was extended to cover other minority ethnic groups. The Swann Report, *Education for All* (1985), confirmed some of the findings of the Rampton Report but also made some of the most wide-ranging suggestions for education in an ethnically diverse society. Among these was the suggestion that children in all schools should be educated for life in a multicultural society. One of the underlying principles of this suggestion was that if children were taught about each other and each other's cultures, this would help to reduce prejudice, especially among white children.

Multicultural Education

The Swann Report's predominant focus on culture set the trajectory of multicultural education along a superficial line in which children learned about the food, clothes and music of different countries without also understanding the structural and institutional inequalities which had been at the core of community campaigns (Troyna, 1993; Sarup, 1986).

Preceding the broadening of multicultural education to include all schools regardless of ethnic composition, schools had attempted to deal with the supposed low self-esteem of black students by including within the curriculum subjects which were deemed to be 'ethnically relevant' and would help black students to acquire a more positive self-identity. In some schools black students were withdrawn from some mainstream subjects in order to attend classes on 'Caribbean culture' or to learn how to play steel drums. This assumption that the problems faced by black students in schools lay with the black students themselves was severely criticized by Maureen Stone (1981), who argued that not only did black students not suffer from low self-esteem, but that teachers were themselves not qualified to teach children the cultures of their homes. This was the job of the parents and not the teachers. Furthermore, by withdrawing students from some lessons, they were being deprived of access to some vital areas of the curriculum, which was compounding and not solving their academic difficulties.

The broadening of multicultural education to include white students and teachers, and the recognition that racism was a factor affecting the education of black students, did not, however, give rise to a radical rethinking of the curriculum or of pedagogy. What in effect took place was an extension of the 'black studies' approach to include white students, so that white students too could play steel drums or learn to cook South Asian or African foods, and wear 'ethnic' clothes. The exoticization of minority ethnic group cultures and customs merely served to reinforce the notion that these cultures were indeed 'Other' and drew the boundary more firmly between 'Them', the 'immigrants' or 'foreigners', and 'Us', the 'real' British. Needless to say, this approach itself came under severe criticism as a form of education that was said to be tokenistic and failed to address the real problems of schools and of communities within them. While multicultural education was an attempt to address the prejudices of white teachers and students, it was not appropriate for tackling and changing inequalities in society (Sarup, 1986). Sleeter (1994) described liberal forms of multicultural education as opportunities for white people 'to project a positive image about groups of color without actually confronting white supremacy'.

Anti-racism

The criticism of multicultural education led to a greater awareness of structural and institutional inequalities, and to a shift from a focus on the alleged 'deficiencies' of minority students and cultures to different manifestations of racism in schools and society. There was greater stress on individual and structural racisms and on the need to educate teachers in particular to explore different teaching strategies which not only allowed for personal examination of racism, but ways in which these new understandings could be incorporated into teaching. 'Race' relations advisers and multicultural advisory teachers also struggled with finding ways to promote anti-racist teaching in schools, and were sometimes accused of adopting strategies which were damaging and counterproductive. MacDonald et al. (1989) commented on the dangers of not including the white working class in any anti-racist policy. A further criticism was that anti-racists functioned with simplistic notions of racism and failed to recognize the complex and contradictory ways in which racism was manifest. Identities, it was argued, are both multiple and complex and defy attempts to reduce them into essential ethnic or racial categories (Rattansi, 1992; Gilroy, 1992).

Critics of anti-racist education were, however, themselves unable to suggest teaching strategies which took account of the complexities and contradictions to which they drew attention (Troyna, 1993). Troyna pointed out the resistance of local education authority administrators to changes in schools and the fundamental lack of commitment of governments to the promotion of equality of opportunity for minority ethnic group students (Troyna, 1993; see also Bagley, 1992; Richardson, 1992; Gillborn, 1998a). Referring to official responses in the USA, Noguera (1999, forthcoming) states that 'The absence of action and attention says more about how these issues are perceived and understood than the rhetoric of individual responsibility and equal opportunities occasionally uttered by politicians in reference to the urban poor.'

Conclusion

Whatever the shortcomings of multicultural and certain forms of anti-racist education,[13] it seems clear that the lack of government commitment to which Troyna and others have drawn attention contributed to teachers' and schools' ambivalence towards the issue of minority education. During the Conservative era, equality issues were not only placed on the back burner, but actively demonized. Attempts among groups who felt themselves increasingly marginalized to restore public attention to equity issues were derided for 'political correctness'. 'Political correctness' came to represent not a caring and inclusive society but one in which supposed political demagogues sought to impose their views at the expense of the majority.

The onset of a Labour government has done little, despite the rhetoric of 'an inclusive society', to challenge the fundamental injustices and inequalities faced by Britain's minority ethnic groups (Gillborn, 1998a; Hatcher, 1998). Gillborn argues that the politics of 'race' and nation which were discussed earlier in this chapter, and which were made explicit during the government of Margaret Thatcher, have been kept alive in the new rhetorics of the Labour government. He points to a few cosmetic changes, such as the funding of some Muslim schools and the retention of Section 11 funding (now Ethnic Minority Achievement Grant), as disguising the lack of commitment of the Labour government to tackle the real issues which confront minority groups in Britain. Labour policy, he argues, is nothing more than 'naive multiculturalism' and is, like the policies of predecessor governments, informed by a deficit view of minority peoples and cultures, an obstacle which prevents real understanding of social justice issues and stymies any attempts to tackle them.

What we would argue for is a radical re-examination of the teacher education programme with full support from government (Cole, 1999). Some teacher education programmes may well include the historical facts about nineteenth-century attitudes towards education for the urban poor in Britain but what lessons do they provide about the colonial attitudes towards subordinated peoples of colour? More importantly, what lessons do they draw in relation to the classist, racist and sexist legacies of these attitudes and beliefs for themselves and the types of teachers they will become?

Haberman (1995, pp. 91–2) suggests five steps which he considers to be essential for teachers-to-be, in order to overcome 'prejudice'. We have adapted his steps by replacing the rather nebulous psychologistic concept of prejudice with racism.

- The first step is a thorough self-analysis of the content of their racism. Those who never get beyond the denial stage should not be allowed near children or youth.
- The second step is to seek answers to the question of source: How did I learn or come to believe these things? Who taught them to me? When? Under what conditions? How much part of my daily life are these beliefs?
- Step three . . . In what ways do I suffer or benefit from my racism?

- Step four is to consider how other irrational dislikes and fears, for example, those related to gender, sexuality, disability or social class, may be affecting the many issues surrounding what we believe about schools and children, and how they learn best.
- Step five is the phase in which we lay out a strategy explicating what we plan to do about our racism and these other dislikes and fears. How do we propose to check them, unlearn them, counteract them and get beyond them?

Within this process, one would need to incorporate the structural and systemic role that schools play in the reproduction of inequality (Apple, 1990), as well an understanding of the history of 'race' and racism (see Chapter 3 of this volume).

These five steps allow for the exploration of complex issues which include the meaning of racism, of the discursive construction of racism, of our own identities as both multiple and complex, of the role of power in defining and conferring privilege, the meaning of 'whiteness', 'blackness', and, most importantly, of the ways in which these issues affect our responsibilities as teachers and the kinds of learning environments which we create for children. We recognize that this is only one of many strategies that are necessary for dealing with unjust and unfair practices in education, but it is time that we stopped looking for problems in the children and their communities and turned our focus more closely not only to the ideologies and practices of teachers, but on teacher educators. Working-class and minority families invest much in education and have been short-changed for far too long.

Notes

1 We put 'race' in inverted commas for the reasons discussed in Chapter 3, Note 1 of this volume.
2 Fryer cites evidence of a large percentage of skeletons of black Africans found among 350 excavated in 1951, dating back to Roman times (Fryer, 1984, cited in Brandt, 1986, p. 7).
3 Todd is citing Fryer's (1984) book *Staying Power* and Visram's (1986) book *Ayahs, Lascars and Princes*. See also Walvin (1973).
4 The following analysis is based on Cole (1992).
5 We use the term 'black' here to refer to people of African descent whether they be from Africa or the Caribbean. The term is also used to refer to people of dual heritage where one parent is of African descent.
6 One of the authors of this article worked as an adviser for multicultural education, and as late as 1989 was helping schools identify books with outdated colonial theories and racist views and images. In addition to history and geography books, story books and well-intentioned books by non-governmental organizations (NGOs) such as Oxfam, and published in the 1970s, presented images that were demeaning to black and minority peoples.
7 We place the term 'Asian' in inverted commas to draw attention to the problematic of subsuming a diverse number of groups under one label. We do, however, also use it without inverted commas where appropriate to show how groups thus labelled have experienced similar forms of stereotyping and been subjected to the same types of educational and cultural assumptions.
8 Section 11 is Section 11 of the Local Government Act (1966). This funding was initially provided to meet the needs of minority ethnic group children in schools, but

was later redefined to cover the language needs of children, or specific LEA projects for minority ethnic group children.

9   In November 1998 the government announced an increase of 15 per cent (making a total of £430 million over three years) for the teaching of minority ethnic group pupils/students, with special help targeted at refugee children and other children for whom English is not their first language. This funding, known as the Ethnic Minority Achievement Grant, has now replaced Section 11 funding.

10   CSEs and O levels no longer exist and have now been replaced by one qualifying examination, the General Certificate of Secondary Education (GCSE)

11   The terms suspension and expulsion were replaced by the term 'exclusion' in the Education (No. 2) Act of 1986.

12   One of the authors of this article had personal experience, as an adviser for multicultural education in the late 1980s, of children being forbidden to speak their home languages as teachers feared that his would 'interfere' with their English language acquisition.

13   The debate between multicultural and anti-racist educators continues to this day (see, for example, Short and Carrington 1996 and 1998; Cole 1998a and b).

References

Advisory Centre For Education (ACE) (1993) *Investigations into Exclusions*, London: ACE

Apple, M. (1990) *Ideology and Curriculum*, London and New York: Routledge

Armytage, W.H.G. (1981) 'Issues at Stake: The Biosocial Background of the 1902 Education Act', *History of Education*, 10 (3)

Bagley, C. (1992) 'In-service Provision and Teacher Resistance to Whole-school Change', in Gill, D., Mayor, B. and Blair, M. (eds), *Racism and Education: Structures and Strategies*, London: Sage

Blair, M. (1994) 'Black Teachers, Black Students and Education Markets', *Cambridge Journal of Education*, 24, pp. 277–91

Blair, M. (1998) 'The Myth of Neutrality in Educational Research', in Connolly, P. and Troyna, B. (eds) *Researching Racism in Education*, London: Routledge

Blair, M. and Bourne, J. with Coffin, C., Creese, A. and Kenner, C. (1998) *Making the Difference: Teaching and Learning Strategies in Successful Multi-ethnic Schools*, London: DfEE

Blythe, E. and Milner, J. (1994) 'Exclusion from School and Victim-blaming', *Oxford Review of Education*, 20 (3), pp. 293–306

Brah, A. and Minhas, R. (1985) 'Structural Racism or Cultural Differences: Schooling for Asian Girls', in Weiner, G. (ed.), *Just a Bunch of Girls*, Milton Keynes: Open University Press

Brandt, G. (1990) *The Realization of Anti-racist Teaching*, Lewes: Falmer

Bryan, B., Dadzie, S. and Scafe, S. (1985) *The Heart of the Race: Black Women's Lives in Britain*, London: Virago

Chancellor, V. (1970) *History for Their Masters*, Bath: Adams and Dart

Chevannes, M. and Reeves, F. (1987) 'The Black Voluntary School Movement: Definition, Context and Prospects', in Troyna, B. (ed.), *Racial Inequality in Education*, London: Tavistock

Coard, B. (1971) *How the West Indian Child is Made Educationally Sub-normal in the British School System*, London: New Beacon Books

Cole, M. (1986) 'Teaching and Learning about Racism: A Critique of Multicultural

Education in Britain', in Modgil, S., Verma, G.K., Mallick, K. and Modgil, C. (eds), *Multicultural Education: The Interminable Debate*, Lewes: The Falmer Press

Cole, M. (1992) *Racism, History and Educational Policy: From the Origins of the Welfare State to the Rise of the Radical Right*, unpublished PhD thesis, Department of Sociology, University of Essex

Cole, M. (1998a) 'Racism, Reconstructed Multiculturalism and Antiracist Education', *Cambridge Journal of Education*, 28 (1), pp. 37–48

Cole, M. (1998b) 'Re-establishing Antiracist Education: A Response to Short and Carrington', *Cambridge Journal of Education*, 28 (2), pp. 235–8

Cole, M. (1999) 'Conclusion: Where Do We Go from Here?' in Cole, M. (ed.), *Professional Issues for Teachers and Student Teachers*, London: David Fulton

Commission for Racial Equality (1997) *Exclusion from School and Racial Equality*, London: CRE

Connolly, P. (1995) 'Boys Will be Boys? Racism, Sexuality and the Construction of Masculine Identities amongst Infant Children', in Blair, M. and Holland, J. (eds), *Equality and Difference: Debates and Issues in Feminist Research and Pedagogy*, Clevedon: Multilingual Matters

Cooper, P., Upton, G. and Smith, C. (1991) 'Ethnic Minority And Gender Distribution among Staff and Students in Facilities for Students with Emotional and Behavioural Difficulties in England and Wales', *British Journal of Sociology of Education*, 12 (1), pp. 77–94

Driver, G. (1979) 'Classroom Stress and School Achievement: West Indian Adolescents and their Teachers', in Saifullah Khan, V. (ed.), *Minority Families in Britain: Support and Stress*, London: Macmillan

Eggleston, S.J., Dunn, D.K. and Anjali, M. (1986) *Education for Some: The Educational and Vocational Experiences of 15–18 year old Members of Minority Ethnic Groups*, Stoke-on-Trent: Trentham

Eysenck, H.J. (1971) *Race, Intelligence and Education*, London: Temple Smith

Fanon, F. (1970) *Black Skins, White Masks*, London: Paladin

Fine, M. (1991) *Framing Dropouts: Notes on the Politics of an Urban High School*, New York: SUNY Press

Foster, P. (1990) *Policy and Practice in Multicultural and Antiracist Education*, London: Routledge

Fryer, P. (1984) *Staying Power: The History of Black People in Britain*, London: Pluto Press

Fuller, M. (1984) 'Black Girls in a London Comprehensive School', in Deem, R. (ed.), *Schooling for Women's Work*, London: Routledge and Kegan Paul

Gillborn, D. (1990) *'Race' Ethnicity and Education*, London: Unwin Hyman

Gillborn, D. (1995) *Racism and Antiracism in Real Schools*, Buckingham: Open University Press

Gillborn, D. (1998a) 'Naive Multiculturalism: Social Justice, "Race" and Education Policy under New Labour', paper presented at the British Educational Research Association annual conference, Belfast

Gillborn, D. (1998b) 'Racism and the Politics of Qualitative Research: Learning from Controversy and Critique', in Connolly, P. and Troyna, B. (eds), *Researching Racism in Education: Politics, Theory and Practice*, Buckingham: University Press

Gillborn, D. and Gipps, C. (1996) *Recent Research on the Achievement of Ethnic Minority Students*, London: HMSO

Gilroy, P. (1992) 'The End of Anti-racism', in Donald, J. and Rattansi, A. (eds) *'Race', Culture and Difference*, London: Sage

Goodlad, J. (1984) *A Place called School: Prospects for the Future*, New York, McGraw-Hill

Green, D. (1982) *Teachers' Influence on the Self-concept of Different Ethnic Groups*, unpublished PhD thesis, cited in Troyna, B. (1993) *Racism and Education*, Buckingham: Open University Press

Haberman, M. (1995) *Star Teachers of Children in Poverty*, West Lafayette: Kappa Delta Pi

Hall, S., Critcher, C., Jefferson, T., Clarke, J. and Roberts, B. (1978) *Policing the Crisis: Mugging, the State, and Law and Order*, New York: Holmes and Meier Publishers

Hatcher, R. (1998) 'Social Justice and the Politics of School Effectiveness and Improvement', *Race, Ethnicity and Education*, 1 (2), pp. 267–89

Hendrick, H. (1980) 'A Race of Intelligent Unskilled Labourers: The Adolescent Worker and the Debate on Compulsory Part-time Day Continuation Schools, 1900–1922', *History of Education*, 9 (2)

Herrnstein, J. and Murray, C. (1994) *The Bell Curve: Intelligence and Class Structure in American Life*, New York: The Free Press

Hiro, D. (1971) *Black British, White British*, London: Pelican

Hobsbawm, E. (1964) *Labouring Men*, New York: Basic Books

Humphries, S. (1981) *Hooligans or Rebels? An Oral History of Working-class Childhood and Youth 1889–1939*, Oxford: Basil Blackwell

Issues in Race and Education (1981) 34, autumn, ILEA

Jensen, (1969) 'How Much Can We Boost IQ and Scholastic Achievement?' *Harvard Educational Review* 39 (1), pp. 1–123

Kelly, E. and Cohn, T. (eds) (1988) *Racism in Schools – New Research Evidence*, Stoke-on-Trent: Trentham

Ladson-Billings (1990) 'Like Lightning in a Bottle: Attempting to Capture the Pedagogical Excellence of Successful Teachers of Black Students', *Qualititative Studies in Education*, 3 (4), pp. 335–44

Lawrence, E. (1982) *Just Plain Commonsense: The Roots of Racism*, University of Birmingham, Centre for Contemporary Cultural Studies, London: Hutchinson

Mac an Ghaill, M. (1988) *Young Gifted and Black: Student–Teacher Relations in the Schooling of Black Youth*, Milton Keynes: Open University Press

Mac an Ghaill, M. (1994) *The Making of Men: Masculinities, Sexualities and Schooling*, Buckingham: Open University Press

MacDonald, I., John, G. and Bhavnani, R. (1989) *Murder in the Playground: The Burnage Report*, London: Longsight Press

MacKenzie, J.M. (1984) *Propaganda and Empire: The Manipulation of British Public Opinion 1880–1960*, Manchester: Manchester University Press

Maclure, J.S. (1979) *Educational Documents: England and Wales 1816 to the Present Day*, London: Methuen

Mangan, J.A. (1986) 'The Grit of our Forefathers: Invented Traditions, Propaganda and Imperialism, in MacKenzie, J.M. (ed.), *Propaganda and Empire: The Manipulation of British Public Opinion 1880–1960*, Manchester: Manchester University Press

Miles, R. (1982), *Racism and Migrant Labour*, London: Routledge and Kegan Paul

Mirza, H. (1992) *Young Female and Black*, London: Routledge

Mortimore, P., Sammons, P., Stoll, P., Lewis, D. and Ecob, R. (1988) *School Matters: The Junior Years*, Wells: Open Books

National Union of Teachers (1992) *Survey of Pupil Exclusions*, London: NUT

Noguera, P. (1999, forthcoming) 'The Role of Research in Challenging Racial Inequality in Education', *Journal of Contemporary Sociology*

Oakes, J. (1985) *Keeping Track: How Schools Structure Inequality*, New Haven: Yale University Press

Office for Standards in Education (OFSTED) (1993) *Exclusions: A Response to the Department for Education Discussion Paper*, London: HMSO

Office for Standards in Education (OFSTED) (1996) *Exclusions in Secondary Schools*, London: HMSO

Rampton, A. (1981) *West Indian Children in our Schools*, London: HMSO

Rattansi, A. (1992) 'Changing the Subject? Racism, Culture and Education', in Donald, J. and Rattansi, A. (eds), *'Race', Culture and Difference*, London: Sage

Richardson, R. (1992) 'Race Policies under Attack: Two Case Studies for the 1990s', in Gill, D., Mayor, B. and Blair, M., *Racism in Education: Structures and Strategies*, London: Sage

Richardson, R. (1993) *Section 11 Funding: Troubled History, Present Campaigning, Possible Futures*, London: Runnymede Trust

Sarup, M. (1986) *The Politics of Multicultural Education*, London: Routledge and Kegan Paul

Semmel, B. (1960) *Imperialism and Social Reform*, London: George Allen and Unwin

Sewell, T. (1997) *Black Masculinity and Schooling*, Stoke-on-Trent: Trentham Books

Shannon, R. (1976) *The Crisis of Imperialism 1865–1915*, London: Paladin

Short, G. and Carrington, B. (1996) 'Anti-racist Education, Multiculturalism and the New Racism', *Educational Review*, 48 (1), pp. 65–77

Short, G. and Carrington, B. (1998) 'Reconstructing Multicultural Education: A Response to Mike Cole', *Cambridge Journal of Education*, 28 (2), pp. 231–8

Simon, B. (1974) *Education and the Labour Movement 1870–1920*, London: Lawrence and Wishart

Sleeter, C. (1994) 'White Racism', *Multicultural Education*, 1 (4), pp. 5–8

Social Exclusions Unit (1998) *Truancy and School Exclusion*, London: HMSO

Stone, M. (1981) *The Education of the Black Child in Britain*, London: Fontana

Swann Report (1985) *Education for All: Report of the Committee of Inquiry into the Education of Children from Minority Ethnic Groups*, London: HMSO

Tizzard, B., Blatchford, P., Burke, J., Farquhar, C. and Plewis, I. (1988) *Young Children at School in the Inner City*, Hove: Lawrence Erlbaum Associates

Tomlinson, S. (1984) *Home and School in Multicultural Britain*, London: Batsford

Troyna, B. (1984) 'Fact or Artefact: The "Educational Underachievement" of Black Pupils', *British Journal of Sociology of Education* 5 (2), pp. 153–66

Troyna, B. (1992) 'Can You See the Join? A Historical Analysis of Multicultural and Antiracist Education Policies', in Gill, D., Mayor, B. and Blair, M. (eds), *Racism in Education: Structures and Strategies*, London: Sage

Troyna, B. (1993) *Racism and Education*, Buckingham: Open University Press

Troyna, B. and Hatcher, R. (1992) *Racism in Children's Lives: A Study of Mainly White Primary Schools*, London: Routledge

Visram, R. (1986) *Ayahs, Lascars and Princes*, London: Pluto Press

Viswanathan, G. (1992) 'The Beginnings of English Literary Study in British India', in Donald, J. and Rattansi, A. (eds), *'Race', Culture and Difference*, London: Sage

Walvin, J. (1973) Black and White: *The Negro and English Society 1555–1945*, London: Allen Lane

Webb, S. (1896) *The Difficulties of Individualism*, Fabian Tract, 69, London

Wright, C. (1987) 'Black Students – White Teachers', in Troyna, B. (ed.), *Racial Inequality in Education*, London: Routledge

Wright, C. (1992a) 'Early Education: Multiracial Primary School Classrooms', in Gill, D., Mayor, B. and Blair, M. (eds), *Racism in Education, Structures and Strategies*, London: Sage

Wright, C. (1992b) *Race Relations in the Primary School*, London: David Fulton Publishers

5   One of Them or One of Us?

Sexuality, identity and equality

Viv Ellis and Simon Forrest

> The forces of inhumanity are overwhelming, but only one's continued opposition
> can make any other order possible, can give an added strength for all those who
> desire freedom and equality to break at last those fetters that seem now so
> unbreakable.
>
> (R. Duncan in Blasius and Phelan, 1997, p. 233)

This quotation, from an essay written in the 1940s by the American poet Robert
Duncan, is an apposite epigraph for this chapter. It is indicative, in a number of
ways, of the content of the chapter, and comes from an essay to which we will return
in our discussion of the key issue of sexuality and identity. First, it identifies a
struggle for human rights, equality and freedom on the part of those oppressed
because of their sexuality. In this chapter we will trace some of the history of that
oppression and consider the implications of recent events and campaigns for the
progress of the struggle for lesbian and gay equality. Second, Duncan's speculation
on the possibility of 'any other order' draws attention to a definition of sexuality as
a cultural field which is subject to both construction and reconstruction as parts of
a historical process. We will consider attempts to define and represent sexuality
and show how this is a peculiarly modern enterprise. Third, decontextualized as
it is, the quotation appears to allow for diversity of sexual potential rather than
delimiting categories such as heterosexual or homosexual. Our discussion will
try to focus on conceptions of sexuality *per se* rather than individual categories,
these categories being relatively recent cultural effects. Finally, the epigraph
actually comes from an essay by a homosexual male which demonstrates that, even
with categories based on sexual behaviour, there is no single or simple identity
across the category, no one homosexuality or heterosexuality. Duncan was arguing
against such separate identities. So although we may try in this chapter to generalize
about sexuality as a cultural field, yet self-consciously hang our comments on
a history of categories, especially (but not exclusively) the male homosexual,
we will inevitably come back to the very problematic nature of the production
of these separate (and multiple) identities (and communities) based on sexual
behaviour.

Defining Sexualities

Definitions of sexuality – medical, legal and otherwise – abound. Some, like Oscar Wilde's famously expedient misreading of Plato in the dock – 'It is that deep, spiritual affection that is pure as it is perfect . . . It is intellectual' (Wilde, 1895, p. 111) – have attempted to side-step the issue of difference in sexual practices. Wilde's 'love that dare not speak its name' also, of course, involved sexual acts, criminalized by the Victorians as 'gross indecency', a crime of which Wilde and his co-defendant, Alfred Taylor (the keeper of a male homosexual brothel), were eventually convicted. The conversion of sexuality to sexual acts subject initially to religious codification, then to the pathologies of medicine and the jurisdiction of the law, is one on which we will focus in our 'history'.

One of the earliest and most detailed attempts at defining sexualities was made by the nineteenth-century German 'sexologist' Karl Heinrich Ulrichs. He was a legal official who took a campaigning position against what he saw as repressive laws against male homosexuals, exemplified by Paragraph 175 of the German Imperial Code: 'Unnatural vice committed between two persons of the male sex or by people with animals is to be punished by imprisonment; the verdict may also include the loss of civil rights' (Ulrichs cited in Blasius and Phelan, 1997, p. 63). From the early 1860s, Ulrichs produced many short publications designed to challenge such legislation, based on conversations and correspondence with individuals throughout Europe. Alluding to Plato's terminology in *The Symposium*, Ulrichs devised a series of categories and sub-categories which set the boundaries for what he thought to be all the possibilities for sexual behaviour. These included: 'Men' and 'Women', whose sexual object-choice lay exclusively in the opposite sex; 'Urnings', or male homosexuals, who could be 'Mannlings' (virile), 'Weiblings' (effeminate) or 'Intermediaries' (a mixed sub-category); through to 'Urningins' (lesbians), 'Uranodionings' (male bisexuals), 'Uranodioningins' (female bisexuals) and 'Hermaphrodites' (sharing the physical characteristics of both sexes). Ulrichs (1994, p. 314) actually defined a range of twelve sexual types if we include all his sub-categories.

Although his intentions were progressive, Ulrich's project lay the ground for the subsequent pathologizing of sexual behaviour in the discourses of medicine and psychiatry which is still powerful today. The tensions between this progressive intention and the pathologizing effect can be seen in this extract from an appeal to the regional governments of North Germany and Austria in 1870:

> That an actual man would feel sexual love for a man is impossible. The urning is not a true man. He is a mixture of man and woman. He is man only in terms of bodily build . . . The urning too is a human being. He, too, therefore has natural human rights . . . The urning is also a citizen of the state. He, too, therefore has civil rights: and correspondingly, the state has duties to fulfil vis-a-vis him as well . . . The state is not entitled to treat the urning as a man without rights, as it has up to now.
>
> (Ulrichs cited in Blasius and Phelan, 1997, p. 65)

The drive to pathologize sexual behaviour was intensified throughout the nineteenth century by, for example, Karoly Maria Benkert (said to be the person who invented the term 'homosexual'), Richard von Krafft-Ebing and, of course, Sigmund Freud. By the middle of the twentieth century, the proposition that sexual behaviour that had been diagnosed as deviant could be treated was commonplace. Aversion therapies based upon a malign behaviourist psychology became part of the medical/psychiatric repertoire and led to the institutional abuse of countless homosexuals, transvestites, transsexuals and others. It was comparatively recently that homosexuality was removed from some catalogues of mental disorders, and only then after a considerable struggle. The anthropologist Gayle Rubin (1993) has shown how medicine and psychiatry multiplied these pathologies in a hierarchy of (deviant) sexual behaviour that continues to be pervasive but, talking of the relative successes of homosexuals in establishing some human rights in some places and in coming out of the medical textbook, notes that '[s]exualities keep marching out of the *Diagnostic and Statistical Manual* and on to the pages of social history' (Rubin, 1993, p. 416).

The work of Alfred Kinsey (Kinsey et al., 1948; 1953) on human sexual behaviour represents a watershed in the modern understanding and definition of sexuality. Kinsey set out to describe and catalogue the sexual behaviour of human beings by interviewing American men and women about their sexual lives and experiences and by observing sexual behaviour in the laboratory. A major achievement of his studies was to show that contemporary preconceptions about the mutual exclusivity of heterosexuality and homosexuality were erroneous. Many of the men and women participating in his study reported both heterosexual and homosexual contacts, leading to Kinsey to develop an analytic scale on which sexual behaviour could be described in terms of one of six points, ranging from exclusively homosexual with no heterosexual contacts to exclusively heterosexual with no homosexual contacts, with grades reflecting more or less homosexual and heterosexual behaviour respectively in between. By looking over study participants' sexual histories Kinsey was able to assign them a place on the scale. Although he found that most of the men and women participating in the study reported exclusively heterosexual contacts, and a relatively small number (a few per cent) reported exclusively homosexual contacts, up to 37 per cent of the men in his sample had experienced a same-sex sexual experience to the point of orgasm in their lifetime. While the findings of Kinsey's work challenged previously held notions of the exclusivity of homosexual and heterosexual sexual behaviour it did so from within the paradigm of existing essentialist beliefs about sex and, as such, was not as progressive as it might at first appear. The focus on sexual acts rather than any idea of sexual identities did nothing to challenge critical perceptions of homosexuality as a deviancy. The discovery that apparently heterosexual men reported homosexual contacts in their youth could be dismissed as either evidence of a periodic 'arrested development' (*à la* Freud), or of a mature heterosexuality overcoming immature homosexual tendencies.

The fallout of essentialist investigations of sexuality via studies of sexual behaviour is still being felt. Most recently, attention has focused on the search for a genetic basis for homosexuality (and presumably, therefore, heterosexuality). This search is hampered by the inability of genetic science to explain ideas of a sexual identity any more satisfactorily than Kinsey's studies. Consequently, evidence from essentialist studies tends to become hostage to the ideologies of its commentators. Homophobic commentators have latched on to the potential existence of a gay gene as offering the possibility of genetic correction of a perceived sexual deviancy. However, some gay lobbyists have welcomed the 'gay gene' as biological proof that they are essentially biologically different to heterosexuals and have not created a deviant social identity for themselves. Between these lines, factions cross sides and, illustrating the political utility of essentialist findings, some gay lobbyists have argued for the rejection of Kinsey's work because it seems to provide too small an account of exclusive homosexuality. Some 'libertarian' right-wing ideologues draw the conclusion that, if homosexuality is genetically determined, then it is a natural state and should be decriminalized. For Kinsey, the reading of his work by the McCarthy-influenced US government at the time was sufficiently negative that funding was withdrawn from his studies.

While sexological surveys continue, the chief development of thinking about definitions of sexuality comes from fields outside the laboratory. Gagnon and Simon (1973) make the significant contribution to a sociology of sexuality by describing sex as a socio-cultural phenomenon rather than a natural act. This means that if sex is a social construct, subject to various meanings and deemed to have different functions at different times and in different places, it can be reconstructed according to social, cultural and political trends, needs and pressures. This 'discovery' prepared the way for the work of Foucault (1978; 1984) who developed an analysis of sexualities as products of cultures and defined by the interaction of the personal with social norms, scientific knowledge, religious and legal doctrine and authority. Subsequently, feminist thinkers and activists have sought to destabilize patriarchal values and practices by challenging the cultural, social and political hegemony of male heterosexuality. By questioning the orthodoxies of gender, its roles and meanings, feminist authors like MacKinnon (1989) have concluded that sexuality is a cultural effect dependent upon constructions of gender. From this analysis flows a critique of the essentialist paradigm which sets up heterosexuality, and all the associated baggage about gendered sexual roles, as the dominant discourse and other sexualities as subordinate varieties.

We might conclude by observing that in setting out a paradigm of particular sexuality through essentialist studies earlier in the century, academics and activists provided the framework and evidence which has made it possible latterly to deconstruct that paradigm. Definitions of sexuality have moved from previously fairly solid ground on which a simple mutual exclusivity of heterosexuality and homosexuality seemed adequate to describe human experience to a shifting terrain on which sexuality appears as a fluid, discursive phenomenon. A contemporary definition would have to acknowledge the complex interplay of social, cultural and intrapersonal factors in the production of a changing identity. We might describe sexuality as that element of identity which contains a sense of a self in which sexual feelings, ideologies, desires and needs are integrated with one another and reconciled with modes of sexual expression and behaviour. Bringing together our feelings, values and desires may be difficult, as may reconciling these with modes of expression and behaviour acceptable to ourselves and others. Without some reconciliation between these aspects of our internal world and ways of acting and interacting, we are vulnerable to feelings of dislocation between who we are and how we live. Reconciling feelings and actions does not take place only at a psychological level but in the context of the social world in which expressions of sexuality are differently valued. The inevitable consequence of this differentiation is that people who cannot reconcile their sexuality with those who are most socially valued can feel they themselves are less valued.

While on the one hand the weakening of prescriptive definitions opens the field for powerful legal arguments for the equalization of treatment of different sexualities, it also has the potential to undermine the resources available to minorities who feel a strong impulse to congregate around one identity label. In short, what is to be the relationship between sexual acts and identity? Can a gay man be gay in thought and not deed (as the Church of England would seem to allow)? Can a heterosexual woman have a homosexual relationship and still feel herself to be heterosexual? At one level, the invention of a sexual identity which depends heavily on representation of the self has reinvigorated the sexual act as a defining idea. As we shall see, history and the contemporary media have both striven to reinject sexual acts into representations of sexuality in order to keep the lines of distinction clear and position us still on the fringes of either reaction or revolution.

Representations of Sexuality

Representations of sexuality are a central feature of late twentieth-century popular culture. However, the possibilities for representation have been contested in a number of areas by special interest groups such as the National Viewers' and Listeners' Association (for example, Mary Whitehouse's attack on the BBC production of Dennis Potter's *The Singing Detective*) and by the manipulation of obscenity laws by police 'vice' squads (such as the seizure of a book of photographs by Robert Mapplethorpe from the library of the University of Central England). Ironically, given its daily content in terms of features, photographs, advertising and readers' letters, the popular press has often seen one of its most important editorial functions to be upholding notional standards of sexual morality.

When the singer George Michael was arrested in a park toilet in Los Angeles in April 1998 and charged with 'lewd conduct', the *Sun* newspaper, in a character-istically intertextual reference, used the banner headline 'Zip Me Up Before You Go Go'. The front-page story described how 'mega-rich George' had exposed his genitalia to an undercover police officer in a park which was 'a haunt for gays but also popular with families'. It went on to describe the park's location as 'less than two miles from the spot where film star Hugh Grant was caught with hooker Divine Brown three years ago' and to point out that the police were monitoring activity in the park after complaints about 'perverts in the gents'. The *Sun* was predictably pathologizing the singer as a 'pervert', to be associated in the public's mind with another deviant male who had been 'tempted' to use the services of a prostitute. George Michael's behaviour in a public toilet was just as much 'bad sex' as Hugh Grant's commercial transaction on the front seat of his car. And both were bad because they had taken place outside (rather than behind closed doors), on the streets of Los Angeles. The newspaper was drawing on its perceived authority to enforce what it saw as moral limits to sexual expression, even for the 'mega-rich' and powerful. This kind of sexual activity, it implied, was bad, dangerous to families and children, and immoral. Similar discourses permeate all aspects of popular culture; similar prohibitions are frequently demonstrated and the punitive consequences for those involved celebrated. A few days later, the singer gave an interview to an American television network in which he chose to identify himself as a gay man and to apologize for the way in which he had been forced to make this identity public. The *Sun* had seen its position justified: George Michael had admitted that he was homosexual, following years of speculation.

Six months later, George Michael released his first single for some time. Entitled 'Outside', it was a celebration of, among other things, sexual acts in public places and the very act of 'coming out'. In the video which accompanied the song, the singer's face is seen in close-up in an ironic parody of viewer seduction. This is followed by a montage of images of sexual acts – (hetero)sexual intercourse in a glass elevator, two young men (one black, one white) kissing in the back of a pick-up truck, male to female oral intercourse, sexual fetishism and cross-generational encounters, sex in the countryside and, of course, sex in public toilets. The final scenes involve George Michael dressed in a Los Angeles Police Department uniform dancing in formation in a urinal that has been transformed from a mixture of tile and ceramics to a camp combination of chrome, glitter-balls and feather boas. At the end of the video, all the characters apart from Michael are rounded-up and bundled into cars by a pair of male LA cops who, when it's all over, spend the final few seconds kissing each other as a shot from a helicopter picks out a neon sign reading 'Jesus Saves' over which the caption 'All Of Us' is superimposed.

This discussion of representations of sexuality by and of George Michael highlights some of the particularly rich contradictions in modern Western culture's definitions of sexuality. In her influential book *Epistemology of the Closet*, Eve Kosofsky Sedgwick (1994, p. 1) describes these contradictions as extremely powerful 'nodes of thought and knowledge' across 'twentieth century Western culture as a whole'. In the *Sun*'s coverage of the singer's arrest, we see what Sedgwick describes as the 'minoritising view' – the question of definition of sexuality (primarily based on simple hetero/homosexual definition) is only a matter for 'a small, distinct, relatively fixed homosexual minority'. Michael had been identified as one of 'them', and the question of identity is only an issue for 'them'. In the singer's own song, we see the 'universalising view'. Here the question is 'an issue of continuing, determinative importance in the lives of people across the spectrum of sexualities' and it is the sheer pleasure of activity across this spectrum that the singer is celebrating. As a public, we have shared in the reprobation of the *Sun* and the possibilities of the song. These are competing discourses which,

Sedgwick argues, both structure and fragment our ways of knowing ourselves and the world.

Sedgwick's book also presents an analysis of the metaphor of 'coming out of the closet' which argues against the view that coming out has 'float[ed] free from its gay origins' and has taken on a more general cultural significance so that it can be commonly used in everyday conversation produced in an enormous range of contexts. Far from it, Sedgwick hypothesizes:

> exactly the opposite is true. I think that a whole cluster of the most crucial sites for the contestation of meaning in twentieth century Western culture are consequentially and quite indelibly marked with the historical specificity of homosocial/homosexual definition.

> (Sedgwick, 1994, p. 72)

We know 'Outside' in this context; we understand the tensions between secrecy/ disclosure and private/public in the lyric as an effect of an attempt at sexual and individual definition. We are able to recognize that our efforts to understand our own identities take place in the realm of competing yet co-existing discourses. This dilemma has been intensified by the need to position oneself in relation to these discourses, in a space created by the very model of the modern homosexual.

Even for those women and men who acknowledge their sexual attraction to people of the same sex, the question of identity is not simple. 'Dykes' or 'queens', butch/femme, 'straight-acting' or 'scene' are just some of the possibilities for self-identification that are open to homosexuals. There is not one homosexual identity but many. However, they all establish their meaning in a relationship with the 'other', whether that be a generic heterosexual other or another homosexuality. To this extent, they are all products of a minoritizing discourse. In his essay 'The Homosexual in Society', Robert Duncan argued against minoritizing discourses which produce a 'ghetto' or 'cult' of homosexual 'superiority'. He criticized what he saw as the triviality and vapidity of a developing homosexual subculture which sought to keep itself separate, secret and in some ways superior to a notional general population. In doing so, he created a simple opposition between being 'human' and being 'homosexual' which could potentially, in some readers' eyes, assign him to the category of self-hating gay man: 'It is hard . . . to say that this cult plays any other than an evil role in society' (Duncan cited in Blasius and Phelan, 1997, p. 231).

Duncan was actually arguing for the as-yet-unnamed act of 'coming out' to the whole of society rather than seeking a 'sense of sanctuary such as the Medieval Jew must have found in the ghetto' (Duncan cited in Blasius and Phelan, 1997, p. 232). He was regretting his own experience of being silent on the political issues and using the 'group language' of the cult. In his final paragraph he does ameliorate his criticism of members of the cult, yet at times his own language – particularly in his comments on camp, tone and 'self-ridicule' – foreshadows that of members of the 'anti-gay' movement in the 1990s. Nevertheless, the final sentence of his argument (used as the epigraph to this chapter) encapsulates the sense of political responsibility every individual must recognize in the struggle for equality, and the importance of self-disclosure, that remains at the heart of radical campaigning organizations such as Outrage.

Sex Has No History

In this section, we will attempt to give an overview of some key events in a history of sexuality and sexual identity. Like any history, it is inevitably partial and the narrative structured from one perspective. The context for our brief discussion is Western societies and cultures, particularly Britain: we will not attempt to consider sexuality in other cultures or anywhere else on the other side of this epistemological border.[1] The history from which we draw most heavily is largely one of legal prohibitions on same-sex activity, most often directed at male homosexuals, and the struggle by oppressed groups for some degree of equality in the eyes of the law. We have chosen to focus on three significant moments in this history, each separated from the preceding by nearly one thousand years. The purpose is not to dismiss the intervening stretches of time but rather to illustrate vividly how mutable are the social conventions around homosexuality. Throughout, we will view sexuality not as some essential expression of biological drives but as a cultural effect produced and changed by different discourses. The subheading to this section, from David Halperin's work, draws attention to this difference between sex ('a natural fact, grounded in the functioning of the body') and sexuality ('the appropriation of the human body and of its physiological capacities by an ideological discourse') (Halperin, 1993, p. 416). By looking at the shifting position of homosexuality in the eyes of the Christian Church, government, science and the law it is clear the extent to which sexuality is solicited by capital in the establishment and maintenance of particular kinds of social relationships between citizens/subjects and of particular kinds of social/moral order. In general, this has meant differentiating homosexuality from heterosexuality and privileging the latter in certain ways. In fact, hetero-sexuality has become the central resource of the capitalist, nationalist order as conservative visions of the heterosexual, 'nuclear' family as the basic building block of society imply. It provides the means for managing rights of succession and the transfer of capital and power, and the foundation for creating a belief in a natural national family. What our history shows us, in part, is the struggle to control that capital.

Although authors like Taylor (1997), have recently begun to explore the prehistory of sex through the study of early representations of the human being and body on artefacts and in paintings, studies of sexuality in history usually start with a number of observations about the supposed predilection of men in ancient Greece to bugger adolescent boys and the apparent acceptance of these 'homosexual', cross-generational relationships. This is either meant to show that homosexuality is the choice of educated and civilized people (one reading of Plato's *Symposium*, where the context for such relationships is educational in intent) or that it is an unspeakable, foreign vice (another reading of the same text by translators and editors of various historical periods who expunged the offending passages in Plato's original). It is clear, however, that the sexual activities which appear to be described in some classical Greek texts were not seen as an expression of any kind of 'sexual identity' that could be defined as homosexual. They were simply acts that took place in a completely different kind of relationship altogether. David Halperin has said that, '[s]ex is portrayed in Athenian documents not as a mutual enterprise in which two or more persons jointly engage but as an action performed by a social superior upon a social inferior' (Halperin, 1993, p. 418). Halperin presents the sexual dynamic of classical Athens as a relationship between a citizen 'penetrator' (male) and 'penetrated' minors. These 'minors' included women, post-pubertal 'free' males not old enough to be citizens and slaves. The penetrator and the penetrated each had separate 'identities' and the participation in the sexual act did not in any way bring them together in any shared identity based upon an identifiable 'sexuality'. Their personal, physical desires were real but 'their very desires had already been shaped by the shared cultural definition of sex as an activity that generally occurred only between a citizen and a non-citizen' (*ibid.*, p. 419).

In his definitive study of Greek homosexuality, Kenneth Dover (1978) describes how Greek society, particularly between 480 BC and 146 BC, revolved around presumptions of the authority of adult male citizens and that sexual relations between men became overt and acceptable. However, these relationships took on a peculiarly stylized form and emotional tone and were largely confined to men of the higher social classes who mixed in more or less segregated groups as part of military and educational training. The central focus was on the development of a bond between an older man, an *erastes* (lover), and a younger man or boy, an *eromenos* (the loved). The older man, it was expected, would feel strong sexual attraction to the younger man, admiring his beauty, agility and physical attributes, and courting him with gifts. The younger man, rather than experience any emotional reciprocity, was expected to admire the older man for his wisdom and experience and look upon him as a model of masculinity. Over time it was anticipated that the relationship would alter as the younger man grew up, all emotional and sexual overtones would dim and the relationship would become one of friends.

The conventions about the emotional nature of the connection between the men in these relationships percolated through to influence the nature of their sexual intimacies. Officially at least, buggery was taboo, and in theory attracted the penalty of being stripped of one's citizenship. Hence, the usual method of intercourse was intercrural, the *erastes* being the active sexual partner. Sexual relationships between men of equal ages were frowned on, as was penetration of the *erastes*. The strict ideals about the nature of the relationship between men and the nature of Greek masculinity would be violated by such actions. As it stands, masculinity was associated with adult male status and sexual licence to be the penetrative and active partner. Another crucial aspect of Greek attitudes to homosexuality is the emphasis placed on restraint. The Platonic stress on transcending the real world and entering the world of Forms, where the universal essence of objects and ideas is arrayed, canonized restraint and emotional control. So, while Plato, and Socrates before him, accept and venerate homosexual feelings and relationships, their consummation is condemned since it shows passion blinding reason. Towards the end of his life, Plato was driven by inexorable logic, profoundly influential on later thinkers, to describe homosexual behaviour as unnatural. In Dover's translation, he writes:

> Anyone, who, in conformity with nature proposes to re-establish the law as it was before Laios, declaring that it was right not to join with men and boys in sexual intercourse as with females, adducing as evidence the nature of animals . . . could, I think, make a very strong case.
>
> (Plato, *Laws*, 836c–e, (trans. in Dover, 1978, p. 166)

In the Roman Empire, as in the Greek, people were not categorized as hetero-sexual or homosexual. While prostitution, both male and female, flourished under official licence, emphasis was placed on the maintenance of culturally and socially sanctioned ideals of masculinity and femininity which resulted in a continuation of the Greek proscriptions of penetrative and penetrated sexual roles. The 'gender-bending' antics of the imperial classes attracted particular opprobrium from the Roman chattering classes. The satirist Juvenal, in his vitriolic *Second Satire*, turns his anger several times on effeminacy among the ruling classes. He castigates the Emperor Domitian for reintroducing tough laws on sexual activity while indulging in incest and sodomy, reserving his harshest judgements for the soldier Emperor Otho, whom, he suggests, betrays ideals of Roman masculinity through his effeminacy:

> Another queen or queer, even nastier/holds a hand mirror his face to show/the very spectre of the pathic Otho/in which he admired his uniform/while sounding the charge at Bedriacum./Is this the lesson of Rome's recent story/'The path of beauty is the path to glory?'
>
> (Juvenal, *Satire II*, 98–103 (trans. Plumb, 1968, p. 36)

Clearly, while censorious attitudes towards certain types of sexuality emerge in Hellenistic cultures the focus falls on twisting and breaking gender roles and not on sexual identity as a separate entity. A new and peculiar moral sensibility is added to these attitudes by the construction of sexuality emerging with early Judaeo-Christian doctrine and finding full voice in the teaching of the Christian Church in medieval Europe (Richards, 1990). Sexual feeling and experience became synonymous with sin. As St Anselm, Archbishop of Canterbury at the end of the eleventh century, wrote:

> There is one evil, an evil above all other evils, that I am aware is always with me, that grievously and piteously lacerates and afflicts my soul . . . The evil is sexual desire, carnal delight, the storm of lust that has smashed and battered my unhappy soul, drained it of all strength and left it weak and empty.
>
> (cited in Richards, 1990)

As the teaching of St Paul stressed, celibacy was therefore the highest achievable ideal and reproductive sex in the context of marriage an acceptable second best. The Church's control of sexual behaviour was extended principally through the establishment of a legal, sacred marriage service which celebrated, sanctified and moralized about the complementary roles of men and women exemplified by the biblical story of Adam and Eve. For women, this resulted in typification as at once inferior, as the product of Adam's body, and evil, for succumbing to the serpent's temptation. This connection between female sexuality and sinfulness made it logical to sanction wife-beating, as a measure for instilling discipline and the forbidding of women from holding public office or undertaking any military service.

The Church's view of the role of sex inside and outside of marriage is illustrated by accounts of confessions and penances for sexual acts. Payer's (1984) work on the penitentials (books guiding priests in determining the gravity of various sins and the consequent scale of penance) shows a broadly consistent religious attitude towards sexual activity. Sexual matters formed the largest single category of offences in most penitentials. Although the details of penances varied, they were generally based on fasting on bread and water and avoiding sex for a number of consecutive days in multiples of ten. The Church pronounced the proper form of intercourse within marriage as penetrative vaginal sex with the man laying on top of the woman. Dorsal intercourse, with the woman on top, would earn three years' penance; anal intercourse seven years'. Sex was encouraged only at night and then partially clothed. Burchard of Worms (d. 1025) graded penitentials as follows: ten days on bread and water for male masturbation by hand, twenty days if it involved a perforated piece of wood. Interestingly, sexual intercourse with a female servant attracted the same penalty, illustrating the indulgence extended to young men and the social position and relative (un)importance of women. Highest penalties were reserved for incest, sodomy and bestiality. Burchard also proscribed the telling of dirty jokes, mixed bathing and fondling.

Medieval theology has no definition of homosexuality as such, only of homosexual acts. In fact, the terms used by St Paul to condemn homosexual sexual acts imply their occurrence only among heterosexual people. The line was very clear. Drawing on the Book of Leviticus (18:22 and 20:13), homosexual sex was ranked alongside incest, adultery and bestiality as the most serious sin. While the Church dealt in sexual acts, there is evidence to suggest that a homosexual subculture centred on male brothels in barbers' shops and bath-houses sprung up in some French and Italian cities in the twelfth century (Boswell, 1980). Along with the emergence of poetry and song extolling the virtues of erotic love between men, an argot is recorded which refers to young gay men as 'Ganymedes', sex as 'The Game', and cruising as 'Hunting'. Perhaps partially in reaction to this emergent subculture, theologians began to conceptualize homosexuality as an insidious inversion of 'natural', God-given laws. They opined that it was inconceivable that God should have been perverse enough to create sexual activities which undermined His own law, so homosexuality must be the product of a deviant, unnatural and ungodly mind. Consequently, consent to homosexual sex was no defence. By the end of the twelfth century, monarchies in England, France and Spain decreed death as a suitable punishment for those convicted of homosexual acts.

The state of illegality and enforced invisibility effectively lasted for a further 700 years. In the years following the trial, conviction and jailing of Oscar Wilde in 1895, although there was no concerted attempt to force a liberalization of the law in Great Britain, homosexuality became visible at the fringes of artistic society. The repression seemed to have been irretrievably undermined by the world wars in which sexual liberalism spread among the ranks of civilians and the armed forces alike. With the advent of peace in 1945, however, sexual morals were supposed to be restored. The prosecution of gay men rose to new heights. In a climate of political retrenchment, the numbers of men arrested by the police and convicted rose threefold. A series of high-profile cases reached a peak early in 1954 with the conviction of Lord Montagu of Beaulieu, Peter Wildeblood, the diplomatic correspondent of the *Daily Mail* and Michael Pitt-Rivers, a wealthy land-owner, for conspiring to incite two RAF men to 'commit unnatural offences'. The case achieved notoriety, not only because of the social status of the defendants but because the prosecution painted a lurid scene of debauchery in a beach hut on the Beaulieu estate. Regardless of the fact that all the men were consenting adults and the discovery that both Montagu's and Wildeblood's homes were burgled in suspicious circumstances during the course of the trial, the defendants were convicted and sentenced to custody. They found themselves at the centre of a public debate about homosexual rights. A popular limerick of the time ridiculed the law: 'An aircraftsman named McNally/Was caught with a lord in a chalet/The judge said my dears/They're patently queers/Give them two years/For being too pally'.

Pressure built for a reassessment of the law fuelled by the Church of England's Moral Welfare Council immediate publication of *The Problem of Homosexuality: An Interim Report*, which stated that although sex between men was undoubtedly a sin, so too were adultery and fornication, neither of which attracted legal censure. A notable Tory MP, Sir Robert Boothby, lobbied the Home Secretary, Maxwell Fyfe, for a Royal Commission on the matter. Contemporaneously, the Hardwicke Society, a senior debating forum for barristers, carried the motion 'The penal laws relating to homosexual offences are outmoded and should be changed'.

Succumbing to the inevitable, the Home Secretary relented to mounting pressure and established the Departmental Committee on Homosexual Offences and Prostitution under the aegis of John Wolfenden, the Vice-Chancellor of Reading University. This committee sat for the first time on 4 August 1954 and heard evidence from over 200 individuals and groups in the course of more than sixty meetings before publishing its report in September 1957. The committee quickly reached the conclusion that while homosexuality might be morally unacceptable, it could not be stamped out by legislation and continued criminalization was legally untenable since it exposed homosexual men to blackmail and represented an indefensible intrusion into personal privacy. Consequently, Wolfenden's report concluded with the recommendation that homosexual behaviour in private between consenting adults (over twenty-one) should be decriminalized. Wolfenden added that it was not the business of law to 'settle questions of morality, to interfere in the private lives of the citizens; it is only when public decency is offended that the law is entitled to step in and institute criminal proceedings'.

The report received blanket coverage in the press. Seven national newspapers with a combined readership of over 60 per cent of the public gave the report favourable coverage; only two condemned it. However, as Wilde observed of the Labouchere Act, it was not public opinion but politicians' fear for their seats which determines what passes to the statute book. As if to prove the veracity of Wilde's observation that, 'It is not so much public opinion as public officials that need educating,' H. Montgomery Hyde was the first, but not the last, MP to be deselected by his constituency committee in the run-up to the 1959 election for supporting the adoption of Wolfenden's recommendations into law. It was observed, 'We cannot have as our member one who condones unnatural vice.' It took seven parliamentary debates on the Wolfenden Report between 1958 and 1967 before the recommen-dations were adopted into law, and only then by passing initially through the House of Lords where members could vote freely without having to concern themselves with constituency committees.

It would be disingenuous to interpret these historical events as evidence of the forces of reaction carving out a homosexual identity rather than any gay identity emerging through the activities of people themselves. The process of the invention of sexuality *per se*, and of a stigmatized gay identity in particular, is a complex interaction of action and reaction. However, authority has managed successfully to corral sexual acts into an identity which contains implications of ungodliness, unnaturalness and even potentially sedition. These themes reappear in near-contemporary inventions of HIV/AIDS as a 'gay plague', and, recently, the *Sun*'s expressed fears about a gay cabal at the heart of the New Labour government. A result of the politicization of sexuality by the state, the Church and the law has been to harden political activism among those affected by such moralizing and sermonizing. The modern gay rights movement has come to focus its attention on deficits in human rights which can only be addressed by the state. In the penultimate section of this chapter we look at three particular instances of contestation about equality of sexualities which illustrate these contemporary concerns.

Sexuality and Equality: Some Current Issues

With the emergence of HIV in the United Kingdom in the early 1980s gay men were subjected to a backlash of stigmatization. The British Social Attitudes Surveys of 1983, 1985 and 1987 showed a rising disapproval of homosexuality. It was, by 1987, clear to Conservative politicians that initiating legislation targeting gay men and lesbians could garner support from the voting public and serve party political ends. By embarrassing Labour-led local authorities which supported lesbian and gay community organizations, partly founded to meet the need for support because of the spread of HIV/AIDS, the Conservative government could dent support for the Labour Party and warn the gay community. As a result, an amendment, known as Section 28, was attached to the Local Government Act passing through Parliament in 1988 which made it illegal for local authorities 'intentionally [to] promote homosexuality or publish material with the intention of promoting homosexuality', or to 'promote the teaching in any maintained school of the acceptability of homosexuality as a pretended family relationship'. Although the Act was vaguely worded and poorly drafted, the effect was to signal an intention to return to the position prior to 1967 in which gay men and lesbians were not to behave as if their relationships were valid or as if they merited equal rights with heterosexuals. Subsequent gay activism has focused on the repeal of Section 28. It is seen by organizations like Stonewall (lobbying for equal rights for lesbians and gay men) as a bar to effective teaching in schools which denies young gay people an appropriate and protective education and as a menace to equal rights repre-sentation. An attempt by Tony Blair's Labour government to repeal Section 28 in February 2000 failed when it was defeated in the House of Lords.

The age of consent provided another similarly important target for activists. The current debate was initiated in large part by the actions of Chris Morris, at the time a sixteen-year-old student, and Euan Sutherland who took their case for equal treatment under the law on sexual consent (which forbade sex between men under the age of eighteen as opposed to under sixteen for heterosexuals) to the European Court of Human Rights. Earlier that year the Court had handed down a preliminary ruling in favour of Lisa Grant, an employee of South-West Trains who had sought equal access to travel and pension rights for her female partner to those extended to heterosexual employees' partners. While the European Court was clearly keen to support equalization of gay rights and public opinion seemed to be untroubled and even supportive, the British Parliament stalled on the important issue of forcing a Bill through the Lords. At the time of European Court Ruling Chris Hart, the director of the Christian Institute, argued that all ages of consent should be equalized but at a higher rather than a lower age and pointed out that 'homosexual subculture' involved 'drugs and exploitation', and saw the lobby for equal rights as a threat to 'the foundation of family life, which the law should support'. In February 2000 the first stage in the lowering of the age of consent for male homosexual sex was achieved in the House of Commons, and the government indicated that it was prepared to use the Parliament Act to ensure that it passed through the Lords.

The right to engage in consensual group and sado-masochistic sex has also featured in the debates on human rights and sexuality. In December 1990 five men, part of an alleged sixteen-man 'homosexual porn ring', were convicted at the Old Bailey under the 1861 Offences Against the Person Act, for assault and aiding and abetting assault. Their action was to engage together in consensual sado-masochistic sex. The jury found that, regardless of their consent, the activities were injurious to the public good. An appeal heard by Lord Lane in February 1991 upheld the convictions, citing the legal precedent of a man found guilty of assault for caning a woman for the purposes of sexual gratification. A legal precedent seems to have been established in relation to sexual activity which makes it not a matter of private mutual consent but of public political interest.

The trigger to Operation Spanner, the police code-name for the arrest of these men, was the seizure of four home-made videos showing images thought to be so shocking that they were handed to the Obscene Publications Squad (OPS). By drawing the defendants, who thought they were innocent of any sexual crime, into an investigation of the making and passing on of the videos, the OPS effectively secured confessions to the assaults. Press interest was inevitably prurient, trading on public current fears about connections between pornography and paedophilia. While the broadsheets fulminated against the 'illiberal nonsense' of the trial (*The Times*) and saw the judgement as setting 'disturbing precedents' (*Independent*), tabloids like the *Daily Star* crowed, 'Porno Perverts Will Kill Warns Top Cop'. The defendants found themselves the victims of a moral panic feeding on fears of a nation-wide conspiracy among gay men seeking to pervert children into sexual activity.

Operation Spanner not only pointed towards homophobia in the police forces but a continuing prurient interest in patrolling the lawfulness of sexual activities and setting boundaries to expressions of sexuality. The collusion between the press and police in building up images of homosexuality, apparently bizarre sexual practices and paedophilia has contributed to continuing concern about gay men preying on boys, a theme recurrent in the recent Lords debate on equalizing ages of consent.

Common Bonds? Lesbian and Gay Equality, 'Race', Class and Gender

The relationship between the history for the struggle for equality in terms of sexuality and the struggle for equality in terms of 'race', class and gender is, at times, contradictory and conflicting. There is insufficient space to enter into this debate fully here but we will make brief comments on some of the problematic areas. First, the possibilities for representations of sexuality have been challenged at times not only by reactionary self-appointed guardians of morality and the state, but by feminists committed to the anti-pornography and lesbian-feminism movements whose starting point has been the exploitation of female subjects by a 'phallocracy' (Frye, 1981; Rubin, 1993). Feminists have also criticized some male homosexuals for appropriating a stereotypical female gender identity which is bound up with notions of 'effeminacy' at the one end of the spectrum and 'camp' at the other.[2] There have also been criticisms of the black community in Britain and North America (from within those communities) for a perceived, endemic homophobia that is, at times, celebrated publicly in popular cultural representations (Harper, 1991).[3] And, often, the emergence of the homosexual, and of homosexuality leading to an identity choice, is seen as a consequence of a process that began with the rise of capitalism and the formation of the working class. Some commentators have explicitly identified an association between the increasing influence of capitalism and the opening up of possibilities for diverse sexual expression. The historian John D'Emilio has said that:

> gay men and lesbians have not always existed . . . Their emergence is associated with the relations of capitalism; it has been the historical development of capitalism – more specifically the free labour system – that

has allowed large numbers of men and women in the late twentieth century to call themselves gay, to see themselves as part of a community of similar men and women, and to organise politically on the basis of that identity.

(D'Emilio, 1983, p. 468)

D'Emilio argues that it was the changes in the nature and role of the family produced by the free-labour market under capitalism that created the possibilities for diversity of sexual expression and the formation of sexual identities. To oversimplify his argument, he believes that, as the family was no longer 'an independent unit of production' (*ibid.*, p. 469), there was no need to produce many children to labour in this unit. It became possible for individuals to live outside the family unit and to realize erotic lives that did not need to find their expression in reproductive sex. Capitalism allows the possibility for individuals to be economically independent, whereas the former model of family-based units of production made this virtually impossible. However, D'Emilio also recognizes that while capitalism makes this independence a possibility, it also values the family highly as a social structure that can, to some extent, guarantee continuity of production and the maintenance of the status quo. Capitalism, he says, forces individuals into families 'at least long enough to reproduce the next generation of workers' and, simultaneously, into the discourses of heterosexism and homophobia (*ibid.*, p. 474).

But it is not possible to say that these discourses are simply a product of capitalism or that the oppression of dissident sexualties is one of its functions. For example, Marxism itself has been appropriated in such a way as to become implicated in pathologizing sexual behaviour, as Simon Edge has demonstrated in his book *With Friends Like These*. The boast made by groups such as the Socialist Workers Party that Bolshevik Russia abolished anti-homosexual laws is profoundly misleading: all Tsarist laws were abolished shortly after the revolution, effectively legalizing murder (Edge, 1995, pp. 37–9). Later Bolshevik legislation and public health documents of the 1920s pathologized homosexuality and made it subject to 'treatment' in state hospitals (*ibid.*, p. 41). Edge goes on to outline a relationship between homosexuals and revolutionary socialists in the latter half of the twentieth century in which issues of class equality are consistently put above those of equality in terms of sexuality to the extent that violent homophobia is put to one side.[4] The very problem with sexuality for the revolutionary left, according to Edge, is that it makes sexual identity inequality an issue in itself rather than assimilating it into the common struggle against capitalist social class inequalities. The notion of a 'gay "identity" or "community" [becomes] a separatist diversion' (*ibid.*, p. 47) to the 'greater' fight against capitalism.

Edge argues instead for the continued development of an autonomous lesbian and gay community on the political left which is able to fight for equality on its own terms, cutting across other categories of social injustice. In doing so, he is echoing Gayle Rubin, who argued for a 'radical theory' of resistance to the discourses of oppression that was not solely based on feminism:

> Sex is a vector of oppression. The system of sexual oppression cuts across other codes of social inequality, sorting out individuals and groups according to its own intrinsic dynamics. Its is not reducible to, or understandable in terms of, class, race, ethnicity, or gender . . . even the most privileged are not immune to sexual oppression.
>
> (Rubin, 1993, p. 22)

The difficulties with locating and assimilating the struggle for lesbian and gay equality within a wider political struggle for equality, focused on inequalities of distributions of wealth and power, are illustrated by the ongoing debate between Nancy Fraser and Judith Butler in the *New Left Review* (Fraser, 1997, 1998; Butler, 1998).

Both authors seek, in Fraser's words, to 'combine an egalitarian politics of redistribution with an emancipatory politics of recognition' with regard to lesbian and gay equality. Both identify the rise of so-called cultural politics as problematic in that it seems to position some issues, like lesbian and gay equality, as ones of 'cultural misrecognition' rather than the social politics of redistribution. As Fraser has pointed out, the issue of lesbian and gay equality seems to be either primarily about one or the other, dependent on one's point of perception. She argues that this apparent difference obscures the relationship between politics of recognition and redistribution for lesbians and gays.

Fraser is sensitive to the difficulties that might come from appropriating lesbian and gay equality within the redistributive struggle, identifying that the solidarity and power that lesbians and gays can draw from grouping around a culturally differentiated identity is difficult to square with putting aside this differentiation in order to unite with other groups of people in a shared political struggle.

Butler has seen Fraser's position as one which ignores the, to her, obvious links between cultural misrecognition and injustices of distribution. Butler suggests that the politics of distribution can only be understood in terms of the reproduction of gender relationships which build up heterosexual norms about relations between men and women and then attach primacy to the 'family' and feed homophobic prejudices and discrimination.

Some socialist activists seem to have made sense of the difficulties exposed in this debate by making a link between the establishment of political and social equality and an end to the misrecognition of all sexual minorities. Identifying Section 28 of the Local Government Act (see the following chapter for a fuller discussion) and the inequality in ages of consent for heterosexual and homosexual men, as particular targets, Vallee et al. (1992), in a *Militant* publication on gay rights, identify the Thatcherite legal and rhetorical bolstering of the 'family' as a tactic for scape-goating a whole raft of minorities and blaming them for the failings of capitalism.

In this chapter we have illustrated that, in our view, there are inextricable links between struggles for cultural recognition and wider struggles for fairer social and economic distribution. There are concrete manifestations of economic inequality, in terms, for example, of the lack of lesbian and gay rights in the area of access to a deceased partner's pension. And where the struggle seems, at first, to be solely about cultural recognition, we are of the view that it is always potentially about a political and economic freedom too, because invisibility can and does impede equal gay and lesbian participation in social actions and institutions.

Conclusion

At the end of October 1998 Ron Davies, the Secretary of State for Wales, resigned from the cabinet following an 'incident' on Clapham Common in which he was robbed. Media speculation about his sexuality was rife, fuelled by both Mr Davies's defiant denials of any sexual nature to his nocturnal perambulations, and his apparent failure otherwise to account for his actions on that night. The following Thursday, the *Daily Mail* proclaimed in its headline, 'Labour's U-Turn on Gay Ban in Schools', alleging that the government was about to withdraw a Bill repealing Section 28 of the Local Government Act, because of 'fears [of] a public backlash over the Ron Davies affair' The unsubstantiated story not only implied that Section 28 has the direct, statutory power to restrict teaching about homosexuality in schools,[5] but drew Ron Davies's sexuality back into question while protesting that it had no such intent. The story carefully quoted Mr Davies's statement to the House of Commons on his resignation in which he stated, 'we are what we are . . . the product of our genes and experiences'. It now seems unclear whether the government will see through its commitment to repeal Section 28 during the lifetime of this Parliament.

The *Mail*'s speculative coverage stirred up general unease about the connection between public office and private sexuality, implying that government business could be derailed by the activities of an individual Labour MP. The insertion of a byline on putative plans to criminalize sexual relationships between teachers and students under eighteen years old encouraged the readership to make a connection between homosexuality, political corruption, paedophilia and schools.

On page five, the same paper carried the tragic story of a schoolboy, Darren Steele, who allegedly committed suicide as a result of persistent bullying, much of it homophobic. The *Mail* reported that, because of his interest in drama and cookery, Darren had been called 'gay boy' and 'poof' by his peers and been subjected to beatings and burned with cigarettes. He had been reluctant to report the incidents to the school for fear of reprisals. The head of the school, addressing the inquest into the death, explained that although the school had firm anti-bullying policies and further measures were under consideration, Darren had seemed happy and had not reported any problems to his teachers. Darren left a note naming eleven boys responsible for the bullying. Following their arrest and questioning by the police, the Crown Prosecution Service determined that there was insufficient evidence to bring any case against them. Darren is one of countless victims of aggression and violence in schools based on an individual's *perceived* sexuality and this is intensified in the climate created by the symbolic (if not legal) power of Section 28.

In this chapter we have attempted to explore the ways in which homosexuality has been constructed as a negative, subordinate collection of activities and identities in relation to heterosexuality. We have demonstrated how the contemporary invention of sexualities has evolved, in part, through the struggles of the repressed, principally gay men and women, against reaction and social authority which has denied them equal rights with straight men. The story of Darren Steele illustrates the extent to which an embittered and hostile heterosexuality still succeeds in driving to the periphery alternative sexual lifestyles and identities. The message is clear that sexuality represents a cultural field in which the personal and private have been made political. Sexuality has been commodified by the interest of the press and made a legitimate concern of the state. As citizens and subjects, we are all implicated in a struggle to make sexual identities for ourselves, and defend those of others. As teachers, it is inevitable that engagement with young people will mean engagement with the political reality of sexualities. To realize the legitimacy of that engagement is only to reflect an awareness that young people are particularly vulnerable to the play of negative constructions of sexualities. And to begin, we must, as Halperin (1993, p. 426) notes:

> train ourselves to recognise conventions of feeling as well as conventions of behaviour and to interpret the intricate texture of personal life as an artefact, as the determinate outcome, of a complex and arbitrary constellation of cultural processes. We must, in short, be willing to admit that what seem to be our most inward, authentic, and private experiences are actually, in Adrienne Rich's admirable phrase, 'shared, unnecessary/and political'.

Notes

1 The anthropologist Gilbert Herdt offers an interesting comparative study of sexualities in different cultural contexts in *Same Sex, Different Cultures* (Oxford: Westview, 1997).

2 These beliefs are reflected in the journalism of 'popular' feminists such as Julie Burchill in her weekly *Guardian* column.

3 See also the coverage in the black British weekly, *The Voice*, following the footballer Justin Fashanu's coming out as a gay man and also following his suicide in 1998.

4 Edge quotes the SWP writer Mark Brown: 'Homophobia divides working class people. Only the working class can destroy the homophobic capitalist system. There can be no gay liberation without socialism' ('Socialism or Separatism?', *Rouge*, 18, London, 1994; Edge, 1995, p. 11).

5 Section 28 places a restriction on local education authorities. The responsibility for sex education in schools, however, lies with the governing bodies of schools. Section 28's power has been symbolic rather than legally exact.

References

Abelove, H., Barale, M.A. and Halperin, D.M. (eds) (1993) *The Lesbian and Gay Studies Reader*, London: Routledge

Blasius, M. and Phelan, S. (eds) (1997) *We Are Everywhere: A Historical Sourcebook of Gay and Lesbian Politics*, London: Routledge

Boswell, J. (1980) *Christianity, Homosexuality and Social Tolerance*, Chicago: Chicago University Press

Burston, P. (1998) *Queen's Country*, London: Little, Brown

Butler, J. (1998) 'Merely Cultural', *New Left Review*, 227, pp. 33–45

Duncan, R. (1944) 'The Homosexual in Society', *Politics* (August); reprinted in Blasius, M. and Phelan, S. (eds), *We Are Everywhere: A Historical Sourcebook of Gay and Lesbian Politics*, London: Routledge, 1997, pp. 230–3

Edge, S. (1995) *With Friends Like These . . . Marxism and Gay Politics*, London: Cassell

D'Emilio, J. (1983) 'Capitalism and Gay Identity', in Snitow, A., Stansell, C. and Thompson, S. (eds), *Powers of Desire: The Politics of Sexuality*; reprinted in Abelove, H., Barale, M.A. and Halperin, D.M. (eds), *The Lesbian and Gay Studies Reader*, London: Routledge, 1993, pp. 467–78

Dover, K.J. (1978) *Greek Homosexuality*, Cambridge, MA: Harvard University Press

Foucault, M. (1978) *History of Sexuality*, Vol. 1, New York: Pantheon

Foucault, M. (1984) *The Use of Pleasure: Volume Two of The History of Sexuality* (trans. R. Hurley), Harmondsworth: Penguin

Fraser, N. (1997) 'Comment: A Rejoinder to Iris Young', *New Left Review*, 223, pp. 126–9

Fraser, N. (1998) 'Comment: Heterosexism, Misrecognition and Capitalism: A Response to Judith Butler', *New Left Review*, 228, pp. 140–9

Frye, M. (1981) 'Lesbian Feminism and the Gay Rights Movement'; reprinted in Blasius, M. and Phelan, S. (eds), *We Are Everywhere: A Historical Sourcebook of Gay and Lesbian Politics*, London: Routledge, 1997

Gagnon, J. and Simon, W. (1973) *Sexual Conduct: The Social Sources of Human Sexuality*, London: Hutchinson

Halperin, D.M. (1989) 'Is There a History of Sexuality?', *History and Theory* 28, pp. 257–74; reprinted in Abelove, H., Barale, M.A. and Halperin, D.M. (eds), *The Lesbian and Gay Studies Reader*, London: Routledge, 1993, pp. 416–31

Harper, P.B. (1991) 'Eloquence and Epitaph: Black Nationalism and the Homophobic Impulse in Responses to the Death of Max Robinson', *Social Text* 28, pp. 68–86; reprinted in Abelove, H., Barale, M.A. and Halperin, D.M. (eds), *The Lesbian and Gay Studies Reader*, London: Routledge, 1993, pp. 159–75

Herdt, G. (1997) *Same Sex, Different Cultures*, Oxford: Westview

Kinsey, A.C., Pomeroy, W.B. and Martin, C.E. (1948) *Sexual Behavior in the Human Male*, Philadelphia: W.B. Saunders

Kinsey, A.C., Pomeroy, W.B., Martin, C.E. and Gebhard, P.H. (1953) *Sexual Behavior in the Human Female*, Philadelphia: W.B. Saunders

MacKinnon, C. (1989) *Towards a Feminist Theory of the State*, Cambridge, MA: Harvard University Press

Michael, G. (1998) 'Outside', London: Sony Music Entertainment (UK) Ltd/Dick Leahy Music Ltd

Payer, P. (1984) *Sex and the Penitentials*, Toronto: Toronto University Press

Plumb, C. (1968) *Juvenal: The Satires*, London: Panther Books

Richards, J. (1990) *Sex, Dissidence and Damnation: Minority Groups in the Middle Ages*, London: Routledge

Rubin, G.S. (1993) 'Thinking Sex: Notes for a Radical Theory of the Politics of Sexuality'; revised edition reprinted in Abelove, H., Barale, M.A. and Halperin, D.M. (eds), *The Lesbian and Gay Studies Reader*, London: Routledge, 1993, pp. 3–44

Sedgwick, E.K. (1994) *Epistemology of the Closet*, London: Penguin

Simpson, M. (ed.) (1996) *Anti-gay*, London: Freedom Books

Taylor, T. (1997) *The Prehistory of Sex: Four Million Years of Human Sexual Culture*, London: Fourth Estate

Ulrichs, K.H. (1994) *The Riddle of 'Man-manly' Love: The Pioneering Work on Male Homosexuality* (trans. Michael A. Lombardi-Nash), Buffalo, NY: Prometheus Books

Ulrichs, K.H. (1997) *Araxes: Appeal for the Liberation of the Urnings's Nature from Penal Law* (trans. James Steakley); new translation of extract in Blasius, M. and Phelan, S. (eds), *We Are Everywhere: A Historical Sourcebook of Gay and Lesbian Politics*, London: Routledge, 1997

Vallee, M., Redwood, H. and Evenden, M. (1992) *Out, Proud and Militant: The Fight for Lesbian and Gay Rights and the Fight for Socialism*, London: Militant Publications

Wilde, O. (1895) Extract from the trial transcript; reprinted in Blasius, M. and Phelan, S. (eds), *We Are Everywhere: A Historical Sourcebook of Gay and Lesbian Politics*, London: Routledge, 1997, pp. 111–12

6 Difficult Loves

Learning about sexuality and homophobia in schools

Simon Forrest

Introduction

Things that could have made a difference:

- open discussion of homosexuality in class (not discussed as a problem);
- open discussion of the oppression of lesbians and gays;
- role models;
- talks by ex-students;
- plays;
- books;
- teachers standing up for you;
- being taken seriously.

(Young lesbian, reported in Rogers, 1994, p. 64)

To learn about homosexualities would be helpful. What is masturbation on the feminine side? To understand what it is like when going through (and having) sexual intercourse would be information. To explore female genitalia deeper would be interesting. What is a period? IN DETAIL

(Anonymous questions in a 'suggestion box' on sex education
from a boy in Year 9)

Why is it that teaching about sex and sexuality in schools fails to satisfy these young people? What prevents teachers from affirming young gay people's identity? Why do teachers steer clear of the answering questions like those on the boy's list? What is the effect of not dealing with these concerns? What issue of equality is at stake here? This chapter addresses these questions by exploring the phenomenon of homophobia in English secondary schools. The aims are: first, to provide some illustrative accounts of how sexuality is imbricated in teaching, learning and extra-curricula aspects of schooling; second, to give a brief description of the statutory requirements and guidance to schools in relation to young people, sex and sexuality; third, to suggest some practical strategies for dealing with questions and concerns like those raised above; and, fourth, to suggest how tackling homophobia within schools addresses a deficit in equal rights.

Becoming Sexual

Adolescence is associated with particular psychological tensions arising from the need to understand dominant social context, norms and proscriptions about sexuality and to reconcile and integrate these with the development of an independent and unique identity (Moore and Rosenthal, 1993). This intellectual and emotional transition is effected by the sexual maturing of the body and how young people interpret and respond to their sexual feelings and experiences. Becoming success- fully sexual, feeling confident and secure about one's sexual identity, feelings and experiences, is critical in feeling positive about one's whole self.

For both girls and boys, being in step with the physical, emotional, attitudinal and experiential development of their peers, and balancing their development with perceived social and parental expectations, makes an important contribution to their feelings of normalcy and confidence. School represents an important arena for learning about social expectations of sexuality and testing peer norms. The formal aspects of schooling deal very little with sexuality but there are many rituals which project powerful messages about how it ought to be experienced. For example, girls may have difficulty in getting hold of sanitary towels or tampons, find there is no soap or hot water in school toilets or locks on the doors. These experiences send out a message that menstruation, a central biological aspect of female sexual identity, has to be unpleasant and potentially shameful (Prendergast, 1994). The experience of sexuality in adolescence may be particularly difficult for young gay people. Feeling outside the norm, liking people one should not, or harbouring feelings which one thinks will be disapproved of can lead to profound emotional and psychological tensions and feelings of lonely difference. The difficulties young gay men may experience trying to juggle with their feelings about themselves and their expectations of familial reactions to their sexual orientation are well illustrated in Tom's account. He describes the tension he feels between trying to preserve his relationship with his parents while maintaining their love and support and expressing his sexuality.

> I felt I was an embarrassment because I thought I was going to bring shame on them. Just seemed so wrong. Wanting to sleep with other men. That was all based on guilt . . . I thought they would see me as someone completely different once I told them I was gay . . . because my family was so important to me, that was my security . . . You know, I thought, I can't afford to lose that, to break it.
>
> (Cited in Frankum, 1996, p. 32)

Becoming sexual is in part about discovering appropriate and meaningful labels for one's identity, feelings and experiences. A problem encountered by young people is successfully fitting the complexities of their experiences within social proscriptions of sexuality as simple dualities: masculine or feminine, straight or gay. This is evident from the hundreds of letters sent to the problem pages of teenage magazines every week (Forrest, 1997a). Almost invariably the 'problem' pages in these magazines carry letters like the following:

Am I Gay?

I'm 16 and really unsure about my sexuality. My friends have turned their backs on me and I've been spending a lot of time with a new friend. The other day he asked me how I felt about him and whether I wanted to go out with him. He makes a move on me every time I see him and I feel scared but felt good when we kissed. How can I stop these feelings? I know my parents would never approve.

Mark, 16, Exeter

She Had Sex with a Girl

I was at a party when I saw my best friend go upstairs with another girl. A little while later I went upstairs into the room where they were and caught them having sex with each other. I freaked out and ran downstairs. I haven't spoken to her since. Will she always be like this?

Rachel, 15, East Anglia
(both in Forrest, Biddle and Clift, 1997, p. 9)

These young people want simple answers, a neat categorization of themselves, of others, as heterosexual or homosexual. Their sense of uneasiness with their experiences flows from preconceptions that there is something fearful and shameful about homosexuality. Their confusion is increased by the contradiction between the visibility of gay and lesbian cultures outside school and their invisibility in school.

Schools and Sexuality

As Epstein and Johnson (1998) point out, sexuality is deeply imbricated in schooling. Through sports and school uniform, for example, boys and girls find their bodies subject to forms of regulation which seek to confine them within strict stereotypes of gendered sexuality. These stereotypes effectively condemn alternative sexualities as inversions or deviance. Here, the ways in which bodies are educated in sexuality are exemplified by looking at boys' engagement with sport and the ways girls' sexuality is managed and regulated by uniform rules. This section concludes with an example of how boys and girls play with knowledge of their stereotypes through role-playing games.

For boys, sport, particularly football, is a powerful medium for learning about male sexuality. At breaks and lunchtimes school playing fields are usually dominated by groups of boys playing football. These games can be rough, physical contests in which social status off the field can be enhanced by success on it. In observing games of football it is apparent that some of the ritualized encounters between boys are primarily about the body and not the football. Prendergast and Forrest (1998, p. 161), in their work on boys' experiences of school, describe a daily ritual:

> Every lunchtime a group of small boys played football on the school fields. They, like other groups of boys, had their particular patch, their place in the

occupation of the school space. A group of bigger boys often joined in with their game and took pleasure in getting the ball and keeping it from the smaller boys, who were unable to push them off or catch them when they ran away. In the game the big boys slid into tackles on the smaller boys, knocking them over. Some of the smaller boys slid into the big boys in return. The big boys laughed and got up. But sometimes the big boys then tackled the smaller boys with real viciousness, intending to hurt them.

Through these encounters boys are learning that size matters. The bodily capital of the male depends on his size and strength, and display of immunity from physical pain. The big boys indulge their smaller peers, initially knocking them over playfully, showing restraint, saving their bodily capital, but when they have had enough of the smaller boys' playfulness they use their added weight and height to hurt them. The account shows how boys engage with each other in games which are about physical hierarchies in which bigger is better. These rituals and their significance do not grow up spontaneously. They are a product of schooling which celebrates sporting prowess as manly. By pitting bigger boys against smaller boys they endorse cultures of male physicality which demean the masculinity of smaller boys.

The segregation of boys and girls for most sports in schools is also significant in inculcating ideas about gendered sexuality. Girls seem to be kept apart in order to protect them from boys' aggressiveness and from physical harm. This relies on a presumption that the female body is intrinsically more vulnerable than the male body. Not only is this false, but girls, in fact, tend to be bigger and more physically mature than boys throughout their early teenage years. That this presumption is chiefly about sexuality is vividly demonstrated by the recent events surrounding Jane Couch's attempts to obtain a licence to box professionally from the British Boxing Board of Control (BBBC). Her claim to be allowed to box was initially rejected on the grounds that women are more vulnerable to injury of their sexual organs. Couch successfully refuted this claim by pointing out that the uterus is more safely protected in the pelvis than the male sexual organs which sit outside the body. However, the BBBC continued to reject her claims, arguing that she might be susceptible to excess aggressiveness as a result of pre-menstrual tension.

Uniform rules are another vector through which schooling impresses orthodoxies about gendered sexualities on young people. This account, from field notes collected while researching gender in schools, illustrates how a headteacher responds to calls from the school council for girls to be allowed to wear trousers. The headteacher seems not to see that making girls wear skirts makes them constantly sexually vulnerable, placing an onus on them to think about how they sit, stand and play so that boys cannot tease them.

> The Head tells us that the School Council are always complaining about uniform rules. They want girls to have the right to wear trousers instead of skirts. He says he thinks it is rather a trivial point on which the Council

meetings always get bogged down. Last year he suggested to the Council that if it was really a matter of equal rights then they ought to lobby for boys to wear skirts too.

In each of these cases, of boys and football and girls and school uniform, it is important to recognize that while rules affecting sexuality are imposed by schools, the students engage with them as part of a wider discourse about sexuality within the peer group.

A final example illustrates how the regulations about the sexual body are taken on board and played with by young people. In this extract from *P'tang, Yang, Kipperbang* (Rosenthal, 1984, p. 21) young people are shown shearing physical intimacy of its real sexual meaning and inverting the rules of heterosexual engagement. Here, Eunice, rather than truly being the target for the boys' sexual interest, performs as though she is, but is, in fact, making them go through the motions. Her own lack of real interest heightens the comedic sense derived from an inversion of normal heterosexuality.

> A couple of girls are stuffing homework into their satchels and making for the door. They completely ignore the end-of-day routine which is being carried out across the room by the windows.
>
> The routine is this: Eunice stands with her back to the wall, blowing bubble-gum, as the boys, their homework in their satchels, form a queue in front of her. Each boy, in turn, then presses his body against Eunice's for a moment with complete absence of passion, then wanders from the room to go home.
>
> As each boy presses against her, Eunice – automatically and unconvincingly – complains: 'Honestly, you're terrible/You boys really!/A girl just isn't safe!/You're horrible . . . it's every night, the same? I'm disgusted with you, I am truly.'

It is evident that the way the body is treated in school carries strong messages about sexuality. In almost every case, heterosexual gender roles are being imposed or reinforced. While student cultures sometimes contest these rulings, they do so by engaging with and in them. They are playful, sometimes inverting the regulations, but they always acknowledge them as the dominant discourse. The discourse presumes that the body is the seat of sexuality and the body is heterosexual, hence sexuality is heterosexual.

Homophobia in Schools

In 1994 Stonewall (the national organization lobbying for lesbian, gay and bisexual civil rights) undertook a survey of lesbian, gay and bisexual experiences of violence, harassment, verbal abuse and avoidance strategies (Mason and Palmer, 1995). Forty-eight per cent of people under eighteen responding to the survey reported experiencing a violent attack, and 22 per cent had been 'beaten up'. Of the violent attacks, 40 per cent had taken place in school and in half the cases the perpetrators of the attacks had been other students. Forty-four per cent of under-eighteens had been harassed by fellow students and 79 per cent had been called names. A young lesbian described her experiences as follows;

> I was 'outed' at school when I was fourteen by some 'friends' who thought I shouldn't need to hide my sexuality . . . People tried to push me off my bicycle in local parks, I had sandbags thrown at me in one science lesson. Fortunately myself and my partner decided to tell some teachers . . . The group of boys who were doing the bullying were given a warning . . . and did eventually stop. However, the girls in my year who I was not close friends with continued to make remarks about us fancying them, and they acted very strangely (embarrassed) when changing for PE lessons.
>
> (Cited in Mason and Palmer, 1995, p. 61)

Through detailed qualitative research, Rivers (1995, 1996) drew four conclusions about homophobic bullying in school. First, young gay people suffer more verbal than physical homophobic bullying, but the effects are equally pernicious. He lists being given nasty stares and looks, vandalism of personal property and being 'sent to Coventry' among the most common experiences. Second, the main sites for bullying are classrooms, corridors, school yards and playing fields, changing rooms and the journeys to and from school. This means that some unavoidable spaces within school are unsafe. Third, about 30 per cent of respondents reported the bullying to teachers or parents. In only 6 per cent of cases did the bullying stop as a result. Finally, Rivers identified the most frequent perpetrators of bullying as groups of boys, then boys and girls together, followed by groups of girls. In half the cases teachers had colluded with the bullying by making snide remarks or failing to challenge homophobic remarks made in class. Douglas et al. (1998) report findings of a postal survey of teachers in 1,000 secondary schools on homophobic bullying, support of lesbian, gay and bisexual students, HIV/AIDS education and the effects of Section 28. This study showed that 82 per cent of responding teachers were aware of verbal and 26 per cent of physical homophobic bullying among students. The majority of teachers reported between one and six incidents in the last term.

Both the Stonewall survey and Douglas's work illustrate the extent to which homophobic bullying is focused on young gay people, but also affects young people perceived by their peers to be gay and those expressing tolerant views about homosexuality. In Douglas's study a teacher reported incidents of homophobic bullying arising simply because of a close friendship between girls.

> Two of three girls who have a very strong friendship bond between them . . . go round together to the exclusion of other girls . . . the other girls have responded by using the word lesbian as a term to bully these girls . . . they will . . . chase them around the playground shouting at them . . . It started to become a kind of physical manifestation as well as verbal if you like.
>
> (Douglas et al., 1998, p. 19)

These studies indicate some of the characteristics of homophobic bullying in schools. It is principally perpetrated by groups of boys, generally takes the form of verbal abuse and is focused on young people who are 'different' because they have a particularly close friendship with someone of the same sex, support gay rights or are openly gay. While a substantial proportion of teachers are aware of homophobia their responses to it are not perceived by young people as particularly effective. There is, in fact, a marked reluctance to report homophobic bullying and assaults. The Stonewall survey found that only 18 per cent of the young respondents reported violent attacks to the police. It is suggested that it is difficult, particularly for gay men under eighteen, to disclose their sexual orientation in reporting attacks upon them in the light of concerns about implying a breach of the law on age of consent. Research also highlights the profound effects of homophobic bullying. Rivers reports truanting as a strategy to avoid the worst situations in school, but respondents in his study often found it hard to avoid school without facing difficult questions at home. Other young people avoid confrontation by concentrating on academic schoolwork with the hope that success will lead to opportunities to escape to safer, more tolerant learning and working environments. Where these strategies prove insufficient to deflect or make homophobic bullying tolerable, Remafedi (1991) shows that experience can be linked to drug use, self-harm and suicide among young lesbians and gay men.

Roots and Causes

> It's a kind of fear really. I think I as a boy I was scared of gay men. How would I cope with the embarrassment if I was chatted up? Would it mean I was gay? I had never met a gay man – it was a stupid belief. But when you're scared, especially of something you actually know nothing about, hatred is a natural reaction.
>
> (Robert, twenty-five, cited in Forrest, Biddle and Clift, 1997, p. 17)

There is no single simple cause of homophobia. However, research reviewed by Clift (1988) indicates that people who hold negative attitudes towards homosexuality tend to report having no homosexual experiences or feelings, little or no contact with gay people, and are negative about sexual relationships outside marriage. In addition, holding negative attitudes towards homosexuality correlates with having strong religious beliefs which disapprove of sex and/or homosexuality and lower social and educational class. Among young people homophobia is more frequently and aggressively expressed by boys than girls and may be associated with the rigidity of models of masculinity (Forrest, 1997b). Attitudes towards sexuality and homosexuality in particular are also heavily shaped by cultural traditions. A recurrent theme has been the linking of homosexuality with moral deviance and disease which threatens the reproductive health of the individual and of the nation. In his writing for boys in the scouting movement, Baden-Powell extended this analysis to make an explicit connection between heterosexual manliness and the survival of the British race and Empire:

> The temptation has to be fought down . . . remember also that you have done this, not only for your own sake, but because you have duty to the nation, to the race that it is, to beget strong, healthy children in your turn; and to do this you have to keep yourself pure.
>
> (Baden-Powell, 1930, pp. 111–12)

Orthodox gender stereotypes are strongly linked to the development of homophobia. The conflation of sexuality and gender is clear when we consider that boys who show their feelings or who are too intimate with other boys are often called 'girls' or 'poofs' by their peers. Equally, girls who are deemed to be too tomboyish run the risk of being called 'dykes' or 'lesbians'. The threat of victimization associated with failure to conform to gender role stereotypes can make young people show homophobic attitudes. For example, boys can prove their heterosexual maleness by showing a bragging sexual interest in girls and rejecting shows of emotions with other boys and men. Boys, particularly, may feel that any expressions of tender feelings is open to interpretation as a sign of latent homosexuality. In contrast, among girls, close friendships which involve embracing, touching and sharing thoughts and feelings are more legitimate.

Ideological and Political Frameworks of School Sex Education

Prior to the Education (No.2) Act, 1986, there were no specific obligations placed on either local education authorities or schools with regard to sex education. The 1986 Act demanded that school governing bodies determine the school policy on sex education and what place, if any, it should occupy in the secular curriculum. The Education Act of 1993 made it compulsory for maintained schools in England and Wales to provide students with sex education subject to their parents' right to withdraw their child, following the precedent of the Education Act of 1944. In May 1994 the Department for Education issued a circular to maintained schools containing detailed guidance on sex education (DfE, 1994). Latterly, under the Education Act of 1996, the existing law on sex education was subsumed within one statute. Why has there been so much political interest in sex education over the last fifteen years? And what is the thrust of this interest?

The increasing involvement of government during the 1980s in describing the aims, limits and content of school sex education has to be seen in the context of an evolving political interest in bringing under increased control the whole system of maintained education. The restructuring of the financial management of schools under, first, local management and, latterly, grant maintenance, and the imposition of a national curriculum represent the two main mechanisms through which the autonomy of teachers and schools has been brought under the dual authority of central government and parents in the form of school governing bodies. The establishment of the Office for Standards in Education (OFSTED) and the gearing up of the parental right to choose have placed increased pressure on schools to be seen to perform successfully in relation to one another. Added to this, the annual publication of 'league tables' implies the creation of consumer culture in education.

These changes have forced schools to concentrate on populist measures of effectiveness. For example, because it was perceived to appeal to potential parents, schools like to be seen to clamp down hard on unruliness, suspected, real or imagined drug use, to impose rigid uniform rules and generally strive to present an orderly face to the outside world, because this implies firm leadership and firm leadership implies success. Such reactionary educational attitudes are, for the most part, supported by parents, the majority of whose children never need to be disciplined or need the support of a liberal regime. Consequently, the social subjects and social education have slipped to the margins of school life and the periphery of the curriculum. Not only are they not perceived to make a contribution to league-table exam success, but a school which highlights social education may be perceived by parents as needing to act to remedy student misbehaviour or poor socialization. Providing social education, particularly on sex and drugs, can also attract negative press and parental attention, as a series of highly publicized scandals has illustrated. For instance, in 1995, a science teacher in a Jewish state secondary school in the north-west was accused of gross misconduct following complaints from parents for answering questions from fifteen- and sixteen-year-olds about oral sex and masturbation during a science lesson on sexual reproduction. While he maintained his innocence, and was subsequently supported by an industrial tribunal in his claim that he had been trying to deal with questions 'openly and honestly', he has not worked in the school again due to an irrecoverable breakdown in relations with his employers. While portions of the daily press were sympathetic to the teacher's case, the populist broadsheets published damaging implications about his sexuality and his relationship with his students. This case vividly illustrates how a school providing a sex education which meets the needs of the students might stand to lose support in the surrounding community. Consequently, schools may feel nervous about tackling the subject and may adopt repressive positions, providing only the basic facts about sexual behaviour as part of science teaching.

Although successive Conservative administrations during the 1980s and 1990s focused on driving up academic standards in schools, there was a parallel, connected effort to regulate and control young people's sexual behaviour. *The Health of the Nation* (Department of Health (DoH), 1992) laid out the government's national health strategy. Within the area identified as 'Sexual Health' a target was set for the 50 per cent reduction of the rate of pregnancies in girls under sixteen years old. This amounted to reducing the rate from 9.5 per 1,000 in girls aged thirteen to fifteen in 1989, the highest rate in Western Europe, to no more than 4.8 per 1,000 in 2000.

For Conservative administrations the aim of reducing teenage conceptions represented the climax of long-running political debates about sexual behaviour and parenthood among young people. The driving concern was welfare spending associated with single parenthood. In a series of highly publicized speeches, a succession of Conservative government ministers characterized absent fathers as irresponsible for failing to provide for the maintenance of their female partners and children, and young single mothers as feckless scroungers who got pregnant in order to jump housing queues and whose intention was to live off benefits (for example, see *Independent on Sunday*, 10 October 1993). This moralistic ideological thrust found specific form and definition in the Thatcherite rallying call to the post-1987 election Conservative Party conference for a return to 'family values'. The sexual behaviour of young people was characterized as a threat to traditional moral values and their attitude towards state benefits and welfare was cited as evidence of the decline. Schools were positioned as front-line agents in attempts to roll back the creeping moral decline. These assumptions about young people, their sexual behaviour and schools played a significant part in shaping the legislation and guidance to schools on sex education.

However, right-wing moralism with regard to teenage pregnancy was tempered by realism demanded by the discovery of significant and rising numbers of infections of people with HIV, the virus which leads to AIDS, in the United Kingdom in the early 1980s. A major effect of the spread of HIV infection was to gear up public concern and awareness of the diversity of sexual behaviour and of the risks associated with it. The importance of school-based sex education about HIV and safer sex as part of the prevention strategy is well known (Wight, 1993). However, moralistic approaches to sex education are not congruent with effective educational interventions in HIV/AIDS prevention. Moralistic approaches cannot accommodate, for example, the need to challenge the stigmatization of gay men, which contributes to their vulnerability to infection, since any tacit acceptance of homosexuality undermines the prescriptions of sexuality involved in promoting a narrow heterosexual preconception of 'family values'.

Political debate about the specific form the legislation and guidance to schools on sex education should take was heated. Not only were aspects of the content contested but there were specific concerns about how the right of parents to withdraw their children could be legally balanced with the interests and wishes of the child. Similarly, teachers' positions in relation to giving contraceptive advice to young people was problematic with respect to the rights of children, particularly those over sixteen, to demand confidential advice from other sources, particularly doctors (Harris, 1996). The 1996 Act represents an uneasy compromise on these points.

The Act makes it a legal requirement that all maintained, county, voluntary, maintained special and grant-maintained schools in England and Wales provide sex education. The government states its belief that 'All pupils should be offered the opportunity of receiving a comprehensive, well-planned programme of sex education during their school careers' (DfE, 1994, p. 3). The Act provides that sex education should be defined as including education about HIV and AIDS and other sexually transmitted diseases but stated, 'the law does not however define what else is included in sex education' (*ibid.*, Annex A). However, teachers are advised to look for advice and guidance on structure and content to be found in *National Curriculum Council Guidance 5 – Health Education* (NCC, 1990). The compulsory provision, under the standing orders for science, and the minimum basic education to be provided to all pupils is as follows:

By the end of the primary school years pupils should have been taught basic facts about living things and, specifically, to be able to name the main external parts [of humans], for example the hand, elbow and knee of the human body; that humans can produce babies and these babies grow into children and then into adults; and to recognise similarities and difference between themselves and other pupils.

By the end of Key Stage Three of the National Curriculum, at the age of 14 years old, pupils should be taught the ways in which some cells including sperm and ova are adapted to their functions; about the physical and emotional changes which take place during adolescence; the human reproductive system, including the menstrual cycle and fertilisation; how the foetus develops in the uterus, including the role of the placenta; that bacteria and viruses can affect health. By the end of Key Stage Four, at the age of 16, pupils should be taught about chromosomes and genes, hormonal control, including sex hormones; the medical use of some hormones, including the control and promotion of fertility; that sexual reproduction is the source of genetic variation and how gender is determined in humans.

The Act also provides information on implementing sex education policy and programmes in schools, referring specifically to the provision of information to parents, their right to withdraw their children, advice to individual pupils on sexual matters, and teacher training (DfE, 1994, pp. 35, 36, 38, 43). The Act provides that information about the school's provision and programme of sex education should be included in the prospectus to parents and an up-to-date policy should be freely available on request. This information should make it clear that parents have the right to withdraw their children from any or all parts of the programme other than those elements which are required by the National Curriculum Science Order. Parents do not have to give their reasons for their decision to withdraw their children or to indicate what, if any, other arrangements they intend to make for providing sex education to their child. The Act acknowledges that if a child sought to contest the decision of their parents to withdraw them from sex education resolution would ultimately have to be sought in the courts. With regard to advice to individual pupils, the Act stresses the distinction between general education about sexual matters and counselling and advice to individual pupils, particularly if this relates to their own sexual behaviour. The Act emphasizes that it is inappropriate for teachers to provide contraceptive advice to pupils under sixteen years of age, although, again, the legal position remains to be tested in the courts. The Act advises teachers to refer pupils seeking contraceptive advice, in the first instance, to their parents and/or a doctor. If a teacher judges that a pupil has embarked on, or is likely to embark on, a course of action which places them at moral or physical risk or is in breach of the law, they should inform the pupil and notify the school's headteacher. In relation to teacher training, the guidance issued in 1994 advised schools to review the in-service training needs of teachers with a primary responsibility for providing sex education and to make use of Grants for Education Support and Training (GEST) for basic curriculum training.

The current guidance stresses a moral framework for sex education. This was defined by the Secretary of State in 1994, John Patten, who insisted that sex education should be provided with balanced and objective information within a framework of values which 'encourage [pupils] to appreciate the value of stable family life, marriage and the responsibilities of parenthood'. This framework was seen to be congruent with wider aims laid out in the Education Act of 1993, to 'promote the spiritual, moral, cultural, mental and physical development of pupils at the school and of society; and . . . prepares such pupils for the opportunities, responsibilities and experiences of adult life'.

The New Labour government maintained the focus of the previous administration on reducing teenage conceptions and centrally dictating the curriculum. However, it remains to be seen what, if any, revisions of policy and guidance will pass on to the statute book as a result of wide-ranging reviews of the pastoral curriculum by the Advisory Group on Personal, Social and Health Education, set up to develop work on the so-called 'fourth R' of relationships education, and the work of the Department of Health-sponsored Health Schools Initiative and the Public Health Strategy laid out in *Our Healthier Nation* (DoH, 1998). However, the fiscal concerns of government with welfare spending, evident from the extension of the 'New Deal' on job creation to single parents, are evidently the same for the current adminis-tration as the preceding Conservative ones.

Despite the extent of political interest in school-based sex education, provision may still be patchy and inconsistent. Teachers may feel under-trained and under-resourced and lack confidence and conviction about the utility of addressing gender, sexuality, relationships and emotional and attitudinal aspects of sex education which lie outside the National Curriculum Orders for Science. A combination of these doubts and concerns and the weak structural position occupied by sex education provision outside the National Curriculum in English and Welsh Schools seem to be chief culprits.

Sex education provision which lies outside the National Curriculum Orders for Science usually occupies timetable space designated for Personal, Health and Social Education (PHSE). This involves an aggregation of social subjects within which sex education may be more or less marginal depending on the prejudices and interests of individual teachers, school management and governance, trends in public concerns and the support of outside agencies like the local police and health services. A good example of the imbalance that can occur is the priority given to drug education in recent years as a result of political, police and health service interest in drug-related crime and health problems. Additionally, PHSE is non-examinable and may be comparatively unimportant to teachers focused on subject specialisms taught towards public examination. PHSE may also be organized in a variety of ways which disperse responsibility and accountability for its provision. The role of PHSE co-ordination in schools often brings with it no budget, and added with the low status of the subject may not seem to have equally high status as other co-ordinating roles. Teachers' confidence to teach PHSE may be undermined because teaching strategies in published resources tend to recommend a partici-pative, child-centred approach to learning which is currently out of favour with educational orthodoxies. The marginal nature of PHSE, the sensitivity of the subjects, and the lack of interest of teachers may all conspire with students' sometimes volatile reactions in the classroom to deter teachers from starting or continuing to provide social education. The tendency of boys in particular to exploit their own and the teacher's embarrassment by misbehaving during sex education within PHSE is well documented (see, for example, Measor et al., 1996). Although sex education has been important to political debates about young people's sexuality, morality and health for over a decade, it occupies a very weak position in the school curriculum. It is difficult not to agree with Stears et al. (1995, pp. 181–2), who described the position of the social subjects within school in the light of a threefold strategy driven by right-wing ideology as

> censoring a critical social perspective within National Curriculum core and foundation subjects . . . by excluding social subjects from the National Curriculum and . . . by garrisoning social subjects into a variety of cross-curricular themes which suggests they lack the credibility of 'real' subjects within the curriculum proper.

Sex education strategies may collude with heterosexual presumptions about sex, and hence stigmatize non-heterosexual sex, by focusing on a definition of sex as reproductive behaviour. The dominant imagery of heterosexual vaginal intercourse interacts with ideals about masculinity and femininity to inform and reinforce homophobia in a potentially pernicious way. Male sexuality is characterized as thrusting, active, urgent and penetrating; female, conversely, as passive, receptive and penetrated. As a result young people can reach the conclusion that same-sex sexual relationships must be pseudo-heterosexual and involve penetration and the partners in roles which mimic heterosexual gender roles. Hence the stereotyping of gay men as effeminate and lesbian women as butch.

The centrality of the vagina and penis as penetrated and penetrating sexual organs effectively delegitimizes some sexual acts. As Jewitt (1996) has pointed out, some sex education material describing human sexual organs fails to label the anus at all, thus making anal sex invisible. An effect of the conflation of sexual acts with heterosexual gender and sex roles is that gender role behaviour is used by young people both to explain and understand sexuality. So male effeminacy can be taken to imply homosexuality. Not only behaviour but the body itself can become suspect. For example, bigger, heavier girls, who do not conform to masculine stereotypes of feminine body shape, can often find themselves labelled lesbian. Finally, since same-sex sexual activity is characterized as a substitute for heterosexual sexual behaviour, it is often portrayed as though it were an arrested sexual development, an immature or displaced heterosexuality. This may lie at the root of preconceptions that gay men and lesbian women are failed heterosexuals who have either never had proper heterosexual sex or else were turned away by bad heterosexual experiences.

In summary, the recent history of sex education in maintained schools in England and Wales is dominated by political and ideological reaction which has stifled teaching. The tendency within schools has been to retrench in the security of provision which is least likely to attract media or parental opprobrium and avoids any potentially contentious issues. The tendency towards a lowest common denominator of providing 'hard' facts about human reproduction seasoned with stern warnings about the moral risks of teenage sexual behaviour has relegated dealing with sexuality critically, as a political and social phenomenon, to the educational sidelines. At the centre of policy and provision lie heterosexual reproduction and the reproduction of heterosexuality, and sexual diversity, feelings and pleasures are at the edge.

Section 28

Section 28 of the (1988) Local Government Act has played a major part in deterring schools from developing a critical perspective on sexuality. Section 28 is briefly referred to within statutory guidance on sex education, where it is stated that

> section 28 . . . prohibits local authorities from intentionally promoting homo-sexuality . . . and from promoting the teaching in any maintained school of the acceptability of homosexuality as a pretended family relationship. This prohibition applies to the activities of local authorities themselves, as distinct from the activities of the governing bodies and staff of school on their own behalf.
>
> (DfE 1994, Annex A)

Section 28 states that a local authority shall not:

(1) intentionally promote homosexuality or publish material with the intention of promoting homosexuality; promote the teaching in any maintained school of the acceptability of homosexuality as a pretended family relationship.
(2) Nothing in subsection (1) above shall be taken to prohibit the doing of anything for the purpose of treating or preventing the spread of disease.

Although schools are explicitly excluded from the provisions of the Act, the effect has been to prevent teaching about homosexuality. This mistaken belief in the scope of the Act is no doubt a result of the context in which it was drawn up and passed on to the statute book. Conservative governments throughout the 1980s made plain their hostility to homosexuality. Whipped by popular press misinformation about HIV and AIDS, public attitudes towards homosexuality hardened throughout the period (Jivani, 1997). Clearly, governmental action against gay men and lesbians would not be greeted by hostility by the public at large and could be used as a party political weapon targeted at Labour-led local government. Many Labour-led local authorities had sought to protect gay men and lesbians from discrimination in the light of hostility stirred up by HIV scares and extended funding to support organizations. By attacking the 'promotion' of homosexuality by these local authorities the Conservative government achieved the dual purpose of warning off the emerging gay community and embarrassing the opposition, which believed that local support of gay causes was not popular with their voting base. The public politicization of sexuality also effectively deterred schools from addressing sexuality and lesbian, gay and bisexual issues. Moreover, in the section of the *Handbook* for OFSTED Inspectors of Schools the Act was misrepresented through a statement to the effect that 'promoting homosexuality through resources or teaching is prohibited' (OFSTED, 1992, p. 13).

However, the exclusion of teaching and discussion about homosexuality from school sex education is becoming increasingly contentious. An increasing number of young gay people report dissatisfaction with the sex education they have received in school.

> I was waiting to hear something about homosexuality, safe sex and different things in sex education. Maybe some information that could help me. But I got nothing. There was nothing.

> It was a gay plague, or it was drug addicts, so naturally they assume that healthy young boys don't grow up to sleep with other men and are very unlikely to use drugs at a Catholic school, so they just didn't tell us anything about it.
> (Tim and Spencer, respectively, cited in Frankum, 1996, p. 23)

The vocalizing of young gay people can be coupled with powerful dissenting voices from legal and health professionals and political lobbyists. As Bibbings (1996) points out, the current position with regard to school sex education may breach the legal rights of young lesbian, gay and bisexual people who are not receiving provision which promotes their well-being in line with the demands of the National Curriculum. In addition, the denial of equal rights may breach the United Nations Convention on Rights of the Child. No less an authority than the British Medical Association (BMA, 1997) has recently pointed out that the failure of current provision to address the needs of young gay men and women may contribute to their vulnerability to health problems. The BMA's recommendations on sex education state,

> Responsible teaching about homosexuality is especially important to meet the needs of young people who may be growing up gay, lesbian or bisexual in view of the risks of mental and physical health problems to which they may be exposed as result of social isolation, bullying and lack of self-esteem, and to educate all young people about the effects of prejudice and stereotyping.
> (BMA, 1997, p. 5)

Clearly, a basically heterosexual and heterosexist sex education is not likely to meet the aims of health strategies seeking to reduce the incidence of HIV infection. It is hard to see how a situation in which young people may get little or no education about HIV and AIDS can be squared with the DoH strategy on HIV and AIDS health promotion which identifies personal, social and health education (including sex education) in school as a key element in HIV prevention and general sexual health (DoH, 1996). The increasing understanding of the importance of equalizing the access of young gay people to sex education on the ground of both health and human rights is well illustrated by the synthesis expressed in the Terrence Higgins Trust report on evidence-based HIV prevention (THT, 1998) which has identified the achievement of equality in school as a key element in HIV prevention. This report subsumed the Stonewall Agenda 2000 for Equality (Mason and Watson, 1997) within it, stating the aim of achieving 'Equal recognition for young lesbians, gays and bisexuals in our schools, an end to homophobic bullying and repeal of Section 28' as one of five key targets for the organization.

Addressing Sexuality in School

It has been said that sexuality is 'everywhere and nowhere' in school (Redman, 1994, p. 1997). This combination of pervasiveness and elusiveness may seem, initially, a deterrent to teachers looking for somewhere to start addressing issues like homophobia and heterosexism. Teachers' priority will, rightly, always fall on what can be done directly in relation to young people. However, in addressing sexuality it may be better to begin at the level of staff training and policy-making. A first step is to achieve some agreement on the need and motives for raising awareness of sexuality within the school. These might include any of the following:

- Young people have a right to accurate information about sexuality. Since sexualities are diverse and not limited to concerns about disease or reproduction, sex education which does not address the diversity of sexualities is not accurate.
- Students frequently discuss and play about sexuality among themselves. To exclude it from the formal curriculum is to collude with the inevitable perpetuation of misinformation which may cause some young people anxiety.
- Attempts to tackle bullying which exclude explicit reference to challenging homophobia and sexism are unlikely to succeed.
- Partly as a result of homophobic bullying, lesbian, gay and bisexual young people need extra support in school.
- The wider school community, including some parents and governors, may welcome attempts on the part of a school to alter sexist and homophobic attitudes among young people.
- The stigmatization of young gay men and the exclusion of relevant information about safer sex from school sex education increases their vulnerability to HIV infection and may also decrease young heterosexual people's awareness of their vulnerability to sexually transmitted infections, including HIV.

A positive step is to assess these motives in relation to existing policy in a relevant area: for example, considering whether anti-bullying policy contains a sufficiently explicit commitment to challenging homophobic remarks; also, whether the way homophobic bullying is dealt with is likely to encourage disclosures from other victims. Within sex education and elsewhere in the curriculum opportunities exist for opening up sexuality for discussion. Teachers can establish sufficiently safe classroom environments for discussion of gender or attitudes towards sexuality in the course of drama, English and history lessons. Harris (1990) provides a detailed guide to suitable resources available to the English teacher. Accounts are readily to hand in the works of Jeanette Winterson (1985) and extracts from *The Diary of Anne Frank* (Frank, 1997) and among collections of gay and lesbian stories and histories (Jivani, 1997). Leaflets which contain accounts of the experiences of young gay men are available from such organizations as the AIDS Education and Research Trust (AVERT) and the Terrence Higgins Trust (THT).

A useful activity for staff may be to collect a selection of leaflets from local and national lesbian, gay and bisexual help and advice services and to use them as prompts to discussion about what information should be made available to students on noticeboards in the school. These same materials can be used by students, along with other service information, within a sex education lesson in order to make a poster or flyer detailing local agencies available to young people. Most materials of this kind are available free in small quantities from the relevant agencies.

Sexuality, Education and Equality

The previous chapter described the 'invention' of sexuality and showed how there has been a movement towards depathologizing and politicizing homosexuality in recent years. Sexual practices have become to a lessser extent the domain of the medical and legal establishment as people have demanded the right to their own sexual identity and to engage in whatever sexual practices they choose. The tendency to liberalization has not, however, been uncontested. Reactionary political and moral forces have sought to champion institutions like 'the family', and establish a strong link between homosexuality and disease, and homosexuality and moral decline. However, the increasing visibility of lesbian and gay people, and the 'outing' of historical figures, makes these positions untenable.

Within education, however, as a result of the combined pressures to scale down social education (seen by the political right as a transgression on personal freedom and the role of the family), to avoid offending parents and making the school vulnerable in the educational market-place and prurient media interest in sex education, the conservative tendency has not been reversed. A gulf has opened between young people's experience of the wider world, in which sexuality is seen as more fluid and pleasure-orientated, and schooling, where it remains fixed to traditional gender-role stereotypes and focused on policing reproductive sex. Currently, young people are being denied a right to an education which equips them for adult life (in transgression of the law). For young gay people, their enforced invisibility and the denial of equal access to basic relevant sex education is a breach of a human right. The prospect of the equalization of the ages of sexual consent and repeal of Section 28 is welcome, but until schools take up the issues in the classroom, changes in the law are unlikely to have any impact on knowledge or attitudes.

Acknowledgments

Thanks are due to AVERT for funding the Talking about Homosexuality in Secondary Schools Project, on which this chapter draws. Also, thanks to Stonewall for the opportunity to make a presentation on the ideas in this chapter at the Equality 2000 conference, 1998, on which this chapter draws.

References

Act of Parliament (1986) *1986 Education (No.2) Act*, London: HMSO
Act of Parliament (1988) *Local Government Act 1988*, London: HMSO
Act of Parliament (1993) *1993 Education Act*, London: HMSO
Act of Parliament (1996) *Education Act 1996*, London: HMSO
Baden-Powell, R.S.S. (1930) *Rovering to Success: A Book of Life-sport for Young Men* (fifteenth edition), London: Herbert Jenkins Ltd
Bibbings, L. (1996) 'Gender, Sexuality and Sex Education', in Harris N. (ed.), *Children, Sex Education and the Law*, London: National Children's Bureau
British Medical Association (1997) *School Sex Education: Good Practice and Policy*, London: BMA Board of Science of Technology
Clift, S.M. (1988) 'Lesbian and Gay Issues in Education: A Study of First Year Students in a College of Higher Education', *British Educational Research*, 14 (1), pp. 31–50
Department for Education (1994) *Education Act 1993: Sex Education in Schools. Circular 5/94*, London: HMSO
Department of Health (1992) *The Health of the Nation – A Strategy for Health in England*, London: HMSO
Department of Health (1996) *HIV and AIDS Health Promotion: An Evolving Strategy*, London: HMSO
Department of Health (1998) *Our Healthier Nation: A Contract for Health*, London: HMSO
Douglas, N., Warwick, I., Kemp, S. and Whitty, G. (1998) *Playing it Safe: Responses of Secondary School Teachers to Lesbian, Gay and Bisexual Pupils, Bullying, HIV and AIDS Education and Section 28*, London: Health and Education Research Unit, University of London
Epstein, D. and Johnson, R. (1998) *Schooling Sexualities*, Buckingham: Open University Press
Forrest, S. (1997a) 'Confessions of a Middle Shelf Shopper', *The Journal of Contemporary Health*, 5, pp. 10–14
Forrest, S. (1997b) 'Talking about Homosexuality in Secondary Schools: What Happens with Boys', *Working with Men*, pp. 4–7
Forrest, S., Biddle, G. and Clift, S. (1997) *Talking about Homosexuality in the Secondary School*, Horsham: AVERT
Frank, A. (1997) *The Diary of a Young Girl: The Definitive Edition* (trans. O. Frank and M. Pressler), London: Penguin
Frankum, J. (1996) *Young Gay Men and HIV Infection*, Horsham: AVERT
Harris, N. (ed.) (1996) *Children, Sex Education and the Law*, London: National Children's Bureau
Harris, S. (1990) *Lesbian and Gay Issues in the English Classroom*, Milton Keynes: Open University Press

Jewitt, C. (1996) *Forum Factsheet 11: Supporting the Needs of Boys and Young Men in Sex and Relationships Education*, London: Sex Education Forum

Jivani, A. (1997) *It's Not Unusual: A History of Lesbian and Gay Britain in the Twentieth Century*, London: Micheal O'Mara Books

Mason, A. and Palmer, A. (1995) *Queerbashing: A National Survey of Hate Crimes against Lesbians and Gay Men*, London: Stonewall

Mason, A. and Watson, M. (1997) *Equality 2000*, London: Stonewall

Measor, L., Coralie, T. and Fry, K. (1996) 'Gender and Sex Education: A Study of Adolescent Responses', *Gender and Education*, 8 (3), pp. 275–88

Moore, S. and Rosenthal, D. (1993) *Sexuality in Adolescence*, London: Routledge

National Curriculum Council (1990) *Curriculum Guidance 5: Health Education*, York: The National Curriculum Council

OFSTED (1992) *The Handbook for Inspection of Schools*, London: Office for Standards in Education

Prendergast, S. (1994) *This Is the Time to Grow up: Girls' Experiences of Menstruation in School*, Family Planning Association

Prendergast, S. and Forrest, S. (1998) '"Shorties, low-lifers, hardnuts and kings": Boys, emotions and embodiment in school', in Bendelow, G. and Williams, S. (eds), *Emotions in Social Life: Criticial Themes and Contemporary Issues*, London: Routledge

Redman, P. (1994) 'Shifting Ground: Rethinking Sexuality Education', in Epstein, D. (ed.), *Challenging Lesbian and Gay Inequalities in Education*, Buckingham: Open University Press

Redman, P. and Mac an Ghaill, M. (1997) 'Educating Peter: The Making of a History Man', in Steinberg, D.L., Epstein, D. and Johnson, R. (eds), *Border Patrols: Policing the Boundaries of Heterosexuality*, London: Cassell

Remafedi, G. (1991) 'Risk Factors for Attempted Suicide in Gay and Bisexual Youth', *Paediatrics*, 87, pp. 869–75

Rivers, I. (1995) 'The Victimisation of Gay Teenagers in Schools: Homophobia in Education', *Pastoral Care*, 3, pp. 35–41

Rivers, I. (1996) 'Young Gay and Bullied', *Young People Now*, 18–19 January 1996

Rogers, M. (1994) 'Growing up Lesbian: The Role of the School', in Epstein, D. (ed.), *Challenging Lesbian and Gay Inequalities in Education*, Buckingham: Open University Press

Rosenthal, J. (1984) *P'tang, Yang, Kipperbang and Other TV Plays*, Harlow: Longman

Stears, D., Clift, S. and Blackman, S. (1995) 'Health, Sex and Drugs Education: Rhetoric and Reality', in Ahier, J. and Ross, A. (eds), *The Social Subjects within the Curriculum: Children's Social Learning within the National Curriculum*, London: Falmer Press

Terrence Higgins Trust (1998) *An Ethics, Theory and Evidence Based Health Promotion Strategy to Reduce the Incidence of HIV Infection through Sex between Men in England*, London: Terrence Higgins Trust

Wight, D. (1993) 'A Reassessment of Health Education on HIV/AIDS for Young Heterosexuals', *Health Education Research*, 8 (4), pp. 473–83

Winterson, J. (1985) *Oranges Are Not the Only Fruit*, London: Pandora Press

7 Disability Discrimination, the Final Frontier

Disablement, history and liberation

Richard Rieser

Introduction

At least 10 per cent of the world's people have a significant, long-term, physical or mental impairment which can and usually does disable them from taking part in the usual educational, social and economic activity in their community. This is due to barriers in attitudes, in the built environment and in the way society is organized, which prevent us from participating on an equal level with others. The reason why most of these barriers exist is because societies have until very recently not recognized that the systematic way in which they discriminate against disabled people, when backed by discriminatory laws and practices of the state, often amounts to oppression. Barnes (1991) gives a full account of the discrimination disabled people encounter in all areas of life. This oppression has developed from our history, from myths and beliefs that attribute characteristics to disabled people which are unrelated to the reality of disabled people's lives. Such collections of attitudes often determine how non-disabled people respond to the 'different' in their midst; how they form stereotypes of the disabled person as saint, sinner, super-hero, freak, fiend, victim, obsessive avenger, isolationist, the butt of jokes, just a burden, or someone to be pitied. The particular form of stereotyped thinking depends on the society's history, its explanation of how it has come to be and the resultant culture.

The dimensions of inequality to do with gender, sexual orientation, 'race' and class all interact with disablement to create additional oppressions for those with one or more of these oppressions. However, until very recently, the arguments for disability equality have often been ignored in the development of thinking about equal opportunities. In this chapter, therefore, I will begin by looking at how disablement is defined and modelled. I will then look at the extent of disability, world-wide and in the UK. Next, I will give a brief history of disablement, including the growth of the Disabled People's Movement and our struggle for civil rights. I will conclude with an examination of stereotypes in the media – images that are continually recycled to maintain prejudice – and at what is being done to counter this.

Two Ways of Viewing Disablement: The 'Medical Model' and the 'Social Model'

The 'Medical Model' of Disability

The 'medical model' sees the disabled person as the problem. We are to be adapted to fit into the world as it is. If this is not possible, then we are shut away in some specialized institution or isolated at home, where only our most basic needs are met. The emphasis is on dependence, backed up by the stereotypes of disability that call forth pity, fear and patronizing attitudes. Rather than on the needs of the person, the focus is usually on the impairment. With the medical and associated professions' discourse of cures, normalization and science, the power to change us lies within them. Often our lives are handed over to them.

Other people's (usually non-disabled professionals') assessments of us are used to determine where we go to school; what support we get; what type of education; where we live; whether or not we can work and what type of work we can do; and indeed whether we are even born at all, or are allowed to procreate. Similar control is exercised over us by the design of the built environment, presenting us with many barriers, thereby making it difficult or impossible for our needs to be met and curtailing our life chances. Whether it is in work, school, leisure and entertainment facilities, transport, training and higher education, housing or in personal, family and social life, practices and attitudes disable us.

Powerful and pervasive views of us are reinforced in language, and in the media, books, films, comics and art. Many disabled people internalize negative views of ourselves which create feelings of low self-esteem and achievement, further reinforcing non-disabled people's assessment of our worth. The 'medical model' view of us creates a cycle of dependency and exclusion which is difficult to break.

'Medical model' thinking about us predominates in schools where special educational needs are thought of as emanating from the individual who is seen as different, faulty and needing to be assessed and made as normal as possible (see Figure 7.1).

The 'Social Model' of Disability

If, instead of focusing on differentness within the individual, the focus were on, for example, all children's right to belong and to be valued in their local school, then we would be asking 'what is wrong' with the school and looking at the strengths of the child. This second approach is based on the 'social model' of disability. This model views the barriers that prevent disabled people from participating in any situation as being what disables them. The social model makes a fundamental distinction between impairment and disability. *Impairment* is defined as 'the loss or limitation of physical, mental or sensory function on a long-term, or permanent basis', whereas *disability* is 'the loss or limitation of opportunities to take part in the normal life of the community on an equal level with others due to physical and social barriers' (Disabled People's International, 1981, in Dreiger, 1989).

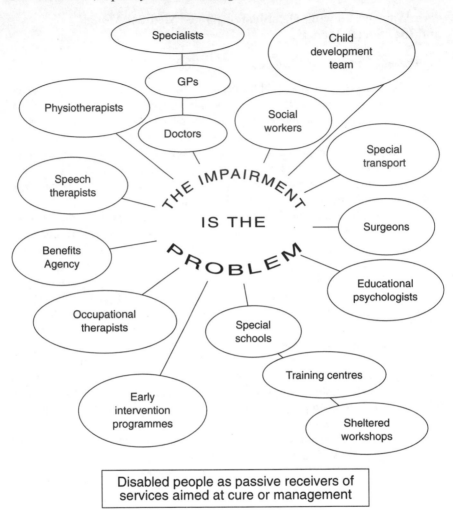

Specialists

Child
development
team

GPs

Physiotherapists

Social
workers

Doctors

Special
transport

Speech
therapists

THE IMPAIRMENT

IS THE

Surgeons

Benefits
Agency

PROBLEM

Educational
psychologists

Occupational
therapists

Special
schools

Training centres

Early
intervention
programmes

Sheltered
workshops

Disabled people as passive receivers of
services aimed at cure or management

Figure 7.1 The medical model

The Disability Movement, which consists of organizations controlled by disabled people, comprises those disabled people and their supporters who understand that they are, regardless of their particular impairment, subjected to a common oppression by the non-disabled world. We are of the view that the position of disabled people and the discrimination against us are socially created. This has little to do with our impairments. As disabled people, we are often made to feel that it is our own fault that we are different. The difference is that some part, or parts, of our bodies or minds are limited in their functioning. This is an impairment. This does not make us any less human. But most people have not been brought up to accept us as we are. Through fear, ignorance and prejudice, barriers and discriminatory practices develop which disable us. This understanding of the process of disablement allows disabled people to feel good about ourselves and empowers us to fight for our human rights (Oliver, 1990; Mason and Rieser, 1994).[1]

I will illustrate the two models of disability, with reference to my own history. I had polio in 1949 which led to the loss of muscle in my left leg, right arm and back. My impairment by the time I was six years old was not major – I could walk, swim, ride a bicycle and so on – but I walked with a limp. However, when I expressed the desire to attend the local primary school, which was all built on one level, the headteacher refused to have me, claiming that I was a fire risk. I was accordingly sent to a school for 'the physically handicapped'. This was my first experience of disablement. The school smelled like a hospital and I did not want to go there. So my parents kept me off school until the London County Council (LCC) agreed to pay for me to attend a private 'progressive' school which was not very good. There I was diagnosed as having 'learning difficulties' and 'behaviour problems'. Seven years later, I chose to leave and went to the local secondary modern, a year below my age group. Again I was disabled by not being allowed to use the lift in the six-storey building, by being bullied and being made to feel bad about myself in PE. Despite this, I did get the necessary O and A levels to enter university, though at some considerable cost to my self-esteem. In all these situations people were disabling me by presenting barriers to my equal participation (see Figure 7.2).

The Disabled People's Movement

The Disabled People's Movement represents the view that the 'cure' to the problem of disability lies in the restructuring of society. Unlike medically based 'cures', which focus on the individual and their impairment, this is an achievable goal and to the benefit of everyone. This approach, referred to as the 'social model', suggests that disabled people's individual and collective disadvantage is due to a complex form of institutional discrimination as fundamental to our society as social-class exploitation, sexism, racism or heterosexism. This leads to discrimination and the internalized oppression we experience. This is not to deny or devalue the discomfort and pain we often experience as a result of having an impairment. Recently a number of disabled writers (Morris, 1993; Crow, 1996; Shakespeare, 1992; Oliver, 1996; Shakespeare and Watson, 1997) have argued that the 'social model' of impairment must include these experiences – for example, pain, discomfort and dying – and that the Disabled People's Movement will only attract larger numbers of disabled people if it takes these ideas and practices on board. There has been understandable resistance from those who experienced their lives as dominated by the 'medical model' and the real problem is that our current 'social model' has not been developed to encompass our experience of impairment and so to develop our own responses to it.

In addition to this, the obsession with finding medically based cures distracts us from looking at causes of either impairment or disablement. In a world-wide sense, most impairments are created by oppressive systems – hunger, lack of clean water, exploitation of labour, lack of safety, child abuse and wars (see below).

Clearly, the 'social model' has important implications for our education system – particularly with reference to primary and secondary schools. Prejudicial attitudes towards disabled people and indeed against all minority groups are not inherited. They are learned through contact with the prejudice and ignorance of others. Therefore, to challenge discrimination against disabled people, we must begin in our schools.

Our fight for the inclusion of all children, however 'severely' impaired, in one mainstream education system will not make sense unless the difference between the 'social' and the 'medical' or individual model of disability is understood (see Chapter 8 of this volume for a discussion of disability and education).

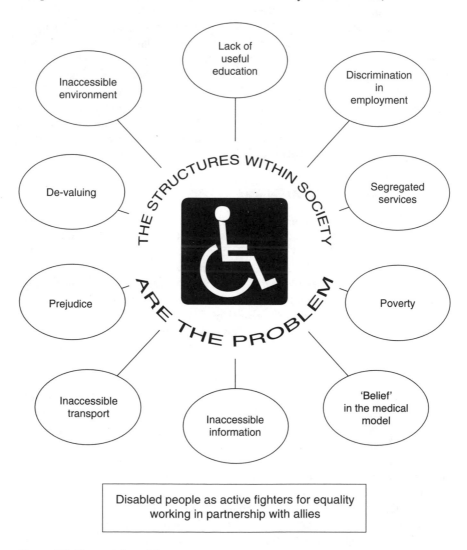

Figure 7.2 The social model

The 'social model' has empowered many disabled people and been important in uniting previously disparate, often impairment-based organizations. The self-representation of disabled people has been important in a situation where organizations 'for' disabled people but run by non-disabled people have sought to do things in our name, but without finding out what disabled people want. The British Council of Disabled People, made up of 136 organizations of disabled people that are run by disabled people, has had a long battle over the last seventeen years to establish itself. This has been particularly hard when large disability charities 'for' disabled people such as the Royal National Institute for the Blind (RNIB), the Royal National Institute for the Deaf (RNID), the Royal Association for Disability and Rehabilitation (RADAR), SCOPE (for people with cerebral palsy) and MENCAP (Royal Society for Mentally Handicapped Children and Adults) get large amounts of government funding to provide services for disabled people, have influence, but do not represent disabled people and are not controlled by them. This was very apparent when the 1995 Disability Discrimination Act passed through Parliament and these organizations welcomed the new law in the face of opposition from disabled people's organizations.

The Disability Discrimination Act was seen by the Disabled People's Movement as weak and full of 'get-out' clauses, such as a 'reasonable' discrimination. In addition, the Act did not create a commission to enforce and support disabled complainants, although this was subsequently promised in the 1998 Queen's Speech. Transport and Education were largely left out of the Act's provisions, and the legislation only applied to employers with twenty or more employees – thus exempting 96 per cent of employers (after pressure, this was reduced to those with fifteen or more employees). The split in the Rights Now Coalition (a group campaigning for civil rights legislation) between the factions 'of' and 'for' us has now been patched up, with the establishment of the Disability Rights Task Force, but there remain strong doubts as to whether New Labour will honour its manifesto commitment to 'comprehensive, enforceable civil rights for disabled people'.

What is Disablement?

World Figures

Disablement, then, is a social process, but many of the attempts to enumerate disabled people do not take account of this; instead, they view it as a medical problem or personal tragedy. In 1996, the United Nations estimated there were at least 500 million disabled people in the world. This was made up of people with the following impairments: 55 million visually impaired (11 per cent), 70 million hearing impaired (14 per cent), 130 million with severe intellectual impairment (26 per cent), 20 million with epilepsy (4 per cent) and 160 million with some sort of mobility impairment (Disability Awareness in Action, 1995, p. 7). Many poor countries do not have information on disability. In some, cultural taboos lead to disabled people being hidden away. In addition, major categories of impairment, such as mental distress, facial disfigurements and deformities, cancer, HIV/AIDS, hidden impairments like diabetes, sickle-cell anaemia, acute asthma and many other conditions which affect physical or mental functioning on a long-term basis, are not included in these figures. If all these groups were to be added, the number would certainly increase significantly to at least 850 million or one in eight. The World Health Organization estimates 10 per cent (Coleridge, 1993, p. 108).

The UN figures also reveal the major causes of impairment. These include: malnutrition (100 million (20 per cent)); accident, war and trauma (including 20 million injured by land mines; 78 million (15.6 per cent)); infectious diseases, such as TB, polio and leprosy (all of which are preventable) (56 million (11.2 per cent)); non-infectious diseases (100 million (20 per cent)); and congenital diseases (100 million (20 per cent)). It has been estimated that 80 per cent of the impairments in the world are preventable as they are caused by poverty, war, hunger and disease. The report gives many examples of self-help projects from around the world, where disabled people have managed to dismantle barriers to their inclusion (Disability Awareness in Action, 1995, p. 9).

It is also clear that the number of people counted as 'disabled' increases as the standard of living increases, showing it to be a social construct. The proportion of disabled people in Austria, for example, is twenty times higher than that in Peru (Coleridge, 1993, p. 105). Local perception, barriers, survival rates and longevity vary considerably from rich to poor countries and will help to explain such variations.

UK Figures

A DfEE Workforce Survey (Winter 1994–5) showed that only 40 per cent of disabled adults of working age (sixteen to sixty-five years old) were working or registered unemployed. The rest – 60 per cent or 2.2 million disabled people – were on benefit and not looking for work. It also showed that, of the 3.7 million disabled of working age adults (up by 1.2 million on the OPCS survey eight years earlier), 41 per cent had no educational qualifications. This compared to the whole working population very poorly, where only 18 per cent had no educational qualifications (cited in Sly et al., 1995).

These figures follow on from a ground-breaking sample survey in the mid-1980s by the Office of Population Census (*6 Reports Survey of Disability in Great Britain*, cited in Martin et al., 1988) that sought to enumerate the number of disabled people in the United Kingdom. This showed that there were at least 6.5 million disabled people in Britain. Of these, 6.2 million were adults (14.2 per cent of the adult population); 41.8 per cent or 2.59 million of these were aged sixteen to sixty-five and 360,000 were five- to sixteen-year-olds. More recent surveys show increases in all categories. The survey did not include under-fives who, given the rise in the birth rate and improved medical techniques, would number at least another 300,000. This is borne out by the 1991 Census which recorded 6.9 million people who were disabled or long-term sick.

To be classed as disabled in this Office of Population Census (OPCS) survey, one had to have a significant impairment that 'restricted or led to a lack of ability to perform normal activities, which has resulted from the impairment of a structure or function of body or mind' (OPCS, 1988, p. xi). Thresholds were set on ten scales such as mobility, hearing, sight, incontinence, lifting, mental ability. Panels of judges developed the scales by examining the responses to narrowly based questions. People were interviewed and asked 'what they normally can do'. Anyone who is disabled has had to learn to do things in an environment and with objects that are not designed for us to use. Second, the questions asked were individualized rather than socialized and did not examine people's impairments against a background of the social and environmental contexts of disabled people's lives.

Criticizing the survey method and the ideology that lies behind it, Mike Oliver (1990) makes the different orientations clear. From the OPCS survey (1986–8), he examines questions that were drawn from the face-to face interviews. The questions were:

1   Can you tell me what is wrong with you?
2   What complaint causes you difficulty in holding, gripping or turning things?
3   Do you have a scar, blemish or deformity which limits your daily activity?
4   Have you attended a special school because of a long-term health problem or disability?
5   Does your health problem/disability affect your work in any way at present?
6   Do your health problems/disability make it difficult for you to travel by bus?

These questions clearly see disability as individualized and are based on 'medical model' thinking. They could have been put in an alternative way that draws on a 'social model':

1   Can you tell me what is wrong with society?
2   What defects in design of everyday equipment like jars, bottles and lids causes you difficulty in holding, gripping or turning things?
3   Do other people's reactions to any scar, blemish or deformity you have limit your daily activity?
4   Have you attended a special school because of your education authority's policy of sending people with your long-term health problem or disability to such places?
5   Do you have problems at work as a result of the physical environment or the attitudes of others?
6   Do poorly designed buses make it difficult for someone with your health problem/disability to use them?

(Oliver, 1990, pp. 7–8)

Abberley (1992, p. 154), in criticizing the surveys, has this to say:

It is a matter of political choice that OPCS surveys were designed in terms of an individualistic 'personal tragedy' approach to disability, rather than to devote significant resources to an exploration of the ways in which it is society that disables impaired people. Whilst there are ways in which we may utilise OPCS data, we must not in doing so lose sight of this most fundamental flaw. Information gathered on the basis of an oppressive theory, unless handled with circumspection, is itself one of the mechanisms of oppression.

Anyone who has followed the pronouncements of the New Labour government in the UK on disability benefits can see the dangers of this oppressive theory. Despite announcing a task force to recommend full civil rights legislation for disabled people, the government allowed the Benefits Integrity Project to whip up pressure generally to cut back on the non-means-tested Disability Living Allowance (DLA) by producing false figures that one in five claimants was bogus. When this was shown to be false they claimed that if everyone who was entitled to claim Disability Living Allowance did, then 8.6 million people would be eligible on the current criteria, thus creating a climate for cut-backs. This time a huge outcry from disabled people and their allies prevented any threat to DLA. The allowance was the one positive thing that came out of the OPCS surveys which showed definitively that disabled people lived in poverty and needed extra money to participate in society. *OPCS Report 2* (Morris and White, 1988) established that disabled people were poorer than any other section of UK society. Now DLA is under threat because the government fails to understand that the barriers in society disable us and until they have been removed we need to be compensated for the extra cost of being disabled.

The History of Disablement

The continuing inequality we face will not be rectified by ramps, lifts and accessible communications, or the outlawing of discriminatory behaviour, welcome as these may be. The well-spring of our oppression comprises deeply held social attitudes that reflect generations of prejudice, fear and discrimination towards disabled people in education, work and social life. The main reasons are negative attitudes and stereotypes which are based on untrue ideas that have been around for thousands of years and which are amazingly persistent.

We can, at any time, all become disabled – develop a physical or mental impairment. Perhaps the need to distance ourselves from this reality makes it convenient to rely on negative attitudes and stereotypes of disability. They are less troubling than accepting the individuality, the joy, the pain, the appearance, the behaviour and the *rights* of disabled people.

Work by anthropologists (Hanks and Hanks, 1948) has established that there is no one way that disabled people are viewed across a wide range of societies. Views ranged from high status to outcast. There appears to be an underlying economic basis, so in societies with more surplus produce, such as agricultural rather than nomadic or hunter-gatherer, there was more acceptance of disabled members of those societies. There was more chance of their being supported as there was surplus food. Invariably, however, this was not the case and some evidence exists that hunter-gatherers have valued disabled members of their societies. A band of

Northern Territory Aborigines carried a member of their band who could not walk with them on their wanderings for sixty years (Davis, 1989). Where an impairment was more commonly occurring, such as blindness in a Mexican village (Gwaltney, 1970), or on Martha's Vineyard, an island off the New England coast with an unusually high proportion of deaf people (Groce, 1985) the whole culture changed to accommodate guiding and signing, respectively. Though no systematic cross-cultural study of the position of disabled people has yet been carried out, it is clear that the individualized tragic view of disability prevalent in modern Western society is not universal.

The Ancient World

To understand the development of this particular view of disabled people, we must go back to ancient Greece, to the beginning of 'Western civilization'. In Greek mythology Zeus and Hera had a child, Hyphaistos, God of Fire, who was born with a 'club-foot'. He was thrown off Mount Olympus into the sea, but, being a god, he survived to return and become the butt of jokes of all the other gods (Garland, 1995). He was a forger of metal and as he grew up his sexual relations with women were frequently fraught with difficulty because of the attitudes of the other gods. His wife, according to Homer, was the beautiful Aphrodite, who deceived him by having an affair with Ares. Here, we witness one of the most pernicious myths about disabled adults – that they are incapable of adult sexual relations.

The Greek and Roman attitude was to worship and adore the body beautiful. This is exemplified by the many perfectly proportioned sculptures of the human body, bodies with 'beautiful' symmetrical features. In representations on vases, tablets, sculptures and so on, there are very few disabled people. The Olympic ideal was to aspire to be like the gods in physique, intellect and morals. This is still often apparent in the Olympic Games, where the Para Olympics and Games for People with Learning Difficulties still segregate disabled athletes, although some sensory-impaired people have recently competed in the main Games.

The cult of the body beautiful was put into practice, particularly among the patrician or ruling classes in ancient Greece and Rome. Aristotle wrote 'that you should take your child off if they are imperfect and get rid of them' (Garland, 1995, p. 15). The status of 'child' was not conferred until seven days after birth, so there was time to dispose of unwanted babies legally. In militaristic Sparta, children were the property of the state and inspected at birth. 'If the child be ill-born or ill-formed', the father was required to expose it at a chasm-like place called Apothetai or the Place of Exposure (*ibid*., p. 14). In Rome disabled infants were meant to be drowned in the Tiber and the games at the Coliseum put on to entertain and pacify the 'mob' included disabled children being thrown under horses' hooves, blind gladiators fighting each other and 'dwarves' fighting women. The rest of the ancient world was not as proscriptive, but nevertheless exposure was widespread. Those with less significant impairments who survived generally led a half-life, disdained and ridiculed, often having to rely on begging. There were exceptions. Even in Sparta, King Agesilaos was afflicted with 'congenital lameness' but this acted as a spur to his ambition and he desired to be first in all things (*ibid.*, p. 40). Clearly, then, exposure did not always occur, as parents do tend to love their children, and many disabled people survived infancy. In Rome, despite the dislike of and cruelty towards people with impairments, there is evidence that at least one emperor was disabled: Claudius may well have had cerebral palsy (*clauditas* in Latin means lameness). Claudius' mother, Antonia, described him 'as a monster of a man, not finished by nature but only half done' (*ibid.*, pp. 40–2). Echoed in Shakespeare's *Richard III*, this develops into an abiding stereotype as the evil and avenging man/monster.

The Judaeo-Christian Tradition

Another seminal source of thinking about disabled people was the Judaeo-Christian tradition that fundamentally disability is a punishment for evil – 'if humans are immoral they will be blinded by God' (Deutoronomy, 27:27); in Exodus (20:5) God tells Moses that retribution for sin will be inflicted on the offspring of the sinners for many generations. In the books of Exodus, Numbers and Deuteronomy, the people of Israel are repeatedly punished for their sinful ways through physical impairment (Rose, 1997).

The Jewish faith, however, has a more complex position, with some parts of the Talmud advocating disability as a holy state and a means of getting to heaven. Similar sentiments are expressed towards those who help disabled people. Some of this is reflected in the parables of the New Testament, but usually with Christ performing miracle cures. Rarely are disabled people accepted as themselves.

The Book of Leviticus (21:16–20) has a clear message that impairment is unclean and polluting, and prevents disabled people from receiving sacraments:

> And the Lord said to Moses none of your descendants throughout the generations who has a blemish shall draw near, a man blind or lame or one who has a mutilated face or a limb too long, or a man who has an injured foot or an injured hand or a hunchback or a dwarf, or a man with defective sight or itching disease or scabs or crushed testicles. He may eat the bread of his God, both of the most holy and of holy things, but he shall not come near the veil or approach the altar, because he has a blemish, that he has a blemish, that he may not profane my sanctuaries.

This message was taken seriously. Until the 1950s people with learning difficulties were not allowed to receive certain sacraments in the Roman Catholic Church.

The Medieval Period

Disabled people were treated in medieval Europe as both saints and sinners. On the one hand, they were 'innocents unstained by normal and sinful human characteristics' (Barnes, 1991, p. 12) who should be offered asylum and alms; on the other, they were evil changelings – the work of the devil (Haffter, 1968).

Martin Luther, the architect of the Reformation, believed that changelings had no soul and advocated that children so 'afflicted' should be taken to the river and drowned. Nevertheless, the bulk of disabled people born into feudal villages or acquiring impairments would have been accepted and did what they could, while those with more severe impairments may have been subject to infanticide.

Veterans of war were often treated better. The first record of a sheltered workshop in Europe was the Congregation of Three Hundred, established in France in 1254 for 300 crusaders who had had their eyes gouged out by Saracens (Ford, 1981).

At times of crisis disabled people were likely to be scapegoated as superstition took over – for example, during the Plague or during the Great Witchhunt of 1480–1680. The 'Malleus Malleficarum' – 'the Hammer of Witches', 1487, written by two priests – was a bestseller in Europe and went to seventy editions in fourteen languages. It includes whole sections on how you can identify witches by their impairments or by their creation of impairments in others; or giving birth to a disabled child. Between 8 million and 20 million people, mainly women, were put to death across Europe and a good proportion were disabled. Three witches were recorded as hanged after an Oxford trial in 1513, one of whom was put on trial because she was a disabled person using crutches (Rieser, 1995, p. 6). Recent research on the treatment of people with learning difficulties, however, suggests that naturalistic accounts of learning difficulties and mental illness were accepted, rather than the disabled people being demonized (Neugebauer, 1996).

The 'disabled witch' comes through in the folklore of Britain and Europe. The Brothers Grimm collected the oral stories of northern Europe and made them into their fairy tales. The witch in *Hansel and Gretel* is deformed, blind, ugly, disabled and carries a stick (this book has been adapted for use with children as young as two years old). There are also storybooks which feature evil imps swapping healthy babies for disabled ones (Rieser, 1995, p. 5).

There are many pictures and stories from medieval times of penitent sinners. Groups of penitent 'cripples' are depicted trying to get alms and, if they wandered around long enough, feeling humble enough, then maybe they would make it in the next life. A very strong message therefore came across. Disabled people were often scapegoated for the ills of society, as in Brueghel's painting *The Cripples*, where the fox tails denote wrongdoing. Outside any medieval church are the deformed ones, the gargoyles; and on the inside are the 'perfectly formed' pictures around the crypt.

Until the seventeenth century those disabled people rejected by their families relied upon the haphazard and often ineffectual tradition of Christian charity and alms – gifts for subsistence (Barnes, 1991, ch. 2). During the sixteenth century the wealth and power of the Church was greatly reduced due to the confrontation between Church and state in England. There was also a growth in those seeking alms due to a rise in population, poor harvests, the beginning of the commercialization of agriculture and immigration from Ireland and Scotland (Stone, 1985). To secure the allegiance of local gentry and magistrates, the Tudor monarchs were forced to make economic provision for people dependent upon charity. The 1601 Poor Law marks the first recognition of the need for the state to intervene in the lives of disabled people. Some two hundred years earlier, the Peasants' Revolt of 1381 had led to a mandate to local officials to distinguish the 'deserving poor' from the 'undeserving poor'. The bulk of relief went to the deserving poor in the form of 'household relief' to people in their homes. Segregation did not really emerge until the nineteenth century (Barnes, 1992, pp. 14–19).

Close examination of Rembrandt's sketches reveals that the beggars are often wearing white head bands. This is because in seventeenth-century Holland the bacillus-leprosy, brought inadvertently on the back of the 'spice trade' from colonies in the tropics, spread quickly around urban areas. An edict was passed by the state that all those who contracted it had to report to The Hague, and once their condition was confirmed they had all their worldly goods confiscated, had to wear a white head band and they and their families had to rely on alms as penitent sinners. Those with leprosy had to live in segregated colonies and their only reward for penance was rehabilitation in heaven (Toth-Ubbens, 1987).[2]

The Eighteenth and Nineteenth Centuries

The development of industrial capitalism and its inherent requirement for workers to sell their labour power meant that those with significant impairments were excluded from the labour market. Those disabled people who were able to work were forced to the bottom rungs of the labour market ladder (Morris, 1969, p. 9). As a result, disabled people came to be regarded as a social and educational problem, and increasingly were segregated out of the mainstream, in institutions of various kinds: workhouses, asylums, colonies and special schools (Oliver, 1990, p. 28). According to Finkelstein (1980), this is Phase Two of disabled people's development, the phase when we were separated from our class origins and became a special segregated group, with disability seen as an impairment, requiring segregation from the labour market as well as social restriction.[3]

Throughout the eighteenth and nineteenth centuries the policy of segregating severely impaired people into institutional settings slowly spread. The main impetus was the change from working as groups or families on the land, down the mines or as cottage industry to factory work. The latter required set rates of working on repetitive tasks for long hours; time was money. By 1834, Poor Law household relief was abolished for the 'non-deserving poor' – the unemployed. The deserving poor were categorized – children, the sick, the insane, defectives and the aged and infirm, the last four being categories of impairment – and provision was uniform across the country. Deterrence was built into relief as a principle of 'least eligibility' was introduced. This meant that those on relief would be less comfortable than an 'independent labourer of the lowest class' before benefits would be granted (Barnes, 1991, p. 16). Charles Dickens and others have vividly described the horrors of the workhouse. Charities increasingly set up asylums for the insane and then special schools for blind and deaf children. This role was taken over by the state from the 1890s (Hurt, 1988).

The 'insane', which included 'idiots', 'lunatics' and the mentally infirm, were, after the 1845 Lunacy Act, able to be detained on the certification of a doctor. This was based on a theory advanced by the medical profession that mental illness had physiological causes that were treatable. This marked the beginning of the medical profession's state-endorsed involvement in the lives of disabled people (Barnes, 1991). This power is still exercised today; as a disabled person, if you want an orange badge, Disability Living Allowance or Incapacity Benefit you have to be examined by a doctor. Disabled people are not trusted in general and here is always a belief that people will pretend to be disabled to get benefits fraudulently, but this does not explain the continual checking of our impairments even when medical science has no solutions and our conditions are stable or deteriorating. Far more disabled people who are entitled to benefits don't claim them than bogus claims from non-disabled people are made; the latter, in reality, being rarities.This symbolic treatment of disabled people who are at the margins of the workforce very much defined who was part of the workforce and who was not (Oliver, 1990).

In the last quarter of the nineteenth century, another strand of thought became highly influential – the eugenics movement. This had and continues to have a disastrous effect on the lives of disabled people. Drawn from the ideas of Aristotle, eugenics thinking first wrongly applied Darwin's theories of natural selection to ideas about racial degeneration and was then applied to disabled people. The birth of disabled children, it was claimed, would weaken the gene pool and out-breed non-disabled people. This, in turn, would weaken the European population in its task of colonizing and controlling the rest of the world (see Chapters 3 and 4 of this volume for a discussion of racism and imperialism).

The Twentieth Century

Traditional myths that there were genetic links between physical and mental impairments, crime, unemployment and other social evils were constantly proposed by the likes of Galton (1883, 1909), Dugdale (1895) and Goddard (1913). They wished to improve the British and American 'races' by preventing the reproduction of 'defectives' by means of sterilization and segregation. In the UK in the 1920s pressure from eugenicists for 'voluntary' sterilization increased (Ryan with Thomas, 1987).

These ideas spread quickly to intellectuals of all political complexions as the century of science got under way: H.G. Wells, Sidney and Beatrice Webb, Bernard Shaw and D.H. Lawrence, Y.B. Yeats, J.M. Keynes, Winston Churchill and Aldous Huxley to name but a few.

> If I had my way, I would build a lethal chamber as big as Crystal Palace, with a military band playing softly, and a Cinematograph working brightly; then I'd go out in the back streets and the main streets and bring them in, all the sick, the halt and the maimed; I would lead them gently, and they would smile me a weary thanks; and the band would softly bubble out the 'Hallelujah Chorus'.

So wrote D.H. Lawrence in 1908 in a letter to Blanche Jennings (Boulton, 1979, p. 81). This was part of an élitist intellectual culture, which included a dislike for the industrial world and the social disorder it had spawned, and eugenicist views towards disabled people (Carey, 1992).

The Mental Deficiency Act of 1913 was the result of eugenicist agitation and it led to the incarceration of 'idiots', 'imbeciles', 'the feeble minded' and 'moral imbeciles', the last category usually referring to young people who had had illegitimate children. Many were incarcerated for life in sex-segregated institutions to prevent them from reproducing. At first it was argued that units or extra classes attached to ordinary schools were best, but soon the eugenicist view prevailed and the early part of the century saw large numbers of segregated schools for 'crippled children, epileptics, educable morons and feeble minded children' (Copeland, 1997, p. 714; see also Hurt, 1988).

A great wave of building ensued after the First World War with large institutions and colonies being erected on the outskirts of towns. Simon and Binet's false science of IQ testing, refined by supporters such as Cyril Burt (1977), was developed to distinguish the educable from the ineducable. An IQ of less than 50 meant you were destined for a mental deficiency institution as a child and probably for life. It is estimated that 50,000 children with no mental deficiency were sent to these institutions prior to 1950, on the false diagnosis of doctors who, at this time, subscribed to bogus theories, such as that someone's intelligence could be determined by their head shape and size (Humphries and Gordon, 1992).

Children perceived to be ineducable, including many with cerebral palsy, Down's syndrome and speech impairments, went to junior training establishments right up to 1972. At that time, some 60,000 children joined the education system in severe learning difficulty schools. Today, many with the same conditions successfully attend ordinary schools.

In the USA, compulsory sterilization was in wide use by the 1930s. Forty-one states had provision for the sterilization of the insane and feeble minded, and seventeen states prohibited people with epilepsy from marrying. In many states women born deaf were sterilized. Twenty-seven states still had these laws until very recently, though they were seldom enforced. In China, some 15 million people with 'mental incapacity' have been compulsorily sterilized under a law that was enacted in 1995. This is an abuse of their human rights and, as the *Guardian* reported in 1997, is a particular outrage since it is known that many of these women have developed their condition from iodine deficiency in their environment.

Recently it has been reported that in Scandinavia and France, mentally defective women were compulsorily sterilized up to the 1980s. This all took place despite the findings of a study carried out for the Wood Committee in 1929 which showed that only 7.6 per cent of patients of one particular asylum had defective parents.

Disabled people are seen as a burden, and at times of economic stress this view intensifies. The Nazis, when they came to power in Germany in 1933, introduced a law for the Prevention of Hereditary Diseases which led to the forced sterilization of more than 300,000 people. Under the Third Reich, propaganda films were made to show how we were a burden on the state. We were the 'useless eaters', and we should be got rid of. In the beginning, voluntary euthanasia was advocated to end the suffering of 'the incurable', but this ultimately evolved into mass murder. One hundred and forty thousand physically and mentally disabled people were murdered in 1939/40 at the hands of the doctors of the Third Reich in six so-called clinics, which were staffed by many of those who went on to run the concentration camps where 6 million Jews were exterminated (Burleigh, 1994).

With cut-backs in the welfare state, the eugenicist argument is currently undergoing a revival in Britain. A recent poll on GMTV revealed that 86 per cent of people who rang in thought that a doctor was right to abort two disabled children. In Holland and Tasmania laws have been introduced to allow voluntary euthanasia. This is indicative of the way in which, through history, people have been socialized to view disabled people. The medical ethics committees are allowing the Genome Project to map the seat of all genetic disorders. Soon science will have the capability to eradicate many forms of impairment.

This brief excursus through the history of disabled people should cause us to ask if normality and uniformity are so important or is it difference that makes life interesting? The medicalization of impairment ignores the social context. In 1972 in the UK a child with Down's syndrome (an extra chromosome) would be deemed ineducable. Today, many such children who have attended mainstream schools are able to sit seven or eight GCSEs and are accepted by their peers. What would their lives be like if prejudice and discrimination were to be eradicated? Yet the medical profession insists on genetically screening all pregnant women over thirty for Down's syndrome with a view to termination if it is identified.

The Struggle for Human Dignity

The oppression of disabled people, over the years, has not gone uncontested. On the contrary, many disabled people have consistently struggled for human dignity and for inclusion in mainstream society. The National League for the Blind and Disabled and the British Deaf Association, for example, were both run by disabled people and, from the 1890s, campaigned for rights. In the 1920s, when unions of disabled veterans were formed all over Britain, sit-ins and occupations were held in an attempt to force the introduction of legislation for disabled people's rights. In the 1920s and 1930s, there were hundreds of thousands of First World War veterans with no rights at all in this country. Even those young people incarcerated in institutions for the blind or deaf had a culture of resistance; for example, when sign language was banned deaf pupils managed to develop their own pigeon sign language.[4]

In 1944 the Disabled Persons Act was passed. This included a quota system, whereby 3 per cent of the jobs in any given business had to be allotted to disabled people. This was to accommodate injured war veterans, and was abolished by the Disability Discrimination Act of 1995. It remains to be seen if this weak Act (see above) is any more effective in getting disabled people into work.

In the 1970s war veterans in the USA started the disability movement there and successfully campaigned until they achieved full civil rights legislation in the

Disabilities Act of 1991 (Dreiger, 1989).[5] In the 1970s in the UK the Union of Physically Impaired Against Segregation was formed. This was initiated by Paul Hunt, who lived in a Cheshire home which he called the new workhouse. He wrote a letter to the *Guardian* (20 September 1972) calling on severely physically impaired people to form a new consumer group to put forward their views. This and a number of other organizations run by disabled people and formed in the 1970s amalgamated into the British Council of Organizations of Disabled People (BCODP). The Council, which supports the 'social model' of disability, now represents some 300,000 disabled people who all control their own organizations. The BCODP also linked a number of the local Centres for Independent Living and Local Coalitions of Disabled People (Campbell and Oliver, 1996). These organizations campaigned for full civil rights legislation. Fifteen attempts were made from 1980 to 1995 to get a Civil Rights Bill through Parliament in the UK. Instead, all that was achieved was the 1995 Disability Discrimination Act. The Direct Action Network of disabled people expressed the frustration of millions of disabled people in a series of actions which brought London and other cities and towns to a standstill. As a result, the Labour government has set up a ministerial task force to advise on the implementation of full anti-discrimination legislation based on the 'social model' of disability. It remains to be seen whether disabled people's aspirations will be finally met. Disabled people are still struggling for the rights to use public transport, to get into buildings, to go to school or college with their friends, to get a job and even to go to the cinema. In October 1998, Glenda Jackson MP announced that £500 million would be spent on making London Transport buses accessible.

Recycling Old Ideas in the Representation of Disabled People

As disabled people, we often feel that the culture we are in characterizes us in a number of false ways that make us seem different to everyone else. Stereotypes of the disabled abound. Thus, there is the 'super-crip' or the disabled person who 'triumphs over tragedy'. Have you ever noticed how often perfectly ordinary things that disabled people do become newsworthy – the blind mountain climber, the boy with cerebral palsy who walked one mile, or the deaf man who was a chess champion? These things are only seen as newsworthy because journalists have a view that disabled people usually cannot or should not be doing ordinary things. The 1996 London Marathon was advertised by Nike showing a man with no legs or arms. The caption was: 'Peter is not like ordinary people. He's done the Marathon.' This plays on two ideas: first, that we are not able to do things; and, second, that we are objects of curiosity – 'freaks' who are worthy of public attention.

We are often referred to as 'cripples'. This comes from an Old German word *kripple*, meaning to be without power. We do not like being called this. President F.D. Roosevelt, the only man to be elected President of the USA four times, had a physical impairment, having had polio in both legs, and was unable to walk unaided. Yet he perfected ways of disguising it, such as never being photographed in his wheelchair. He once observed that 'the American public would never vote for a president who was a cripple'. He may well have been right.

With the development of the printing press in 1480, at a time when most people in Europe could not read, cartoons and other graphic representations became popular ways of making political and moral comments to a mass audience The old ideas of the Greeks became recycled: humankind was created by gods who were physically perfect. Since human beings were created in the gods' own image, the less physically perfect were less worthy. Evil, moral weakness and powerlessness were depicted by caricatured disabled people. For example, in an attempt to discredit Richard III, historians portrayed him as a disabled and vengeful mass murderer. However, when his portrait which hangs in the National Portrait Gallery was X-rayed, it was discovered that the king's hump had been added sixty years after his death. Modern film-makers often make their villains disabled. Little changes.

One need only look at pirates. From Lego to Stevenson's Long John Silver or Blind Pew, or Barrie's Captain Hook in *Peter Pan*; nearly all have eye patches, hooks and wooden legs. All these disabled pirates do not accord with historical reality. Pirates had a system of simple social security long before anyone else. They had common shares in the common purse so, if they were injured during the course of their endeavours, they would retire to a tropical island with as much money as they wanted. They were unlikely, therefore, to go on trying their luck as an impaired pirate (Greenwich Museum private exhibition, 1994). Yet in the nineteenth century a number of writers became obsessed with disabled and evil pirates. In previous centuries pirates had been socially acceptable as they plundered and built up the British Empire. For example, Daniel Defoe wrote a bestseller about a certain Captain Singleton, pirate, popular hero and, on his return, thrice Lord Mayor of London. But pirates outlived their usefulness as privateers who expand the Empire, and after the Battle of Trafalgar the Royal Navy could do the job on its own (Rieser, 1995).

Many charity adverts are designed to create fear. Take, for example, the one depicting a girl living 'under the shadow of diabetes'. She probably did not even know she was 'in a shadow' until she found herself up on the billboards of England for three years. She was simply injecting insulin every day and that was all right. Other charity advertisements use black and white imagery to make us look pitiful (for a detailed analysis of how charities use images of disabled people to disable us, see Hevey, 1992).

There is, however, some cause for cautious optimism. The Invisible Children Conference, for example, jointly organized by Save the Children and The Alliance for Inclusive Education, was an exciting and thought-provoking day held in London on 1 March 1995 and attended by more than 150 key image-makers. The conference decided that 'disabled people should be shown as an ordinary part of life in all forms of representation, not as stereotypes or invisible'. The 1 in 8 Group, which grew out of this conference, has issued the following useful guidelines to the media. There are ten main stereotypes of disabled people: the disabled person as:

- Pitiable and pathetic: e.g. charity advertisements and telethons, concepts like *Children in Need* and characters like Tiny Tim in *A Christmas Carol* or Porgy in Gershwin's *Porgy and Bess*.
- An object of violence: e.g. films such as *Whatever Happened to Baby Jane* or *Wait until Dark* which set the style for countless TV films.
- Sinister or evil: e.g. Shakespeare's *Richard III*, Stevenson's *Treasure Island*, the films *Dr Strangelove, Dr No, Hook* or *Nightmare on Elm Street*.
- Curios or exotica: e.g. 'freak shows', images in comics, horror movies and science fiction, films such as *The Hunchback of Notre Dame* or *X-Men*.
- Super crip or triumph over tragedy: e.g. films like *Reach for the Sky*, the last item on the television news – featuring a disabled person climbing a mountain, for example.
- Laughable: e.g. films like *Mr Magoo, Hear No Evil, See No Evil* and *Time Bandits*.
- Having a chip on their shoulder: e.g. Laura in the film *The Glass Menagerie*. This is often linked to a miracle cure as in *Heidi* and *The Secret Garden*.
- A burden/outcast: e.g. as in *Beauty and the Beast* set in subterranean New York, or the Morlocks in the *X-Men*.
- Non-sexual or incapable of having a worthwhile relationship: e.g. Clifford Chatterley in *Lady Chatterley's Lover, Born on the Fourth of July*, O'Casey's 'Silver Tassie' or the film *Life Flesh*.
- Incapable of fully participating in everyday life: our absence from everyday situations, not being shown as integral and productive members of society.

(Biklen and Bogdana, 1977, amended by Rieser and Mason, 1992)

Images: The Way Forward From and For Disabled People

- Shun one-dimensional characterizations and portray disabled people as having complex personalities and being capable of a full range of emotions.
- Avoid depicting us as always receiving; show us as equals – giving as well as receiving.
- Avoid presenting physical and mental characteristics as determining personality.
- Refrain from depicting us as objects of curiosity. Make us ordinary.
- Our impairments should not be ridiculed or made the butt of jokes.
- Avoid sensationalizing us, especially as victims or perpetrators of violence.
- Refrain from endowing us with superhuman attributes.
- Avoid *Pollyanna*-ish plots that make our attitude the problem. Show the societal barriers we face that keep us from living full lives.
- Avoid showing disabled people as non-sexual. Show us in loving relationships and expressing the same range of sexual needs and desires as non-disabled people.
- Show us as an ordinary part of life in all forms of representation.

- Most importantly, cast us, train us and write us into your scripts, programmes and publications.

(Rieser, 1995, p. 44)

There was general agreement at the Invisible Children Conference that to continue to portray disabled people as invisible or one-dimensional reinforces the discrimination and isolation disabled people experience in all aspects of life. This can include becoming targets for bullying and physical attack. It was felt that children are particularly affected by the images to which they have access. Unfortunately, most children and young people rarely meet disabled children in their schools and form their views of them mainly through the media. The inclusion of disabled people in producing and creating images and the portrayal of disabled people as 'real people' is crucial. It was felt now is the time to achieve this.

With a very few welcome exceptions – such as the children's television serial *Grange Hill*, the BBC drama *Skallagrigg* or Channel 4's *ER*, and the films, *Four Weddings and a Funeral, Shine* and *Muriel's Wedding* – disabled characters and images are largely absent, or when they do appear they are presented in a negative and stereotypical way. Change can occur. Twenty years ago Asian, black and other minority ethnic people were in a similar position. Now the necessity for their inclusion is taken for granted. Lack of portrayal of disability in our society is not accidental. Western culture from Greek and Roman times, reinforced in Renaissance Europe, has seen 'the body beautiful' as an ideal, and those with physical or mental imperfections have been seen as being in receipt of divine retribution. Such ideas are deeply embedded in myth, legend and classical literature. Today's celluloid entertainment culture reinforces the tendency to judge people by their appearance. The 1 in 8 Group has concentrated on changing the perceptions of image-makers, particularly in film and TV. There has been some shift in the TV soaps, which now include disabled characters, but these are not usually played by disabled actors. To keep the industry aware of these issues, the 1 in 8 Group organizes an annual Raspberry Ripple Award for good and bad portrayal.[6]

In the next chapter I will examine how both traditional thinking about disabled people and the 'social model' impact on the English education system, one which has grown out of the oppressive history of disabled people and 'medical model' thinking, predominant in special needs education. I will argue that inclusive education, rooted in an understanding of these diverse processes, is the way forward in eliminating both disadvantage and prejudicial attitudes.

Notes

1 Mason and Rieser (1994) is for teachers and school governors.
2 This book is written in Dutch, with an English summary.
3 In Phase 1, disabled individuals were part of a greater feudal underclass. In Phase 3, which is just beginning, disability comes to be seen solely as *social restriction*. The surplus value generated in capitalist societies, combined with modern technology, means that we can be exploited as workers by capitalism in much the same way as

non-disabled people. However, it also means that we can make the case *not* to be segregated either in the world of work, or more generally in the mainstream society.

4 The book *Out of Sight* contains first-hand oral histories and photographs of life in special schools and institutions in the first half of this century (Humphries and Gordon, 1992).

5 This is a good account of the international development of the Disabled People's Movement.

6 Norden (1994) gives a fascinating account how the image of disabled people has been developed through Hollywood, while Pointon (1997) provides a very useful handbook on how the disability movement has developed a critique and a response to the way disabled people are shown in the media. These ideas could also be useful to educationalists in the way they reproduce and interpret images of disabled people in the classroom.

References

Abberley, P. (1992) 'Counting us Out: A Discussion of the OPCS Disability Surveys', *Disability, Handicap and Society*, 7 (2), pp. 139–56

Barnes, C. (1991) *Disabled People in Britain and Discrimination*, London: Hurst

Biklen, D. and Bogdana, R. (1977) 'Media Portrayals of Disabled People: A Study of Stereotypes', *Inter-racial Book Bulletin*, 8 (6 and 7), pp. 4–9

Boulton, J.T. (1979) *The Letters of D.H. Lawrence Vol. 1 1901–1913*, Cambridge: Cambridge University Press

Burleigh, M. (1994) *Death and Deliverance: Euthanasia in Germany 1900–1945*, Cambridge: Cambridge University Press

Burt, C. (1977) *The Subnormal Mind*, Oxford: Oxford University Press

Campbell, J. and Oliver, M. (1996) *Disability Politics: Understanding our Past, Changing our Future*, London: Routledge

Carey, J. (1992) *The Intellectuals and the Masses: Pride and Prejudice amongst the Literary Intelligentsia, 1880–1939*, London: Faber & Faber

Coleridge, P. (1993) *Disability, Liberation and Development*, Oxford: Oxfam

Copeland, I. (1997) 'Pseudo-science and Dividing Practices: A Genealogy of the First Educational Provision for Pupils with Learning Difficulties', *Disability and Society* 12 (5), pp. 709–22

Crow, L. (1996) 'Including all our Lives: Renewing the Social Model of Disability', in Barnes, C. and Mercer, G. (eds), *Exploring the Divide: Illness and Disability*, Leeds: The Disability Press

Davis, A. (1989) *From Where I Sit: Living with disability in an Able Bodied World* London: Triangle

Disability Awareness in Action (1995) 'Overcoming Obstacles to the Integration of Disabled People', UNESCO sponsored document for the World Summit on Social Development, Copenhagen, March 1995

Dreiger, D. (1989) *The Last Civil Rights Movement*, London: Hurst

Dugdale, R.L. (1895) *The Jukes: A Study in Crime, Pauperism, Disease and Heredity*, New York

Finkelstein, V. (1980) *Attitudes and Disabled People: Issues for Discussion*, New York: World Rehabilitation Fund

Ford, B. (1981) 'Attitudes towards Disabled Persons: An Historical Perspective', *Australian Rehabilitation Review*, 5, pp. 45–9

Galton, F. (1883) *Enquiries into Human Faculty*, New York

Galton, F. (1909) *Essays in Eugenics*, London: London Eugenics Society

Garland, R. (1995) *The Eye of the Beholder: Deformity and Disability in the Graeco-Roman World*, London: Duckworth

Goddard, H.H. (1913) *The Kallikak Family: A Study in the Heredity of Feeble-mindedness*, New York: Macmillan

Groce, N. (1985) *Everyone Here Spoke Sign*, London: Harvard University Press

Gwaltney, J. (1970) *The Thrice Shy: Cultural Accommodation to Blindness and Other Disasters in a Mexican Community*, London and New York: Columbia University Press

Haffter, C. (1968) 'The Changeling: History and Psychodynamics of Attitude to Handicapped Children in European Folklore', *Journal of Behavioural Studies*, 4

Hanks, J. and Hanks, L. (1948) 'The Physically Handicapped in Non-Occidental Societies', *Journal of Social Issues*, 4 (4)

Hevey, D. (1992) *The Creatures Time Forgot: Photography and Disability Imagery*, London: Routledge

Humphries, S. and Gordon, P. (1992) *Out of Sight: The Experience of Disability 1900–1950*, Plymouth: Channel 4 Books

Hurt, J. (1988) *Outside the Mainstream: A History of Special Education*, London: Batsford

Martin, J., Metzler, H. and Elliot, D. (1988) *OPCS Report 1: The Prevalence of Disability among Adults*, London: HMSO

Mason, M. and Rieser, R. (1994) *Altogether Better*, London: Comic Relief

Morris, J. (1991) *Pride against Prejudice*, London: Women's Press

Morris, J. (1993) *Independent Lives: Community Care and Disabled People*, London: Macmillan

Morris, J. and White, A. (1988) *OPCS Surveys of Disability in Great Britain Report 2, The Financial Circumstances of Disabled Adults Living in Private Households*, London: HMSO

Morris, P. (1969) *Put Away*, London: Routledge

Neugebauer, R. (1996) 'Mental Handicap in Medieval and Early Modern England: Criteria, Measurement and Care', in Wright, D. and Digby, A. (eds), *From Idiocy to Mental Deficiency: Historical Perspectives on People with Learning Disabilities*, London: Routledge

Norden, M.F. (1994) *The Cinema of Isolation: A History of Physical Disability in the Movies*, New Brunswick, NJ: Rutgers University Press

OPCS (1988) *Surveys of Disability in Great Britain*, London: HMSO

Oliver, M. (1990) *The Politics of Disablement*, London: Macmillan

Oliver, M. (1996) *Understanding Disability from Theory to Practice*, London: Macmillan

1 in 8 Group (1995) 'Disability in the Media Broadsheet' 78

Pointon, A. with Davies, C. (1997) *Framed: Interrogating Disability in the Media*, London: British Film Institute Publishing

Rieser, R. (ed.) (1995) 'Invisible Children: Report of the Joint Conference on Children, Images and Disability', London: Save the Children

Rieser, R. and Mason, M. (1990/1992) *Disability Equality in the Classroom: A Human Rights Issue*, London: DEE

Rose, A. (1997) 'Who Causes the Blind to See?: Disability and Quality of Religious Life', *Disability and Society*, 12 (3), pp. 395–405

Ryan, J. with Thomas, F. (1987) *The Politics of Mental Handicap*, London: Free Association Books

Shakespeare, T. (1992) 'Renewing the Social Model', *Coalition*, September, pp. 40–2

Shakespeare, T. and Watson, N. (1997) 'Defending the Social Model', *Disability and Society*, 12 (2), pp. 293–300

Sly, F., Duxbury, R. and Tilsley, C. (1995) *Labour Force Survey*, London: DfEE

Stone, D. (1985) *The Disabled State*, London: Macmillan

Toth-Ubbens, M. (1987) *Lost Images of Miserable Beggars: Lepers, Paupers, Guex*, Lochem-Gent: Uitg.Mij. De Tijdstroom

8   Special Educational Needs or Inclusive Education

The challenge of disability discrimination in schooling

Richard Rieser

Introduction

When I first had Kim he was my son.

A year later he was epileptic and developmentally delayed. At eighteen months he had special needs and he was a special child. He had a mild to moderate learning difficulty. He was mentally handicapped.

I was told not to think about his future.

I struggled with all this.

By the time he was four he had special educational needs. He was a statemented child. He was dyspraxic, epileptic, developmentally delayed and had complex communication problems.

Two years later, aged six, he was severely epileptic (EP), cerebral palsied (CP) and had complex learning difficulties.

At eight he had severe intractable epilepsy with associated communication problems. He was showing a marked developmental regression.

He had severe learning difficulties.

At nine he came out of segregated schooling and he slowly became my son again. Never again will he be anything else but Kim – a son, a brother, a friend, a pupil, a teacher, a person.

(*Kim* by Pippa Murray, in Murray and Penman, 1996)

The great majority of children with special educational needs (SEN) will, as adults, contribute economically; all will contribute as members of society. Schools have to prepare all children for these roles. That is a strong reason for educating children with SEN, as far as possible, with their peers. Where all children are included as equal partners in the school community, the benefits are felt by all. That is why we are committed to comprehensive and enforceable civil rights for disabled people. Our aspirations as a nation must be for all our people.

So wrote David Blunkett, Secretary of State for Education and Employment, in his foreword to the government Green Paper *Excellence for All Children:*

Meeting Special Educational Needs (DfEE, 1997, p. 4). Blunkett is himself a disabled person who attended a special school for the blind and left without any formal qualifications. He had to attend evening classes, while working full time, to gain the necessary qualifications to go to university. The government's commitment to developing inclusive education is, in principle, clear. However, it lacks an understanding of how deeply 'medical model' thinking (see Chapter 7 of this volume) permeates the world of education. In addition the government is easily deflected by those wishing to maintain the status quo of segregated provision. For example, in the Green Paper, a continuing but 'redefined role of special schools to develop a network of specialist support' is proposed (DfEE, 1997, p. 49). Nevertheless, the expectation of the forthcoming period in education is that an increasingly wide diversity of pupils will be educated alongside their peers in mainstream classrooms.

If inclusive education is to be effective, teachers have to adopt 'social model' thinking about disabled people (see Chapter 7 of this volume). They must analyse the growing documentation of good practice, but they should also be aware of the barriers which prevent inclusion. These include physical barriers, communication barriers, social barriers, attitudinal barriers, educational barriers and institutional barriers. By physical barriers I mean the separate special school system and inaccessible school buildings and equipment; communication barriers are to do with lack of appropriate signing, Brailling and augmented communication, a lack of the use of plain jargon-free language, or of appropriate computers and other aids. Social barriers are separate classes or units, or 'discrete' courses within mainstream provision, which can lead to isolation and a lack of non-disabled friends. Attitudinal barriers include ignoring, bullying and devaluing us; denying the history, experience or culture of disabled people. Educational barriers consist of inadequate and inappropriate staffing levels, training or material resources within mainstream schools to address the real teaching and learning needs of all. Institutional barriers are the rules, regulations and procedures, including inappropriate testing, targets and examinations, that discriminate against disabled people. Finally, emotional barriers are to do with low self-esteem, lack of empowerment and the denial of the chance to develop worthwhile reciprocal relationships.

The term 'disabled' includes people with: physical impairments; sensory impairments (deaf people, blind people); chronic illness or health issues, including HIV and AIDS; all degrees of learning difficulties, including specific learning difficulties such as dyslexia and speech and language impairments; and impairment based on emotional and behavioural difficulties. It also includes people with hidden impairments such as epilepsy, diabetes, sickle-cell anaemia; children labelled as 'delicate'; people who identify as 'disfigured'; people of diminutive stature and people with mental distress. All are excluded by barriers, though not all have impairments.

The Fixed Continuum of Provision

In Chapter 7 I examined society's historical response to difference and how, in the early part of the twentieth century, as a result of eugenicist thinking, segregation and separation of adults and children with physical and mental impairments became the norm. I also argued that people became identified by their impairment and were thus the target of professional interventions under 'medical model' approaches, which, for the sake of efficiency, were provided in specialized settings. These processes have led to a geographically discrete and fixed continuum of provision in most local education authorities (LEAs). In many parts of the country a child is assessed independently of their local school and community. From this assessment they will be placed where their 'need' can best be met, often in a school for that type of need away from their peers, segregated with other children with that particular need or impairment (see Figure 8.1).

This continuum of provision is very often located in the schools and institutions that were expressly set up in the past to segregate young disabled people from their

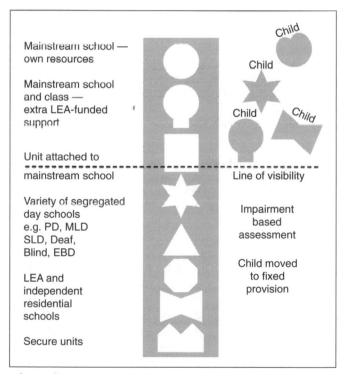

▲ In the fixed continuum the disabled child is slotted and moved according to an impairment based assessment

Figure 8.1 The fixed continuum of provision
Source: Mason and Rieser, 1994

Table 8.1 Number of children in special schools in England and Wales, 1897–1998

Date	Number of children
1897	4,739
1909	17,600
1914	28,511
1919	34,478
1929	49,487
1939	59,768
1947	40,252*
1955	51,558*
1965	70,334*
1967	78,256*
1977	135,261*+
1987	107,126*+
1998	106,426*+

Notes: * hospital schools not included; + includes severe learning difficulty

Source: Cole, 1989, based on Chief Medical Officer, Ministry of Education, DfEE circular 9/13 1998 for England, only includes statemented children in maintained and non-maintained independent schools and PRUs and special schools.

communities. A brief examination of the factors that led to a separate special school system will be useful to understand the social forces that led to the separation of children with more severe impairments (Mason and Rieser, 1994; Cole, 1989). Despite the good intentions of legislators, this has remained remarkably stable in the last twenty years (see Table 8.1).

The Origin of Special Schools

Following the Forster Education Act of 1870, School Boards were set up to provide elementary education for all. The Act did not specifically include provision for disabled children. For the next fifteen to twenty years, most disabled children were in units attached to elementary schools, or not at school at all. Elementary classes were large and instruction was based on the 'Official Code' with rote learning and memory tests. Teachers were paid by results. Large numbers of children made little or no progress and the scale and complexity of learning difficulty and impairment in the population became apparent for the first time. Some progress was made in providing specialist tuition for blind and deaf children in the aforementioned units. For example, by 1890 in Scotland and by 1893 in England and Wales, all blind children aged between five and sixteen and all deaf children between seven and sixteen were sent to school as of right. Much of this provision was made by extending existing elementary schools. No such rights to education applied to the much larger group of 'physically and mentally defective' children. In 1913, the Mental Deficiency Act was passed. Consistent with eugenicist thinking, this required LEAs to ascertain and certify which children aged seven to sixteen in their area were 'educable defectives' and which were 'ineducable defectives'. In 1914 and 1918, respectively, rights to education were provided for those considered 'educable mental and physical defectives'. However, prior to this, many LEAs had made some such provision. In 1921, under strong eugenicist pressure, five categories of disablement were identified: blind, deaf, mental defective, physical defective and epileptic. Children thus labelled were certified and provided for only in separate schools or certified classes.

Following the increasing popularity of IQ testing in the 1920s and 1930s, the Spens Report recommended a tripartite system. The 1944 Education Act established secondary schools for all, but segregated into grammar, secondary modern and technical. Entry at 11-plus was based in part on IQ tests. Selection by ability prompted selection by 'disability' and the growth of special schools, the number of children in which rose sharply when eleven categories of children based on impairment were introduced. These were blind, partially sighted, deaf, partially deaf, delicate, diabetic, educationally sub-normal, epileptic, maladjusted, physically handicapped and those with speech defects. Regulations prescribed that blind, deaf, epileptic, physically handicapped and aphasic children were seriously 'disabled' and *must* be educated in special schools.

It was hoped that the majority of other categories would receive their education in ordinary schools. However, as a result of overcrowding, prejudice, misinterpretations of the legislation and teacher resistance this did not take place. In fact, it was not until the 1950s that large numbers of new special schools were opened. This continued throughout the 1960s and 1970s. Throughout this period, as new demands were made on teachers, nearly always without additional resources or training, the pressure to exclude more children became greater. In 1965, Circular 10/65 was introduced with the intention of abolishing selection at 11-plus and of instituting a system of comprehensive education, the aim being to cater for the needs of all children regardless of gender, 'race', class or ability. Ironically, this led to a further rise in the number of children in special schools, as a result of a fear over declining standards. In addition, economic cuts meant that the majority of comprehensives stuck to streaming rather than mixed-ability teaching and never catered for the full ability range. This is because effective mixed-ability teaching requires more preparation and planning time, and staffing cuts made this difficult. Even so, over the next thirty years, comprehensives proved to be the most effective way of educating the whole cohort, and where there was mixed ability there was overall the greatest exam success (Benn and Chitty, 1997).

In 1970, in England and Wales, the last 60,000 children who had been considered ineducable under the terms of the 1913 Mental Deficiency Act secured the right to education, but with the label 'Educationally Sub-Normal (severe)' (later 'Severe Learning Difficulty') attached to them. Some 400 new special schools were created largely out of the old junior training centres, which were where 'ineducable children' previously received training. Similar moves took place in Scotland in 1974.

The 1976 Education Act was intended to provide schooling for all categories of disabled children in mainstream schools. The then Secretary of State decided not to introduce it, however, owing to resistance from special schools and some LEAs, and the economic cost.

The 1981 Education Act, following the 1978 Warnock Report, again stressed the need for children with special educational needs to be educated in mainstream schools where possible, and introduced the principle of integration. However, no extra resources were made available, and despite some significant moves in some parts of the country, and some excellent examples of good practice, the proportion of the segregated school population has not declined significantly (1.41 per cent in 1977, 1.35 per cent in 1988 and 1.29 per cent in 1997). In addition, owing to local variations in LEA policies, there is an eightfold difference in your chances of going to a mainstream school if you have a statement of special educational need depending on where you live (Norwich, 1997).

The good practice in some areas has been matched by an increase in the percentage of pupils in special schools in other areas, particularly in the period from 1988 to 1991. There is little doubt that the 1988 Education Reform Act has increased the pressure in some schools to segregate disabled children, especially when schools have not already established good integration policies and allocated resources accordingly. Publication of test results is making many schools more selective about their intakes. This has affected non-statemented children with special educational needs, as there is no additional funding earmarked for them and they are not recorded in published results. Statemented children who have earmarked resources attached to them are a more attractive proposition to locally managed budgets, allocated by inflexible, cost-cutting formulae.

The Audit Commission/HMI report, 'Getting in on the Act' (1992), which examined the effectiveness of the 1981 Act, clearly identifies an unmet demand among two-fifths of special school parents who want their children educated in mainstream schools. If mainstream schools demonstrated their ability to include more disabled children, a far larger number of parents would choose these for their children. The Audit Commission report also indicated that, as well as local authorities failing to implement the provisions of the 1981 Act adequately, central government was failing to provide financial incentives. The initiatives following the more inclusionist Green Paper in 1998 are for the first time directing government resources to inclusion.

But the impact of discrimination in education goes much deeper. As Colin Barnes (1991, p. 28) put it after having completed a survey of government reports on education for the Disability Movement:

> Institutional discrimination against disabled people is ingrained throughout the present education system. The data shows that most of the educational provision for disabled children and students remains basically segregative, is dominated by traditionally medically influenced attitudes and commands a low priority as a whole. As a result, rather than equipping disabled children and young people with appropriate skills and opportunities to live a full and active life, it largely conditions them to accepting much devalued social roles and in so doing condemns them to a lifetime of dependence and subordination.

Unfortunately, both the 1993 and 1996 Education Acts kept the 'get-out' clauses of the 1981 Act, with respect to special needs provision. These clauses, which have so often been used to compel disabled children, against their and their parents'/carers' wishes, to attend special schools (Mason, 1998), stipulate 'that educating the child in a school which is not a special school is compatible with:

a   His [*sic*] receiving the special educational provision which his learning difficulty calls for,
b   The provision of efficient education for the children with whom he is educated, and
c   The efficient use of resources.

The difficulty with these stipulations relates to who defines 'efficient' and what values, model and understanding do they bring to these stipulations? Are the parents'/carers' wishes a response to failed assimilation and their own disempowerment?

Each of these clauses is based on a value judgement and there is a remarkable variance from school to school and LEA to LEA over which children it is felt can integrate. It is clear that it has much more to do with attitudes and commitment than anything else. It is also clear that where integration has been planned and resourced, and where all staff have developed it as a whole school policy, it is much more successful (Hegarty and Pocklington, 1981; Booth et al., 1992; Booth and Ainscow, 1998; Sebba, 1997).

The New Labour government (DfEE, 1998) has agreed to review the statutory framework for inclusion. However, the fundamental point is that this legislation does not guarantee the right to an education in the mainstream, if you want it. It is still concerned with assessing the individual, rather than assessing to what extent schools have removed the barriers to inclusion, inherited from the past. So long as these stipulations remain, disabled children will always be threatened with being compelled to go to a special school when the political climate shifts, when there are insufficient resources, or if the school has failed to meet their needs. There is a wider symbolic problem. As long as there are institutions called special schools, mainstream schools and teachers will not feel they have to change their buildings, ethos or teaching and learning strategies to accommodate disabled children. All of us involved with education must engage in the ongoing task of changing deep-seated attitudes and discriminatory behaviour if we are to create an inclusive future in which all will benefit.

Segregated education has not been good for disabled people. Hirst and Baldwin (1994) carried out a major comparative survey of the lives of young disabled and non-disabled people (aged thirteen to twenty-two) which showed stark differences in lifestyle. Most telling was an index of self-esteem which clearly showed that those who attended special schools had a significantly lower score than disabled people who attended mainstream schools, and their scores were also significantly below those of non-disabled people.

Table 8.2 Unequal opportunities growing up disabled

	A Disabled	B Non-disabled
Living with parents	92%	86%
Gone on holiday with friends	25%	52%
Had a spare-time job	22%	32%
Looked after siblings	34%	57%
Had own key	51%	76%
Paid work	35%	67%
Had a boy/girlfriend	30%	40%
Difficulty making friends	35%	20%
Satisfactory network of friends	57%	74%
Self-esteem score	7.3+	8.5*
Internal locus of control	8.8	9.3*

Notes: Group A: 400 disabled people on OPCS category 1–10; Group B: 726 non-disabled people; all respondents aged 13–22.
+ Self-esteem score of those in special schools, 6.2; those in mainstream, 7.5.
* Response score to 12 questions – 6 agree and 6 disagree.

Source: Hirst and Baldwin, 1994.

Table 8.3 Difference in GCSE results for Year 11 students in special and mainstream schools in England, 1995/6

| Schools | 5 or More A*–C | | 5 or more A*–G | | 1 or more A*–G | |
	1995	1996	1995	1996	1995	1996
Mainstream	46.34%	48.42%	84.88%	87.22%	91.25%	93.40%
Special	0.47%	0.46%	3.70%	4.15%	15.32%	16.29%

Notes: There were 5,013 schools in total: 3,985 mainstream secondary and 1,028 special; figures given are percentage of age group.

Source: Gary Thomas (1997) 'Exam performance in special schools', Bristol: Centre for Studies on Inclusive Education (using DfEE 1995/6 secondary school performance league tables).

In addition, Gary Thomas et al. (1997) analysed GCSE results by type of school and found that 70 per cent of special schools do not enter any pupils for GCSE. He went on to show that 93 per cent of mainstream Year 11 students get at least one A*–G grade, whereas only 16 per cent of Year 11 students in special schools get at least one A*–G grade. This is particularly shocking if one considers the largest group of pupils in special schools are labelled as having 'Moderate Learning Difficulty' (nearly 55,000), and that in mainstream schools they would all be entered for GCSE.

The Language We Use

The inheritance of the past conditions current attitudes, policies and practices towards disabled children and young people in society and within education.

This is nowhere more clearly demonstrated and symbolized than in the language used. Take, for example, the negative connotations associated with 'cripple' (without power), 'sufferer', 'invalid' and 'handicapped' (commonly used as a noun to describe children, when it is actually a verb meaning imposed disadvantage from beyond the person).

We wish to be known as 'disabled people' in recognition of the common oppression we face regardless of our specific impairment. People with learning difficulties reject 'mental handicap', wishing to be known as the former. We reject the inhumanity and 'medical model' thinking involved in labelling and identifying people by their impairing condition. Calling someone a 'Down's' or 'spina bifida' child makes the child no more than their condition. Using 'the blind', 'the deaf' or 'the disabled' to describe us diminishes us. We wish to be known as blind people, deaf people or disabled people. If it is necessary to identify a particular impairment, one should say, for example, 'child [or person] with Down's syndrome'.

Within education, impairing condition labels such as 'epileptic' and 'diabetic' and evaluative labels such as 'educationally sub-normal' or 'physically handicapped' have been replaced by labels based on bands of need and derived from Warnock, for example, 'MLD' ('mild learning difficulty') or 'SLD' ('severe learning difficulty'). Inevitably, since children are assessed to fit these categories of need, they become known by their label, and their destination, which tends to be specific separate provision.

In 1991 the Department for Education produced five categories of staffing provision, linked to impairment. These are now increasingly widely used and children are becoming labelled, for example, as 'PMLD' ('profound and multiple learning difficulties') – the most severe category of need with the best staffing ratio. This has reinforced the idea of a continuum of fixed provision in separate schools. We must reject the legacy of the past that has excluded us. We have to recognize that all children and adults have a right to be included in mainstream education and society as a fundamental human right (Mason and Rieser, 1994; Rieser and Mason, 1992).

A Constellation of Services Supporting Inclusion

In the fixed continuum of provision, the disabled child is slotted in and moved around according to an impairment-based assessment (see Figure 8.1 above). In contrast, the constellation of services provides what the child and the class teacher need in mainstream schools. This includes a variety of services, resources and specialists who bring their expertise to the child rather than vice versa. This conception allows for the development of inclusive schools (see Figure 8.2). It also provides much greater flexibility but, because it is new and unknown, it is seen by many professionals as threatening. These two figures show the transition we wish to achieve from an education service structured on the 'medical model' to one based on the 'social model'.

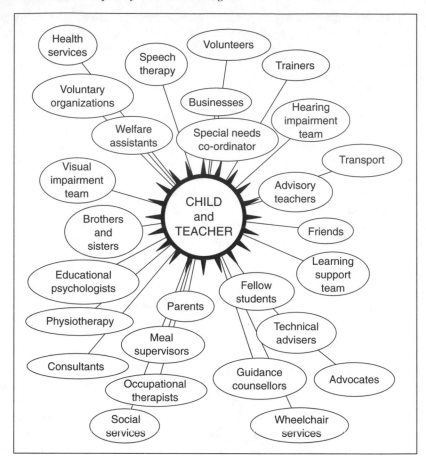

The constellation of services provides what the child and the class teacher need in ordinary schools, from a variety of services, resources and specialists. This conception allows for the development of inclusive schools.

Figure 8.2 The constellation of services
Source: Mason and Rieser, 1994

Integration and Inclusion

Integration

Integration is a matter of location and there are at least four variants:

- Periodic integration: children from special schools are bussed into a mainstream school at a regular time each week for 'integration', or an 'integration event' is organized.
- Geographical integration: disabled children may be educated in units or schools

on the same campus or site as their non-disabled peers, but do no
socially.
- Social integration: disabled children may share meals, playtime and
  with non-disabled peers, but are not taught with them.
- Functional integration: disabled and non-disabled children are ta
  same class.

What all forms of integration have in common is the assumption of some form of assimilation of the disabled child into the mainstream school. The school remains largely unchanged and the focus is on the child fitting in. As we have seen, if the child is unable to do this, the law can be used to direct her/him to a special school or unit.

Inclusion

Inclusion, on the other hand, is about a child's right to belong to her/his local mainstream school, to be valued for who s/he is and to be provided with all the support s/he needs to thrive. Since mainstream schools are generally not organized in this way, it requires planned restructuring of the whole school. This restructuring should be seen as an extension of the school's equal opportunities policy and practice. It requires a commitment from the whole staff, the governors, parents/carers and pupils/students. Inclusion is not a static state like integration. It is a continuing process involving a major change in school ethos and is about building a school community that accepts and values difference.

In order to become inclusive, schools should adopt a 'social model of disability'. They must identify the barriers within the school's environment, teaching and learning strategies, attitudes, organization and management that prevent the full participation of disabled children and, as such, are part of the social oppression of disabled people. Functional integration is a precondition for the development of inclusion and disability equality. It does not, in itself, achieve it. The index of inclusion schooling – a pilot project being developed by the Centre for Studies of Inclusive Education (CSIE 2000), Professor Mel Ainscow at Manchester University and Professor Tony Booth at Canterbury Christ Church University College – allows schools, through a process of self-assessment by all stakeholders, to self-evaluate their progress from integration towards inclusion. Having been piloted in 21 schools, this is being promoted by the DfEE and a copy is being sent to every school in England. It will enable schools to find out how inclusive they are and will set targets for improvement as part of the school self-review and development plan process.

Inclusion depends on the extent to which all children get what they need to grow and develop, and how open the teacher and the children in the class are to learn and respect each and every child's experience. This sounds idealistic, but the alternative is to continue to reproduce the status quo, with its built-in discrimination against disabled children. Inclusion fundamentally challenges the traditional approach which regards impairment and disabled people as marginal, or an 'after-thought', instead of recognizing that impairment and disablement are a common experience of humanity and should be a central issue in the planning and delivery of a human service such as education.

Mike Oliver, an educationalist and a leading member of the Disability Movement, drew out the differences between integration and inclusion in a paper he gave during National Integration Week in May 1992:

Old Integration is:	'New' Integration or Inclusion is:
a state	a process
non-problematic	problematic
a professional and administrative approach	politics
changes in school organization	change in school ethos
teachers acquire skills	teachers acquire commitment
curriculum delivery must change	curriculum content must change
legal rights	moral and political rights
acceptance and tolerance of children with special education	valuation and celebration of disabled children and children with learning difficulty
normality	difference
Integration can be delivered	Inclusion must be struggled for

Inclusive education should be the guiding principle. We should be working towards a system and an ethos where mainstream schools should accommodate all children regardless of their physical, intellectual, social, emotional, linguistic or other conditions.

Central to inclusive education is the involvement of disabled people in the consultation, planning and implementation of it. Examples already exist of the successful inclusion of children with every type and severity of impairment in mainstream schools in the UK. Many changes in school organization and practice have been necessary to make this happen, but from all such changes the non-disabled majority of children have benefited.

The best way of facilitating such whole school change is to hold whole staff INSET courses run by disabled Disability Equality Trainers with recent experience of the education system. This should be followed up by a representative working and monitoring group to work through the checklist below and regularly report back to all staff.

Pupils/students need to be involved in this process through whole class discussion, assemblies and pupil/student councils. Parents/carers of disabled children are often disempowered by professional interventions which have threatened or broken their relationship with their disabled child. Parents for Inclusion are developing training to address this issue. The LEA, Social Services and Health Service need to provide the support and additional resources to the school to help overcome the barriers to inclusion.

The inclusion process is part of school improvement and developing more effective comprehensive schooling for all. Goals need to be built into the School Development Plan to be met over a five- or ten-year time-scale and their achievement must be monitored.

What follows are some of the necessary changes that schools, teachers, governors, non-teaching staff, parents/carers and pupils/students have to undertake to become inclusive.

A Whole School Policy on Disability Equality and Inclusion

a Access audit of the school environment. Carry out a full access audit of your building. Involve pupils/students. Cost and set targets of major and minor works to be included in the school development plan. Involve the governors in pressing the LEA for access works. Money is available through the Schools Access Initiative.

b Audit access to the learning environment. Audit software and hardware suitable for supporting learning difficulties. Maintain up-to-date information on adaptations, for example, signing, Brailling, vocalizing, voice recognition, touch screen, laptops, switching. Make lessons multi-media. Make sure visuals can be described or subtitled if necessary.

c Ensure disability issues are in the curriculum. When planning a curriculum unit, topic or module think of including a disability dimension. Build up resources and literature that are non-discriminatory and include disabled people in a non-patronizing way (see guidelines in Chapter 7 of this volume). Promote the 'social model' of disability.

d Disabled people are positively portrayed. Ensure all children have access to positive images of disabled adults and children in non-stereotyped activities and roles. Make sure the school has a range of picture or reading books that do this (see selected reading list at the end of this chapter). Involve disabled adults from the community in activities and lessons.

e Diversify the curriculum. When planning the curriculum, use a wide variety of approaches to draw on different strengths and aptitudes of the pupils/students. Build up a resource bank of ideas and lessons allowing time for joint planning and review. Check teaching and learning strategies and targets are appropriate for the needs of all children in the class.

f Develop collaborative learning and peer tutoring. The pupils/students comprise the biggest learning resource in any school. Involve them in pairing with children of different abilities and groups. All children benefit from these approaches.

g Effective team approach for learning support and curriculum planning. Ensure that learning support is effectively co-ordinated throughout the school and in each classroom. Allow time for joint planning in the school day, involving teachers and learning support assistants. Develop the skills and confidence of the learning support assistants to carry out different roles in the classroom with groups of children.

h British Sign Language. When a school includes deaf children, make use of British Sign Language translators and teachers. Offer deaf children the chance to work with native signers. Offer hearing children the chance to study sign language as part of the curriculum. Give a positive value to different forms of communication. For deaf and partially hearing children, it is important to understand their need for induction loops, lip reading and good room acoustics.

i Accessible communication with parents/carers. Recognize that not everyone communicates by written or spoken English. Audit the communication needs within the school and of parents and provide notices, reports, information and directions in the relevant format, for example, large print, Braille, tape, videos in British Sign Language, computer disk and pictograms, and use symbols for people with learning disabilities.

j Be critical of disablist language. Examine language used in teaching and by other pupils. Much of it is disablist and impairment derived. Develop a critical reappraisal through disability equality training, assemblies and in class.

k Challenge impairment-derived abuse, name-calling and bullying as part of the school behaviour policy. Introduce effective policy to prevent abuse, name-calling and bullying because of physical, mental or sensory differences. Make this part of your school anti-bullying policy.

l Involve all pupils in developing behaviour policy. Policies devised with pupil/student involvement and based on principles of self-regulation and mutual respect are the most effective. Cultivate developmental discipline. Sometimes it is necessary for adults to take a lead in setting up circles of friends and buddy systems. All children should remain on roll even if for some time they are out of class. Devise systems where distressed children can take 'time-out' and talk to sympathetic adults. Have access to counselling and psychiatry.

m Develop a whole school ethos on accepting difference. Use events like assemblies, plays and sports days to demonstrate this, as well as in day-to-day functioning.

n Develop empowerment and self-representation of disabled pupils/students. Set up structures through which disabled pupils/students can express their views, develop self-esteem, and have some influence on school policies. Involve disabled adults in this process. Develop training in self-advocacy.

o Physical Education. Ensure PE and sporting activities involve all pupils/students, develop collaboration and encourage all pupils to improve their personal performance. Use adaptation and creative imagination to succeed in this.

p Transport and school trips policy. Make sure this includes all. Ensure that transport to and from the school for disabled pupils fits in with the school day and cater for attendance at after-school activities. Allow the disabled child's friends and siblings to use transport to break down isolation. Ensure no pupil is excluded from a trip or visit because their access or other needs are not met. This means careful advance planning and pre-visits.

q Have an increasing inclusion ethos in the school development plan. The school should examine every aspect of its activity for barriers to inclusion and, describing how this is to be achieved, then set a series of targets for their eradication.

r Include outside specialist support. Plan the work of speech, physio- and occupational therapists in a co-ordinated way which best supports pupils'/students' curriculum needs and reduces disruption to their learning and social needs.

s Policy on administering medication and personal assistance. Devise a policy on administering routine medication which is easy for pupils/students to use and develop systems that maintain their dignity on personal-hygiene issues. Have a system for handling medical emergencies which is easy for everyone to use.

t Maintain equipment. Ensure that specialist equipment is properly maintained, stored and replaced when necessary. Mobility aids, for example, wheelchairs and walking frames, should be regularly checked and staff trained in their proper use.

u Increase the employment of disabled staff. The Disability Discrimination Act now applies to employment in most schools. Revise the equal opportunity employment policy to increase the employment of disabled teaching and non-teaching staff. There is Access to Work money available for disabled employees from Placing, Assessing and Counselling Teams (PACT) officers at Job Centres. All children need disabled adult role models.

v Disability equality training and ongoing INSET for staff and governors. Organize a programme of in-service training for teachers, support staff and governors to help them move towards inclusion and disability equality. Ensure all staff are involved in and understand the process of inclusion.

w Governing body representation. Appoint a governor to have a brief for special educational needs, with the whole governing body involved in developing inclusion policy. Try to get disabled governors.

x Consultation with and involvement of parents/carers. Ensure there are effective arrangements for involving parents/carers in all parts of their child's school life, including any decisions that have to be made. These arrangements should involve counselling and support in helping a child towards independence. With their permission, maintain information about parents/carers who are themselves disabled, so that their access and other needs can be met.

Moving Towards Inclusion

In many schools the largest barriers to including pupils/students with needs that have not previously been catered for at the school are the fears and attitudes of the staff. These can best be addressed by putting disablement into an equal opportunities framework and by having whole staff disability equality sessions which should be led by disabled disability equality trainers (Disability Equality in Education offer such training – see References). This should be followed by an audit of the barriers in the school, the development of an action plan to minimize the barriers and incorporation of the plan into the school's SEN policy (CSIE, 1996, 2000).

Sometimes particular information about children's impairments is required and this can be most usefully obtained from the children themselves or their parents. They are experts on their impairments.

Sometimes medically based professionals such as occupational therapists, physiotherapists and speech therapists can be useful in providing certain procedures or specialist equipment and practices. But it should always be remembered that the child is at school to learn alongside his or her peers and wherever possible this support should be given in class and in the least disruptive way. Often these other adults can benefit groups of children in the class.

There will often be learning support assistants in the class, usually to support particular children. The more they can be involved in joint planning, the more able they are to make a positive contribution to the learning and teaching in the class, not just for their particular pupil. The class or subject teacher has to take a lead in co-ordinating the activities of all these adults and making their activities part of the educational activity in the class. The SENCO (special educational needs co-ordinator) can play a vital role in developing such working partnerships.

For inclusion to work best requires a child-centred pedagogy in well-structured mixed-ability classrooms. There are many pressures from OFSTED, the government and the league tables to set and stream. But these are moves that undermine an inclusive ethos and can often replicate segregative practices within one institution, leading in the longer term to a drop in overall standards. A mixture of teaching styles can meet these competing pressures: whole class teaching with peer tutoring; collaborative groups; individual or paired work; and joint teaching with another class. The more flexible the teaching style, the more likely to include a wider variety of pupil/student needs.

Many teachers say they are in principle in favour of inclusion, but it requires a massive increase in resources to be possible. It must be remembered that one-seventh of all education budgets is spent on special educational needs. There is a need for increased capital investment in the school building stock to make it accessible, and, thanks to the Within Reach Campaign organized by SCOPE and the NUT, this is beginning to happen. But the major problem is that the majority of SEN spending is in the wrong place – some 1,200 special schools for 100,000 children. LEA development plans will have to identify over the coming period how these resources can be reallocated to mainstream schools in a planned way to enhance inclusion. The important point here is that LEAs should agree to ring-fence all resources and posts to special educational needs as they transfer them to the mainstream. LEAs must also set up adequate monitoring and advisory teacher posts to ensure that the resources put into mainstream schools are being used to further inclusion and meet the needs of children with SEN.

The London Borough of Newham (Jordan and Goodey, 1996) provides a useful indicator of how such moves towards inclusion can occur in a poor, multi-cultural, inner-city area. In 1984 a group of parents of disabled children ran for and were elected on to the council with the express wish of seeing the ending of segregated special education. They achieved their aim in a council policy which recognized the rights of children, whatever their needs, to learn together. The borough's latest policy has a goal of making it possible 'for every child, whatever special educational needs they may have, to attend their neighbourhood school'. Between 1984 and 1998 the number of special schools in the borough was reduced from eight to one and the number of children segregated in special education dropped from 913 to 206. Parents/carers are becoming increasingly confident in the ability of their neighbourhood school to meet diverse needs and teachers have signed an agreement on inclusive education.

This was achieved in an educational and political climate that was hostile to this process. Resourced schools were set up to meet certain needs in mainstream schools as a response to parental/carer concerns. These are now planned to be phased out as Newham moves to inclusive neighbourhood schools. The process from the start envisaged radically changing mainstream schools rather than fitting children with SEN into the existing system. An independent report commented that having to cater for children with serious learning difficulties helped schools make better provision for all pupils (Rouse and Florian, 1996). This was borne out in 1997. Newham schools had the biggest improvement nationally in the GCSE results of all students in grades A–G, a trend that continued in 1998 and 1999. Many children labelled as having severe learning difficulties are now passing exams. In addition, the numbers of exclusions have been falling while they have been rising in most other parts of the country. The LEA has now appointed four monitoring officers proactively to address this process of developing inclusion from integration.

It will help to understand the inclusion process to give a thumbnail sketch of two inclusive schools.

The first is one of seventeen resourced mainstream schools in Newham. It is a purpose-built inclusive school with funding for thirty-six statemented children with severe and profound learning difficulties. In addition, there are six other statemented children. Free meals are provided for 59.6 per cent of the children and the school has a multicultural intake. There are four wings: Nursery and Reception, with 120 pupils; Years 1 and 2, with 120; Years 3 and 4, with 120; and Years 5 and 6, with 96 pupils. The additional teaching staff are organized in teams with the class teachers to give six teachers in each wing. In Key Stage 1 there are also six support staff who work as part of the team. The children choose when and what they will do each day, though they must do reading, writing and maths. They keep their own diaries and these are used as the IEP (individual education plan) for statemented children. In each wing there is a practical room, a reading room, a writing room, a finding-out room for science, geography and history and a quiet room. There are no breaks but all children do a PE activity every day, including various sports and physiotherapy. The lunchtime is a continuous sitting and there are many clubs then. The children all seem engaged in learning and are very pleasant to each other, while the support staff are deployed across the teams to meet particular needs. All staff 'change' children and administer medicines if parental permission is given. Each team has a team leader. In the wings one teacher is responsible for one part of the curriculum for the week for all 120 children. In Years 5 and 6, this is for half a term. The additional resourcing allows for shaping teams to meet the needs of all the children. The school has eight extra teachers and fourteen extra support staff, giving a staff of fifty. There is now an excellent account of school change with respect to teaching and learning for inclusion written by staff and pupils at the school (Alderson, 1999).

The second school is a comprehensive high school with 1,100 Year 8 to Year 11 pupils, with ten forms of entry. It is an additionally resourced mainstream school for thirty-six physically disabled students. They have a head of learning development, 8.4 full-time teachers, 1 part-time (two days a week) teacher, 8 learning assistants and a clerical assistant. There is a learning development room where staff from the department work and it is open to any student to come to ask for help at lunchtime or after school. Next door is a physio/resource/changing/toilet/ shower suite. In addition to the thirty-six students for the resourced provision, the learning development department leads on the identified learning needs of the 247 students on the special needs register. The building has been adapted so all rooms are accessible. The school has developed collaborative/partnership teaching in which departments make bids to work with teachers from the learning development department for a term or a year. The purpose of this is to develop a shared understanding of all the arrangements and practice involved in working together, joint planning and evaluation. Time is essential for this process. This is achieved by timetabling learning development teachers and subject teachers to have non-contact periods at the same time, and these are ring-fenced so they are never asked to cover. The collaboration includes shared aims, the joint preparation and presentation of resources and shared responsibility for group discipline, marking and report writing. I visited a science, music and art class and saw the inclusive practice in process. Having disabled students in the class seemed natural to all the students. The teaching staff all seemed happy with the arrangements and talked of their benefit to everyone, and how the department's flexibility gave them all the support they needed.

Thomas et al. (1998) have analysed the Somerset Inclusion Project, which drew its inspiration from a special school in Canada (Shaw, 1990). The Somerset Project centred on the Princess Margaret School for Physically Disabled Pupils. In 1992 it was a day and boarding special school. However, on closing in 1997, it had managed to include the vast majority of its pupils successfully in mainstream schools. Ninety staff were retrained and relocated to support the children in the mainstream. The study gives many insights into the management of change, not least because one of its authors, Dave Walker, was the headteacher of Princess Margaret and effectively oversaw a process which was to leave him without a job.

In conclusion the authors state that:

> with vision and careful planning special schools can successfully change their
> work in such a way to enable their mainstream partners to include children
> even with serious disabilities. One of our clearest findings has been that while
> many mainstream staff were highly sceptical about the inclusion project before

it started, they had changed their views entirely after several months of seeing it in practice and were fulsome in their support of inclusion.

(Thomas et al., 1998, p. 198)

Conclusion

While it certainly helps to have a government or an LEA that is sympathetic to it, inclusion is fundamentally a school-based process. Mel Ainscow (1994, 1995, 1998) has argued that inclusion is part of the process of developing school effectiveness. 'Moving' schools, those that are open to change, which are usually non-hierarchical but with strong leadership, are much more able to develop inclusive practice. 'Stuck' schools, on the other hand, have hierarchical structures, poor leadership and lack of involvement of staff in charge, and are much less likely to be able to undergo the restructuring that is necessary to become inclusive. Certainly the variance in inclusive practice between similar schools would support this. Teachers deciding what type of school they want to work in would do well to remember this distinction.

The thinking of the disability movement, the development of the 'social model' and the voice of disabled people who have experienced segregated and integrated education are essential in the development of inclusion. The Salamanca Statement (UNESCO, 1994) recognizes this crucial role: 'encourage and facilitate the participation of parents, communities and organizations of disabled people in the planning and decision making processes concerning the provision for special educational needs'.

Inclusion is a process of school change that benefits not only disabled people but the entire school community. Eventually society will experience a reduction in prejudice and discrimination against disabled people as difference becomes part of everyone's experience and disabled people become part of the community in their own right.

References

Ainscow, M. (1994) *Special Needs in the Classroom: A Teacher Education Guide*, London: Jessica Kingsley

Ainscow, M. (1995) 'Education for all: Making it Happen', *Support for Learning*, 10 (4), pp. 147–57

Ainscow, M. (1998) 'Reaching out to all Learners: Opportunities and Possibilities', keynote presentation at North of England Education Conference, Bradford

Alderson, P. (1999) *Learning and Inclusion: The Cleeves School Experience*, London: David Fulton

Barnes, C. (1991) *Disabled People in Britain and Discrimination*, London: Hurst

Benn, C. and Chitty, C. (1997) *Thirty Years on: Is Comprehensive Education Alive and Well or Struggling to Survive*, London: Penguin

Booth, T. and Ainscow, M. (1998) *From Them to Us: An International Study on Inclusive Education*, London: Routledge

Booth, T., Swann, W., Masterton, M. and Potts, P. (1992) 'Diversity in Education' and 'Curricular for Diversity in Education', *Learning for All*, London: Routledge

Centre for Studies of Inclusive Education (1996) *Developing an Inclusive Policy for Your School*, Bristol: CSIE

Centre for Studies of Inclusive Education (2000) 'Index for Inclusion: Developing Learning and Participation in Schools', Bristol/CSIE.

Cole, T. (1989) *Apart or a Part?: Integration and the Growth of British Special Education*, Milton Keynes: Open University Press

DfEE (1997) *Excellence for all Children: Meeting Special Educational Needs*, London: HMSO

DfEE (1998) *An Action Programme for Special Educational Needs*, London: HMSO

Hegarty, S. and Pocklington, K. (1981) *Educating Pupils with Special Needs in Ordinary Schools*, Windsor: NFER

Hirst, A. and Baldwin, S. (1994) *Unequal Opportunities Growing up Disabled*, London: HMSO

Jordan, L. and Goodey, C. (1996) *Human Rights and School Change: The Newham Story*, Bristol: CSIE

Mason, M. (1998) *Forced apart: The Case for Ending Compulsory Segregation in Education*, London: Alliance for Inclusive Education

Mason, M. and Rieser, R. (1994) *Altogether Better*, London: Comic Relief

Murray, P. and Penman, J. (1996) *Let Our Children Be: A Collection of Stories*, Sheffield: Parents with Attitude

Norwich, B. (1997) *A Trend towards Inclusion: Statistics on Special School Placement and Pupils with Statements in Ordinary Schools England 1992–96*, Bristol: CSIE

Oliver, M. (1992) 'Talk given to Greater London Association of Disabled People', Integration Week, May 1992, Bristol: CSIE

Rieser, R. and Mason, M. (1990/1992) *Disability Equality in the Classroom: A Human Rights Issue*, London: Disability Equality in Education

Rouse, M. and Florian, L. (1996) 'Effective Inclusive Schools: A Study in Two Countries', *Cambridge Journal of Education*, 26 (1), pp. 71–80

Sebba, J. with Sachdev, D. (1997) *What Works in Inclusive Education?*, Essex: Barnardos

Shaw, L. (1990) *Each Belongs: Integrated Education in Canada*, Bristol: CSIE

Thomas, G., Walker, D. and Webb, J. (1998) *The Making of the Inclusive School*, London: Routledge

UNESCO (1994) *The Salamanca Statement and Framework for Action on Special Needs Education*, Paris: UNESCO

Selection of Recommended Inclusive Children's Books

3–8 Years

Bunnett, Rochelle, *Friends at School*, Star Bright Books. Letterbox*. Beautifully photographed images capture warmth of an inclusive classroom as children play together.

Dowling, Dorothy and Dowling, Jack, *Learning Together ABC: A Fingerspelling Alphabet with Signs for Deaf and Hearing Children*, Sheffield: 18 Blackstock Drive.

Foreman, Michael, *Seal Surfer*, Anderson Press. Letterbox. As the seasons change we follow a special relationship between a disabled boy, his grandfather and a seal.

Hearn, Emily, *Race You Franny*, *Good Morning Franny*, *Franny and the Music Girl*, Women's Press of Canada. Third book: Letterbox. Adventures of a wheelchair-using girl.

Hill, Eric, *Spot Goes to School*, National Deaf Children's Society. Sign Language book.

Larkin, Patricia, *Dad and Me in the Morning*, Albert Whitman. Letterbox. Lovely book about a deaf boy and his dad, signing, lip reading and squeezing hands as they share a dawn walk.

Merrifield, Margaret, *Come Sit by Me*, Women's Press of Canada. Letterbox. HIV/AIDS.

Naidoo, Beverley, *Letang's New Friend*, *Trouble for Letang and Julie*, *Letang and Julie Save the Day*, Longman. Second book: Letterbox. Letang, just arrived from Botswana, befriends wheelchair-using Julie.

Sakai, Kimiko, *Sachiko Means Happiness*, Children's Book Press, Letterbox. Sachiko's acceptance of her grandmother's Alzheimer's with warm and gentle illustrations.

Wilkins, Verna, *Boots for a Bridesmaid*, Tamarind. Letterbox. Story of Nicky and her wheelchair-using mum.

Wilkins, Vera, *Are We There Yet?*, Tamarind. Letterbox. A family day out at a theme park with Max, Amy and wheelchair-using Dad.

9–14 Years

Brown, Christy, *Down all the Days*, *My Left Foot*, Pan (over thirteens).

Harris, R.H., *Let's Talk about Sex*, Walker Books.

Keith, Lois, *A Different Life*, Live Wire/Women's Press. Excellent novel about a fifteen-year-old girl adjusting to not being able to walk and how she learns to be strong (over twelves).

Keith, Lois, *Mustn't Grumble*, Women's Press. Excellent book in which thirty-six disabled women write about their lives (over thirteens).

Stemp, Jane, *Waterbound*, Hodder Headline. An excellent book written by a disabled author, *Waterbound* is the story of a time in the future when eugenics has triumphed . . . or has it? The discovery of disabled siblings beneath the city leads to a revolution (over tens).

* Books available from Letterbox Library, 2nd Floor, Leroy House, 436 Essex Road, London N1 3QP. Tel: 0207 226 1633.

9   Class and Class Analysis for the Twenty-first Century

Tom Hickey

Is your class simply a question of your wealth? Is it, alternatively, more to do with your social background, or your education, or your lifestyle? Is it a question of what kind of job you do, and, if so, is that because of the income you earn from doing it, or the status that it enjoys? Is social class an objective or a subjective matter – are you a member of a class irrespective of what you think, or by virtue of the class in which you believe yourself to be? And, however defined, are members of subordinate classes properly to be treated as victims, and discriminated against in favour of the interests of equality? Alternatively, perhaps the question itself is misconceived. Is the question of class a dead letter at the end of the twentieth century, irrelevant for both politics and social analysis?

The Postmodernist Moment

Postmodernism adopts an affirmative answer to the last of these questions. Postmodernist theories erupted into disputes within the social sciences in the 1980s to challenge the 'discourse' of class analysis, and the 'terrorizing totalizations' of grand theory in general, and Marxism in particular. Historical explanations that sought patterns, uniformities and ultimate causes, or social theories which grounded themselves on definitive characterizations of epochs and the mechanisms of epochal change, were abandoned. Expressive of their moment, and of the disillusionment of their authors in the feasibility of any alternative to the existing social order, these postmodernisms survive now after their moment has passed.

Class politics is ended, the postmodernist declares, and people no longer think about society in class terms. In a 'postmodern world', sub-units of populations are only distinguished, we are urged to believe, on the basis of the unstable characteristics of 'lifestyle choices'.[1] No longer are social groups locked into segmented labour markets by their social backgrounds so as to constitute economic classes. The development of the capitalist market economy, it is argued, has finally suppressed the vestiges of traditional discriminations so that now there is open and unfettered competition between individuals in an undifferentiated labour market. Failure and success are no longer the consequences of social structures and social processes; they are the fruits of individual effort and ability, and are even experienced as such in a privatized and individualized world where group solidarities and identifications based on class no longer exist.[2] Postmodernism is thus a liberal rhetoric for the twenty-first century. If class divisions, and the different interests they express, are denied by postmodernist theorists, so too is class conflict and class struggles. Class is no longer an organizing principle for social action, it is claimed.

Yet these claims persistently collide with the inconvenient details of contemporary political history. At the *fin de siècle*, for example, in response to the development of a global economic crisis, we see a resurgence of trade unionism in Western Europe, the eruption of class-based upheavals in South East Asia, and the popular rejection of political parties associated with the liberal espousal of the free market in the 1980s and 1990s. In Britain, for example, 87 per cent believe income differences between rich and poor to be too great, 69 per cent think that social class affects one's life opportunities 'a great deal' or 'quite a lot', and 59 per cent think that big business operates for the benefit of its owners '*at the expense of* the workers.[3] Furthermore, the evidence shows these perceptions to be well founded. Far from being of declining importance, social class remains the prime determinant of educational attainment, and a major determinant both of the age of death and of general levels of health.[4]

Nevertheless, the postmodernist argument is that the identities which people have in such a world are *adopted by choice*, or by virtue of a non-economic oppression; they are *not ascribed* by the economic position that people occupy. It is around these oppressions, of gender, ethnicity, disability, sexual orientation and locality, and with concern for environmental degradation, maltreatment of animals and global injustice, that 'new social movements' form. These are movements for enlightenment, cultural change and social reform relevant for today and tomorrow; they are not 'yesterday's campaigns' based on issues of class. These social movements are the stuff of the future's politics. Such is the postmodernist prognostication.[5] It is the purpose of this chapter to argue against this fragmentation of politics by suggesting both its double falsity, both as description of the contemporary world and as explanation of it, and its ineffectuality as a strategy for overcoming the oppressions of that world.

This hostility to the idea of class only arises with any fervour, however, when the concept is used as part of a general explanatory scheme. The more astute postmodernist critic realizes that the 'class' to which he or she is so opposed is not a casual identification of some contingent, empirical correlations. With sociological classifications of social class there would be little difficulty. These usually segment the population according to the status of the occupations pursued. These divisions are then used for a variety of purposes from market research (e.g. is an area a promising location in which to site a Waitrose rather than a Tesco supermarket) to voting behaviour. Such schemes are not designed to *explain* social phenomena but rather to act in a purely *descriptive* manner. In this they differ sharply from the models devised by Karl Marx and Max Weber. These are the models of society, and the theories of class embedded in them, that raise the ire of postmodernists. It is to these that we must turn for a developed theory of class.

Marx: 'Class' and Historical Materialism

Historical Materialism was the first systematic attempt to identify *structures* that constrain human behaviour, and determine the circumstances in which humans *become* the social beings that they are. As such, it was a radical break with tradition as both philosophy and social theory. It was a break from the natural rights tradition (from Plato and Aristotle to Aquinas) in which social regulations and codes are rationally binding on human behaviour in virtue of an absolute, and presupposed, human nature and idea of what was Good. It was a break from the empiricist tradition (Locke and Hume), which had treated knowledge as derivable only from observation, and from social contract theory (Hobbes and Locke), which took membership of a society to be evidence of the implicit consent of the governed to the authority of the sovereign power. It was a break from the romantic philosophical tradition that had invested humans with an *inner* power both to determine the Good and to construct laws that met its requirements (Kant), or which treated all phenomena and events as part of an integrated, organic totality that was unfolding according to the plan of an objective (i.e. natural) reason (Fichte, Schelling, Hegel). Historical Materialism, by contrast, was materialist in that humans were treated as material beings who had to satisfy their basic needs for survival and reproduction as a species before they could do anything else; it was historical in that the possibilities for social and economic organization in the present were always set (in the sense both of 'restricted' and 'made possible') by the circumstances that had been inherited from the past.[6]

The young Marx, concerned with the issue of human freedom and emancipation, believed himself to have discovered in 'the proletariat' (or working class) not only a social group with its own *interest* in the overthrow of the political and economic order, but a group whose structural position in modern society provided its members with the *power* to do so. It was the first exploited class in human history to have this potential. It was also a social group which was unable to liberate itself from exploitation without liberating the whole of humanity from its various oppressions. In the early 1840s, both Marx and Frederick Engels turned their attention to the class structure of nineteenth-century European capitalism, and to the struggles between the contending classes to which it gave rise. This focus was to enable them to develop a theory of history, Historical Materialism, whose central distinctive feature was the identification of class struggles as the social dynamic throughout human history. The concept of class used by these authors, and by their followers today, cannot be understood independently of this theory of which it is a part.

For Marx and Engels, as they argued in *The Manifesto of the Communist Party* (Marx and Engels, 1969, p. 108), '[t]he history of all hitherto existing society is the history of class struggle'. By this they did not mean that there were no other interesting or significant features of past and existing societies that were significant for their histories. Their claim was that in order to understand any of these other features adequately, and to grasp why whole societies developed for a period and then decayed and were replaced by successors, required appreciating them in the knowledge of their central feature – the struggle between the direct producers of wealth, on the one hand, and the minority of rulers whose existence depended on the appropriation of part of that wealth, on the other. Indeed, it was the precise way in which the ruling minority extracted a surplus from the work of the direct producers and appropriated it for its own use, the mechanism of 'exploitation', that constituted the defining property of each type of human society. Slave societies differed, they argued, from feudal societies, and these from capitalist societies, not simply by the degree of deprivation and degradation of the direct producers but by the mode of surplus extraction: in the first, by constituting the producers as *the property* of the master, and hence also all that is produced by them; in the second, by the enforcement of traditional *legal rights and duties* entitling the lord to a share of peasant production; and in the third, by contracting with workers, as legally free agents, that they will *exchange in the market* their power to work for a period in return for an agreed wage, and then create goods in that period which would be the property of the capitalist, and whose value exceeded that of the wages that the producers would be paid.

Marx's model of society and history had three key features. First, the claim that it is the economic structure (i.e. the social relations of production, or which class has direct control of the means of production) that is the real foundation of society, and hence that it is '[t]he mode of production of material life [which] conditions the social, political and intellectual life process in general' (Marx and Engels, 1969, p. 503). Second, that there have been in human history a sequence of different modes of production, each characterized by a distinctive method of taking a surplus from the wealth produced by the efforts of the direct producers, of which the capitalist mode is merely the latest, but not the last, despite its appearance of permanence and naturalness. Third, that the class relations in any given mode of production (the 'relations' of production) would bear a definite relationship to the level of development of the techniques used to produce (the 'forces' of production). This was a dramatic and exciting vista on the human condition, whose scope and ambition have never been, and may never be, matched.[7]

All societies that evolved beyond a primitive stage, they argued, generated a class of rulers who would extract from the labour of the producing class as much as possible of what was surplus to the survival needs of the producers. The exact nature of this process of surplus extraction, and the character of the producing and exploiting classes involved in it, would depend on the way in which access to (i.e. ownership or effective control of) the means of production (tools and raw materials – the 'instruments' and 'objects' of human labour) was distributed between classes. This distribution of the means of production – which class owns or controls them – constituted what Marx called the 'relations of production'. Classes are defined then in terms of their relationship to the means of production. In the capitalist mode of production, the bourgeoisie has exclusive ownership or control of the means of production, from which the proletariat has been excluded.[8] This contrasts with pre-capitalist, feudal society where, though exploited by a feudal ruling class, the peasantry as the class of direct producers did have direct access or legal entitlement to work the land and to own seed-corn, plough and draft animals, their 'objects and instruments of labour'.

Throughout the different types of human society thus defined, ruling classes exist on the basis of their capacity to extract and appropriate a surplus from the direct producers. This was the process that Marx referred to as 'exploitation'. In this technical usage, the term did not mean, as it tends to be used today, the *excessive* benefit derived by the most ruthless employer but that *all* employers in a capitalist system are exploiters since all profit, however large or small, constitutes the successful extraction of surplus from the direct producers. They remain so even when running their operations at a commercial loss since their role and position is predicated on profit-seeking. In such a case they are merely *unsuccessful* exploiters. Through their accumulation of wealth and the power attached to it, ruling classes develop the ability to enshrine their position in cultural tradition, in dominant belief systems and in legal constraints, thereby justifying the *enforcement* of their appropriation rights should that prove necessary. It was the behaviour of these contending classes in the different societies in human history (masters versus slaves, lords versus peasants, capitalists versus workers), each pursuing its own interest, that constituted 'class struggle' – the struggle over the distribution of the social surplus between the classes.

Attempts to intensify surplus extraction were, of course, resisted by the producing class, sometimes in open conflict, more often in resentment and sullen resignation and protest. Not until the development of the capitalist mode of production, however, and the emergence of the modern proletariat as the directly producing class, was there the opportunity for the producers to resist the process as such. In pre-capitalist societies, class divisions were typically obscured by social position and social status, by legal rights and obligations, by the weight of tradition and custom and the hierarchy of orders and ranks to which they gave rise. It was only with capitalism that class divisions came to the fore, and those who were objectively members of the classes that Marx's theory had identified could more easily identify for themselves the commonality of their positions; only as capitalism further developed did the increasing polarization of society into the two main classes, bourgeoisie and proletariat, enable each to see its class interests more clearly.

Capitalism is a social system that has thus produced a class with an *interest* in its overthrow. By concentrating this class in workplaces that facilitated the association of its members, and inducing mutuality and interdependence by its continuous pressure for further division of labour, it also created a class with the potential *political power* to achieve that overthrow. The system had, in Marx's words, produced its own gravedigger by creating the proletariat (Marx and Engels, 1969, p. 119); it was a system of production that 'begets its own negation with the inexorability which governs the metamorphoses of nature' (Marx, 1978, p. 715). Only with the development of capitalism, moreover, was there an increasing socialization (interdependence) of otherwise geographically dispersed and functionally discrete human activities; and only with capitalism did human productive techniques (both knowledge and technology) reach a level at which their capacity to satisfy the evolving needs of humanity no longer required the exploitation of one human by another. It was in this sense that Marx held the capitalist mode of production to be simultaneously the best and the worst thing to have happened to humanity.

This did not mean that class interests were always, or even normally, perceived with clarity. Those workers who did band together in mutual self-defence did so, most often, only on a temporary basis, or in defence of a sub-class, sectional interest – as employees of *this* company, as workers from *that* industry, as engineers or nurses or teachers. The recognition of a common position, and of shared interests as employees in a particular firm or industry, did not typically translate into a generalized consciousness of class. When it did so, it would be the result of the educative effect of prolonged struggle, of the formation of class-based political organizations, of an intractable political and economic crisis of the capitalist order. It was these that *could*, but would not automatically, give rise to an awareness of the historic role of the proletariat. In other words, *generalized* class consciousness would not be the norm, but rather the exception, and the prelude to social revolution.

It was for this reason that Marx distinguished between the notion of a class 'in itself' (i.e. those subject to the same objective economic and social conditions, and occupying the same structural position in relation to the process of exploitation) and a class 'for itself' (i.e. knowing the common interests of the whole, and identifying with it). Outside periods of social revolution, only a small minority of the subordinate class or classes would be possessed of the latter. The majority, under the influence of the dominant ideology of the society (the ideas encouraged and funded to conduce to the interests of the ruling class), would be subject to a 'false consciousness' about its true position. While 'class', for Marx, was on the one hand a relational and objective concept (classes exist *analytically* in so far as they endure common circumstances, and hence have identifiable interests incompatible with those of other classes), it also had an important subjective element, in that classes only exist *in reality* when they have some level of self-consciousness, and begin *to act* in pursuit of their class interests.[9]

Each succeeding type of society in history, defined and differentiated from each other by their distinctive relations of production, had its own cultural artefacts and traditions, its own legal order, its own political institutions and processes, and its own set of dominant ideas about what is right, good and proper. These cultural, legal, political and ideological processes had their own histories, of course, so that the precise legal duties and obligations in feudal France did not match those in feudal England, and the exact features of the political institutions today in the capitalist United States do not replicate those in capitalist India. As instances of slave or feudal or capitalist modes of production, however, all of these societies needed their non-economic aspects to share one feature and acquit themselves of one primordial role, whatever their national traditions and peculiarities – to be compatible with, and to facilitate the development of, the relations of production. There was, Marx claimed, using an architectural metaphor, a requirement for correspondence under normal circumstances between these 'superstructural' features of any type of society or mode of production and its economic 'base'.

Whatever the peculiarities of national culture and politics at any stage, then, a supportive relationship between them and the sphere of production was identified by the model as a requirement for stability. Capitalist relations of production had a requirement, at least in a weak sense, for a legal, political and ideological superstructure compatible with them, one that would facilitate rather than 'fetter' the reproduction and further development of capital. Compatibility was not inevitable, however, and normal circumstances did not always obtain. Neither human society nor its history had the character of inanimate machines or biological organisms in which each part of the whole was mechanically or naturally related to each other by its definite function. Superstructural levels *could* evolve in ways that were incompatible with, or sub-optimal for, the dominant relations of production because they were, after all, the consequences of human decisions and human action; and human beings often make mistakes, or act in ignorance of the consequences of their behaviour. But such infelicity would then tend to impair the efficient functioning of the economic base, giving rise to a tension or contradiction that could only be resolved by a change in one or the other. Feudal laws hampered the development of capitalist relations of production until the social revolutions of the eighteenth and nineteenth centuries swept them away; capitalist productive dynamism has created the technological, social and economic conditions necessary for an egalitarian and properly human social order (communism) but the fruition of that possibility requires the culture, laws and institutions of liberalism which defend the private ownership of productive assets to be similarly swept away.[10]

Class struggle is treated by Marx's model as *endemic* to the capitalist system. It is ineradicable and perpetual, though it does not always, or even typically, take the form of open conflict or expressed hostility. It arises ineluctably from the tension generated by the zero-sum game between the wage income to labour and the profits to capital, where a benefit to one is at the cost of the other. The objective interests of the bourgeoisie and the proletariat are incompatible, and therefore generate not a tendency to permanent hostility and open warfare but a permanent tendency towards them. The system is thus prone to economic class conflict, and, given the cyclical instability of its economy, subject to periodic political and economic crises. At these moments the possibility exists for social revolution, for the transition from the oppressive and exploitative, competitive and alienating conditions of the order of capital to a realm of human freedom in which humanity as a whole, through a radically democratic structure, engages collectively in satisfying its needs, ordering its priorities, and constructing new needs, aspirations and challenges to strive for and to overcome.

Marx and the Class Structure: Mapping Past, Present and Future

Marx's description of the class structure of nineteenth-century capitalism (the stage of capitalism's adolescence in Europe) was, naturally, only accurate in detail for its period. The continuing relevance, or otherwise, of the model depends on its fundamental categorizations and relational properties rather than on these details. So how has the structure of developed capitalist society changed in the last century?

Between the bourgeoisie and the proletariat, Marx argued in the nineteenth century, lay an intermediate layer of those who neither exploited wage labour nor were exploited as wage labour. These were self-employed artisans, own account traders, the professions, and so on. They were neither workers nor capitalists, not on principle or out of choice but because such was the nature of employment opportunities at that stage in the development of capitalism. Marx referred to this group as the 'petty bourgeoisie'. His expectation was that, with the further development of the mode of production, this intermediate layer would diminish in importance, some graduating into the ranks of the bourgeoisie proper but most being proletarianized as the ambit of capital expanded to draw more skills into the direct process of extracting surplus value. Within the proletariat, he also distinguished between those who were formally and regularly employed and those in the 'lumpen proletariat'. The latter consisted of those outside regular employment, and at the margins of society, forced by the lack of opportunities to exist in a twilight world of bare subsistence, migrating in and out of petty criminality, and unable to develop a sense of belonging, of class consciousness, and of class solidarity. Politically, Marx argued, the tendency would be for the two chief classes, bourgeoisie and proletariat, to develop parties and programmes serving their distinct interests. While attracted to the liberal and individualist ideology and rhetoric of the bourgeois parties in normal circumstances, the petty bourgeoisie and the lumpen proletariat could be drawn towards the socialist programme of the proletariat at times of economic or social crisis, when the dominant political ideas seemed to offer no solution.

Changes in the balance of occupations, in their rewards and statuses, and in their functions in the last hundred years mean that a Marxian class map at the end of the twentieth century differs interestingly from Marx's nineteenth-century map. Most notably, it contains the category of 'new middle class', which consists of employees in what have been described as 'contradictory class locations' – those who are paid a wage or salary by capital but who, by virtue of the nature of their occupations, are not part of the proletariat.[11] This group can usefully be subdivided into those who work as middle or junior managers for capital and those who retain a large degree of autonomy (i.e. who operate largely independently of direct managerial supervision) because of the kind of work that they do. Managers supervise and direct the labour force, and determine the detailed deployment of *given* resources. This distinguishes them from the senior executives who make strategic determination of *the level* of those resources, and who are, in consequence, members of the capitalist class. The category of autonomous employees, by contrast, those whose jobs do not entail as a prime function the direction of labour or the administration of budgets and resources, includes university lecturers, senior company accountants, hospital doctors, research engineers and scientists, senior social workers, and so on. These employees earn their livings by the selling of their labour power for a wage or a salary but, unlike members of the proletariat, control neither the labour of others nor the deployment of capital. For those so located in the occupational structure, different aspects of their employment conditions are shared with different classes: they are, like the proletariat, wage labourers by remuneration, but are possessed usually of all the petty-bourgeois vanities by virtue of their possession of some control over their own labour process. They also tend to share the attitudes and aspirations of the petty bourgeoisie, and its fluctuating political allegiances.

The proletariat, in this contemporary map, continues to possess its traditional characteristics and properties. Its objective interests are incompatible with those of the owners of capital; it is internally differentiated by deep divisions of educational background (from minimal to higher level), skill attainment, income and cultural interests, and by divisions of gender, ethnicity and nationality; but it is occasionally forced by circumstances to transcend these divisions when the reality of its common interests takes precedence over its typically sectionalist consciousness. In these respects, it is no different to the proletariat of the nineteenth century.

Confusions, however, abound. What Marxists refer to as the 'lumpen proletariat' is often described today by non-Marxists as an 'underclass'. The difference is significant. In the first place, the 'underclass' designation excludes its members from the proletariat. It also implies that all other classes share a common feature (being 'included' in society) that distinguishes them from the long-term or periodically unemployed (who are said to be 'excluded'). Thus members of the bourgeoisie, of the new middle class and of the proletariat are all treated as one social grouping, with interests that differ from those of the 'underclass'. This view is captured by the descriptive slogan, 'A two-thirds, one-third society', and in Britain is institutionalized by the government's 'Social Exclusion Unit'. By contrast, Marxists argue that this is an empirically false and theoretically misleading characterization. First, the interests of a marginalized group vary directly not indirectly with level of struggle and the success of the proletariat as a whole. The struggle of the better-organized sections of the working class benefit all in raising the general level of wages, by defending the number of jobs, and by influencing government welfare policy. Second, there is no reason in principle why workers on short-term contracts and other forms of casual employment should not be drawn into the organized working class. Indeed, they may have a very special interest in becoming part of it. Third, much social commentary generates a systematically distorted picture of advanced societies by conflating those who are marginalized and demeaned by unemployment and casual labour with those who are only seeking part-time employment or a series of temporary contracts. Most of those included as part of a marginalized 'underclass' are members of the proletariat who are in part-time or short-term employment by choice, or are keen to secure full contracts. In either case, their interests are not opposed to those of full-time, permanently contracted workers as is implied by the 'underclass' designation. The size of the truly marginal section of society is, therefore, systematically overestimated. Fourth, the deep divisions of incompatible class interests within the 'two-thirds of society' (between the bourgeoisie and the proletariat) are ignored by the analysis.

If the size of the marginalized sector of society is overestimated by much contemporary analysis, the size of the working class is underestimated. 'White-collar' employees in all sectors are often excluded from the category, and treated as if they are part of the middle class. A similar theoretical fate befalls all those in the service sector in other empirical and theoretical studies. Thus, the senior civil servant in charge of a department of government and the manager of one of its offices, on the one hand, and all of the secretaries, clerks and minor officials engaged in largely routine tasks for less than the average wage, on the other hand, are both treated as if they are members of the same class by virtue of the *non-manual* character of their work. Similarly, cleaners, cooks, nurses, radiographers and junior hospital doctors will find themselves excluded from the proletariat, and sharing a class category with the managers and strategic administrators of the quasi-privatized hospital trust, or the health authority, by virtue of sharing the same sectoral location for the expenditure of their efforts. The phrases 'white-collar occupations' and 'service-sector employment' mask the class divisions that fissure the practices and economic activities to which they refer.

The practical political consequences of these theoretical differences cannot be overemphasized. The description and analysis of social trends offered by contemporary sociology depicts a working class in numerical decline, and suffering a loss of social and political cohesion, as a result of economic de-industrialization and of fragmenting and diverging interests within the working class. If such were the case then not only is Marx's account of the historical evolution of human societies seriously flawed, his characterization of the proletariat as a class with an historic mission is, and must always have been, mistaken. It was never, and could not have been, the agency of human emancipation if this role was one it could perform only with the characteristics it happened to possess for a few decades at the end of the nineteenth century. Moreover, if it was flawed as a political project because the cohesive features of the proletariat were historically contingent, then the effect of this has no less an impact on Marx's class analysis as an explanatory model. If the proletariat was to be defined by the sociological characteristics it happened once to have, rather than by reference to the exploitative relation in which it stands to the bourgeoisie, then the conflict between those classes could hardly explain social change over extended periods and between 'modes of production'. Indeed, with the character and dynamics of the 'economic base' no longer determinable in terms of class relations of production, other aspects of society could hardly be explained by reference to it.

It is, however, a contested trend. The Marxist observes that the purported trend is only 'identified' on the basis of a definition of the concept of class derived from the status hierarchy of different occupations, i.e. the working class is only in numerical decline if it is defined to include only manual occupations, or 'productive' as opposed to service-sector labour. Alternatively, if it is treated as wage labour, and even with the new middle class excluded, it remains the large majority of the population in advanced societies, and constitutes a rapidly growing class as a proportion of the world's population once the development of capitalism in underdeveloped societies and their integration into the global capitalist economy are considered.[12] Moreover, the existence of sharp divisions (of income levels, political allegiances and social attitudes) within the working class can only be interpreted as evidence for a process of class fragmentation if one presumes the existence of a 'golden age' of political and social cohesion. Historically, there was no such period. The proletariat, argues the Marxist, has always suffered from such sectional divisions. The real issue, she argues, is whether Marx was correct in claiming that the proletariat shared common *objective* interests, and in predicting periodic and cyclical economic and political crises in which these interests *could* take precedence over sectional interests in determining class consciousness. If so, then the sociologists' trend is false, and is part of a tendentious theoretical argument. It is itself part of bourgeois ideology.

Marx: Interpretation and Critique

Marxism is also condemned for being an 'economism', and for providing a 'class reductionist' analysis of social phenomena. By 'economism' is meant the explanation of a society's operation or its features by reference to the requirements of its economic processes. This is considered by critics to be illegitimate as an explanation because it ignores the political, social, ideological or cultural determinants of the social phenomenon being studied. What is strange about the criticism is that, though addressed *to* Marxism, it does not seem to address Marxism. Marx never constructed his explanations of historical features of societies or social events as naive reductions to their economic effects on production. He was insistent on the need for detailed political, historical and cultural analysis, and was himself a rigorous exponent of that method. It was in response to crude 'economic reductionism' that he once declared, in a letter to Kugelmann, that if that was Marxism, then, 'I am not a Marxist!' But while cultural and political practices and institutions had their own histories that needed detailed study in themselves to be understood, that autonomy was only partial. All such social phenomena could only exist in so far as the conditions for social reproduction had been satisfied, and all of these political and cultural features of a society would have an effect on the efficiency of material production. To trace those relationships between the economic base and features of the superstructure was not to exhaust *everything* that needed to be included in an explanation of them but it *was* to provide an ineradicable feature of any adequate explanation.

'Class reductionism' is closely related to 'economism'. Marx is accused of 'reducing' all the features of human social experience to the mere appearances or reflexes of the class division of society. Thus it is argued, for example, that the oppression of women is explained by Marxists in terms of its function for the reproduction of capital, and consequently the specificities of that oppression are ignored or minimized. In a seemingly innocent inversion of the normal application of the word, these critics affirm that Marxism 'privileges' class. Once subjected to analysis, however, this turns out to mean no more than an objection to Marx's use of the model he thinks appropriate for social explanation. On the presumption that the criticism is not directed at the process of 'reducing' the complex world to key variables that can be modelled (otherwise it is an objection to *all* scientific endeavour in both the natural or the social worlds), it can only be an objection to the use of class analysis.

Marx and Marxists did and do explain oppression by reference to its operation in a particular society, and in capitalism that means its contribution to the reproduction of capital. In the case of sexist behaviour and institutions (as in the case also of homophobia), the mechanism connecting these oppressive features with the requirements of capital is the role of the family in the reproduction of the labour force. But that connection is indirect. The Marxist does not argue that personal and institutional prejudices are reproduced in people's heads and in their customary behaviour by the unmediated needs of the economy. Culture is the agency by which these values and reflexes are transmitted. Culture, however, exists not in a vacuum but in conditions of material production.

It is for this reason that an Historical Materialist account of female oppression is incompatible with a feminist account to the extent that the latter relies on patriarchy theory. Theories of patriarchy explain social development by reference to male interest in the maintenance of female oppression, and this is treated as a transcendent feature of human experience, constant across different types of society. Historical Materialism explains social development by reference to the requirements of surplus extraction by the ruling class from the labour of the direct producers. All forms of oppression are explained in relation to that insistent demand. Thus, the oppression of women will take different forms in different societies, and in no society will the nature and impact of oppression be the same for all women irrespective of their class.[13] With women from different class backgrounds experiencing oppression in radically different ways, and targeting different objectives as part of its eradication, the generic and undifferentiated category 'women' does not identify an effective agency of social change. Moreover, argues the Marxist, though many working-class men may enjoy the effects of an unequal division of domestic labour which has survived from the nineteenth century, the main beneficiary of oppressive practices and ideas is capital, not men. Oppressions, in dividing the working class, operate to secure the reproduction of capital; they construct social conflict between men and women, or black and white, or skilled and unskilled, dissolving or distorting the conflict between capital and labour. It is in this sense that the Marxist argues that the *whole* of the working class suffers from oppression, and has an objective interest in opposing it; and is the only agent of change that combines the potential power to effect social change with an objective interest in so doing. The Historical Materialist does not assume that she possesses the analytical tools necessary for a *complete* account of women's oppression which would require, among other things, the insights provided by cultural theory and psychoanalysis. She does, however, insist that these insights be read against the backdrop of, and in relation to, the demands of material production.

Weber: Class, Status and Power

It might be no exaggeration to claim that Max Weber's life work was the attempt to construct a social theory that would be an adequate alternative to Marxism. Weber recognized that partial accounts of disparate social phenomena were no alternative to a 'grand theory' of society and history that could link the variety of social events and institutions, demonstrating their interconnection. This is what Marxism had achieved, and if it was to be successfully opposed (as Weber was convinced it must be, because he believed it to be scientifically mistaken and found it politically uncongenial), a superior theoretical system was required. Like Marx then, Weber's theoretical endeavour was ambitious, and his conceptualization of class was similarly rooted in, and conditioned by, his overall theoretical system. He was also similar to Marx in never addressing himself to a detailed investigation of the concept of class in a dedicated volume.

For Weber, social distinctions and divisions had to be understood as the complex interaction of three influences: economic class, social status and political power.[14] Classes were composed of those who have similar life-chances as determined by their relative advantage or disadvantage in the market, and a common cause of that market position either through ownership or non-ownership of property or through the possession of skills or a good education. The boundaries of social classes were defined by the extent and ease of social mobility: a social class position is defined by Weber as all those situations between which the mobility of individuals is relatively easy, and typical in practice. The classes that Weber identified in this manner were, on first appearance, very similar to those isolated by Marx. Weber's classes were: the working class, the petty bourgeoisie, specialists and managers, and those privileged in the market by virtue of their property, skills or education.

Class, for Weber, was only one source of social differentiation, however, and not necessarily the prime source. Social status and political power were also operative, and might in some historical situations be more important determinants of social standing than class. Status expressed the prestige in which a group was held, or honour bestowed on it, and might, in some circumstances, also determine the material reward delivered to its members by the rest of society. It was certainly taken by Weber to provide the members of status groups with the main ingredient of their identity, and an orientation to the world and way of being that could be captured by the cultural concept of 'lifestyle'. Class and status situations could be mutually reinforcing (e.g. where the possession of property itself bestows high status), or contradictory (e.g. where ostentatious wealth ('new money') is disdained as the result of the demeaning commercial activity that generated it).

The benefits accruing to status groups, moreover, and indeed the rights and duties of those in particular class situations, were significantly affected by the exercise of political authority. It is by legal right, established through the exercise of political influence, itself won as the outcome of the contest between political parties, that status groups achieve entitlement to material benefits, and that organized classes alter market conditions in their favour. The relationships between economic class, social status and political party were complex interdependencies: 'classes and status groups influence one another and they influence the legal order and are in turn influenced by it' (Weber, 1948, p. 938). Thus, far from the legal order and cultural phenomena being, in however complex a way, reflections of the class divisions of society, as Marx had argued, they became in Weber's analysis *independent* variables; not the secondary consequences of the evolution of economic class divisions, but rather originary, causal factors in their own right. If the legal order laid down the framework, enforced by the state, which defined the rights of individuals in property, the duties of citizens or subjects, and the ritual and material entitlements of status groups, then law was the primal determinant of social division. Since the legislative framework is moulded, typically at the margin, but cumulatively, by the victors in the political process, there is a sense in which 'politics is in command'. Inverting the causal direction suggested by the materialist, it is here the subjective aspiration and intent of self-conscious social groups, organized in political parties, that determine objective structures. This is the sense in which Weber might reasonably be described as a subjectivist; *not*, that is, in the naïve sense of believing individuals to have *chosen* their class position, or that classes only exist to the extent that they happen to share a sense of identity. If Weber is properly described as a subjectivist it is because he is a social *constructivist* in his account of social division: we *make* our social divisions through witting or unwitting action in the political arena; we are not simply reflections of them, or made into the beings that we are by them.[15]

The concept of power is, of course, what underlies the whole of Weber's analysis. It is the ubiquitous quest for power that provides the prime motivation for human striving for access to resources through the achievement of an economic position, high status or the possession of political influence. It is a concept that remains inadequately theorized or explained in Weber's work, however. Nowhere is it adequately explained by him why power-seeking should be accepted as the *defining characteristic* of human beings. Even were it shown to be a demonstrable aspect of human personality in nineteenth- or twentieth-century Europe (an achievement which neither Weber nor Foucault accomplished) it would still remain as an unsatisfactory element in the account of human being unless it was shown conclusively (or at least argued persuasively) that this fact of human existence was *necessary*, an essential component of human nature, and therefore in no sense dependent on the contingent social and cultural conditions of capitalism, feudalism or any other historically specific society.

Choosing between Theoretical Accounts

There are three key distinctions between the Marxian and the Weberian models: (1) the status of class divisions in determining the general conditions of human existence in capitalist societies; (2) the conformity of class consciousness or class actions with class interests; and (3) the arena in which classes are constituted.

For Marx, it is class division in capitalist society, and more precisely the economic conflict between bourgeoisie and proletariat, that is the determining, or primary, division. For Weber, economic classes constitute only one expression of the way in which power is differentially distributed between groups. For Marx, the open or covert, witting or unwitting, struggle over the economic surplus stamps its mark indelibly on all human relations, cultural forms and social institutions. For Weber, all social phenomena have complex genealogies to which class conflict only makes a partial, and sometimes negligible, contribution. Second, for Marx, while classes have an objective existence and their own objective interests, identifiable by social analysis, they may not be aware of those interests, and may not act in a manner consistent with them (they may, for example, be subject to a 'dominant ideology' that leads them to a 'false consciousness' of their position). For Weber, there is only the evidence of class action *as it happens to occur*, provoked by and expressive of its contingent circumstances. What happens in society as a matter of fact, what classes *actually do*, is the sole source for social commentary, and the sole source of evidence available to the social scientist. For Weber, then, there is no defensible ground, or Archimidean point, from which consciousness or action could be judged to be 'false'. Third, in Marx's theory the decisive confrontation takes place *at the point of production* where value is produced, and where the surplus is extracted. For Weber, it is the deployment of resources *in the market* that distinguishes between economic classes.

Subtending these substantive distinctions is a major methodological difference. While, for Marx, human beings have some definite and unchanging aspects of their natures (material beings with physiological needs, psychic beings with emotional and sensuous needs, consciously creative (i.e. 'labouring') beings), they are in other respects *socially* constructed. They communicate and are mutually dependent because they share a culture that predates them, and into which they are socialized. That culture is geographically and historically specific. Humans are, therefore, profoundly historical beings. Their detailed qualities and powers vary from society to society. To understand humans is consequently, for Marx, to explain the structural aspects of the society that made them the beings that they are. Adequate explanations, for Marx, are *structural* explanations.

Weber, by contrast, is a methodological individualist. He does not deny the existence of a social structure embodied in the institutions, practices and culture of society but argues that an identification of the features of a social structure does not exhaust the problem of explanation. For methodological individualists, structures are only the unacknowledged conditions and unintended consequences of individual action. An adequate explanation must account for structures in terms of the actions that created and preserve them, and therefore the *meanings* that individuals invest in (and the reasons they have for) their behaviour. Methodological individualists ask how and in what sense social structures exist *other than* as the effects of a multitude of individual behaviours that are guided by the meanings and motivations of their subjects. Methodological collectivists, such as Marx, ask how and in what sense individuals exist *at all* except as the powers and limitations bestowed on them by the structure and culture of the society into which they are born.

Verdicts

A theory of class for the twenty-first century resides in the choice between these alternatives. The abandonment of class analysis of any kind is merely the strained and self-serving response of a postmodernist prejudice against scientific analysis in general. As in earlier debates, the verdict on Marxism and Weberianism can only be, in one important sense, a matter of speculation. Given that there is neither empirical evidence that could refute the veracity of either model nor a conclusive argument yet devised that could demonstrate their incoherence or inconsistency, it is only the jury of history that will be able to find for one or the other. We, on the other hand, trapped this side of that future historical moment of revelation, must make a choice on the basis of which theory best explains the historical development of civilization, and best incorporates salient contemporary events into that explanation. With the late twentieth-century re-emergence of cyclical crises as a feature of global capitalism, and the re-eruption of class struggle as a systemic constraint on the ambitions and conceits of the bourgeoisie and of its political representatives, this author believes Marx to have won that contest.

For educators, moreover, it should be clear that the concept 'working class' in any coherent usage cannot simply be a designation for those whose children might have been subjected to environmental deprivation, or for those who should be treated as victims. In every classroom in the state system, the large majority of pupils will be the children of the working class in Marx's sense of the term. A significant minority of them, in the 1990s in contrast to the 1890s, will be destined for successful completion of higher education. For the majority of that sub-set, however, a degree will not transport them out of the working class but rather transform them into wage labourers with high-level skills. As members of that class they will carry, as did their forebears, a political potential of historic importance. It is a potential, however, of which they might spend their lives in ignorance.

Notes

1 For the relationship between lifestyle and class background, see Adonis and Pollard (1997); for the debate between lifestyle and class as the basis for contemporary social differentiation, see Crompton (1998).

2 For some of the more inventive speculations to this effect, see Bauman (1992, 1993), Rorty (1993), and Lyotard (1984).

3 *British Social Attitudes*, No. 14, Dartmouth Publishing 1997/8.

4 For the impact of class position on voting behaviour, health and education in Britain, see Abercrombie et al. (1996) and Hamnett et al. (1989) and Adonis and Pollard (1997). For social class and the National Lottery, see Adonis and Pollard.

5 For the argument proposing such 'new social movements' as *substitutes* for class-based political movements, see Pakulski (1995), Melucci (1995), Maheu (1995), and Coole (1998); for its critique, see Callinicos (1992, 1996), German (1981, 1997), Marabele (1993), Meiksins Wood (1986), Shawki (1990) and Smith (1994).

6 Appreciating its position in the intellectual tradition is not just useful for an understanding of the genesis of Historical Materialism, it is indispensable in making a properly reflective assessment of it. It is so because a rejection of *some form* of Historical Materialism thus defined entails a commitment either to some modern version of the three traditions he rejected, or to an incoherent postmodern relativism.

7 For the original texts in which the argument was first elaborated, see Marx and Engels (1970). For an elaborate and extended contemporary exposition, interpretation and defence of it, see Cohen (1978); and for criticisms of this particular elaboration from a Marxist perspective, see Callinicos (1979). For a Weberian critique of Historical Materialism, see Giddens (1981); for responses see Wright (1983, 1989), and Callinicos (1989); for Giddens's retorts, see Giddens (1985, 1989). For a post-modernist critique, see Laclau and Mouffe (1985); for a response see Géras (1990).

8 That the exact features of a capitalist class or a working class do not, in reality, match

these pure, ideal forms is not a shortcoming of the theory or of its concepts. That the working class includes those who have sources of income other than wages (e.g. rental income from a lodger, dividends from some shares in a privatized utility, clandestine receipts from 'moonlighting' as a petty-bourgeois cabbie or jobbing plumber in the evenings) does not threaten the coherence of the theoretical concept 'working class'. Marx himself noted that the emergence of the joint stock company in the nineteenth century had begun a process that would progressively remove capitalist production from the direct control of individual capitalists, and would have been unsurprised to learn that today's major shareholders are pension funds, some of which, as mutual funds, are under the *nominal* ownership and control of the workers who pay into them.

9 For the clearest original expression of this view, see Marx (1977, 1978).

10 This should not be confused with the 'communism' of the Stalinist states of Russia, Eastern Europe and China in which Marx would have recognized none of his vision of a society of democratically self-governing, free and equal producers.

11 For the development of the concept, see Wright (1978); for the elaboration of the argument here, see Callinicos and Harman (1989).

12 For recent estimates, see Callinicos and Harman (1989).

13 The issue is complicated by the fact that there are those who, in describing themselves as 'socialist feminists', do *not* subscribe to patriarchy theory but rather use an historical and materialist analysis.

14 For an application to contemporary society, see Scott (1996).

15 Weber never went this far, or was never so explicit about the implications of his system, but the logic of the situation seems compelling. It is a logic that has been drawn out and developed by a number of Weberian sociologists since; see Dahrendorf (1959), Giddens (1973, 1986), and Barbalet (1986).

References

Abercrombie, N. et al. (1996) *Contemporary British Society: A New Introduction to Sociology*, Oxford: Polity

Adonis, A. and S. Pollard (1997) *A Class Act: the Myth of Britain's Classless Society*, London: Hamish Hamilton

Aronowitz, S. (1992) *The Politics of Identity: Class, Culture and Social Movements*, London: HarperCollins

Barbalet, J. (1986) 'Limitations of class theory and the disappearance of status: the problem of the new middle class', *Sociology*, v.20, n.4, pp. 557–75

Bauman, Z. (1992) *Intimations of Postmodernity*, London: Routledge

Bauman, Z. (1993) *Postmodern Ethics*, Oxford: Blackwell

Bottomore, T. (1991) *Classes in Modern Society*, 2nd edn., London: HarperCollins

Brenner, J. and M. Ramas (1984) 'Rethinking Women's Oppression', *New Left Review*, no.144, pp. 33–71

Callinicos, A. (1982) *Is there a Future for Marxism?*, London: Macmillan

Callinicos, A. (1983) *The Revolutionary Ideas of Karl Marx*, London: Bookmarks

Callinicos, A. (1987) *Making History: Agency, Structure and Change in Social Theory*, Oxford: Polity

Callinicos, A. (1989) 'Anthony Giddens: A Contemporary Critique' in *idem*. (ed.) *Marxist Theory*, Oxford: Oxford University Press

Callinicos, A. (1991) *Against Postmodernism: a Marxist Critique*, Oxford: Polity

Callinicos, A. (1992) 'Race and Class', *International Socialism*, 55, pp. 3–51

Callinicos, A. (1996) *Race and Class*, London: Bookmarks

Callinicos, A. and C. Harman (1989) *The Changing Working Class: Essays on Class Structure Today*, London: Bookmarks

Cohen, G.A. (1978) *Karl Marx's Theory of History: A Defence*, Oxford: Oxford University Press

Coole, D. (1998) 'Master narratives and feminist subversions', in J. Good and I. Velody (eds) *The Politics of Postmodernity*, Cambridge: Cambridge University Press

Crompton, R. (1989) 'Class theory and gender', *British Journal of Sociology*, n.40 (4), pp. 565–87

Crompton, R. (1998) *Class and Stratification: An Introduction to Current Debates*, 2nd edn., Oxford: Polity

Dahrendorf, R. (1959) *Class and Class Conflict in Industrial Society*, London: Routledge

Eagleton, T. (1992) *Ideology: An Introduction*, London: Verso

Géras, N. (1985) 'The Controversy about Marx and Justice', *New Left Review*, 150, pp. 47–85; and in Callinicos (ed.) (1989) *op. cit.*

Géras, N. (1990) *Discourses of Extremity: Radical Ethics and Post-Marxist Extravaganzas*, London: Verso

German, L. (1981) 'Theories of Patriarchy', *International Socialism*, 12, pp. 39–55

German, L. (1997) *Sex, Class and Socialism*, 2nd edn., London: Bookmarks

Giddens, A. (1971) *Capitalism and Modern Social Theory: An Analysis of the Writings of Marx, Durkheim and Max Weber*, Cambridge: Cambridge University Press

Giddens, A. (1973) *The Class Structure of Advanced Societies*, London: Macmillan

Giddens, A. (1981) *A Contemporary Critique of Historical Materialism: v.1*, London: Macmillan

Giddens, A. (1985) 'Marx's Correct Views on Everything', *Theory and Society*, n.14, pp. 281–6

Giddens, A. (1986) *Social Theory and Modern Sociology*, Oxford: Polity

Giddens, A (1989) 'A reply to my critics', in D. Held and J. Thompson *Social Theory of Modern Societies: Anthony Giddens and his Critics*, Cambridge: Cambridge University Press

Good, J. and I. Velody (eds) (1998) *The Politics of Postmodernity*, Cambridge: Cambridge University Press

Hamnett, C. et al. (1989) *Restructuring Britain: The Changing Social Structure*, London: Sage

Harman, C. (1986) 'Base and Superstructure', *International Socialism*, 32, Spring, pp. 42–69

Harvey, D. (1989) *The Condition of Postmodernity: An Enquiry into the Origins of Cultural Change*, Oxford: Blackwell

Held, D. and J. Thompson (1989) *Social theory of modern societies: Anthony Giddens and his critics*, Cambridge: Cambridge University Press

Holton, R. (1996) 'Has class analysis any future?' in D. Lee and B. Turner *Conflicts About Class*, London: Longman

Holton, R. and B. Turner (1989) *Max Weber on Economy and Society*, London: Routledge

Joyce, P. (ed.) (1995) *Class*, Oxford: Oxford University Press

Laclau, E. and C. Mouffe (1985) *Hegemony and Socialist Strategy: Towards a Radical Democratic Politics*, London: Verso

Larrain, J. (1982) *Marxism and Ideology*, London: Macmillan

Lee, D. and B. Turner (1996) *Conflicts About Class*, London: Longman

Lyotard, J.-F. (1984) *The Postmodern Condition: A Report on Knowledge*, Manchester: Manchester University Press

Maheu, L. (ed.) (1995) *Social Movements and Social Classes: The Future of Collective Action*, London: Sage

Marabele, M. (1993) 'Beyond Racial Identity Politics', *Race and Class*, v.35, n.1

Marx, K. and F. Engels (1969) *The Manifesto of the Communist Party*, Moscow: Progress

Marx, K. and F. Engels (1970) *The German Ideology*, London: Lawrence and Wishart

Marx, K. (1971) *A Contribution to the Critique of Political Economy*, London: Lawrence and Wishart

Marx, K. (1977a) 'The Eighteenth Brumaire of Louis Bonaparte', in K. Marx *Selected Writings*, Oxford: Oxford University Press

Marx, K. (1977b) 'The Poverty of Philosophy', in K. Marx *Selected Writings*, Oxford: Oxford University Press

Marx, K. (1978) 'The Class Struggles in France', in K. Marx and F. Engels *Selected Works*, vol. 1, Moscow: Progress

Meiksins Wood, E. (1986) *The Retreat from Class: A New 'True' Socialism*, London: Verso

Melucci, A. (1989) *Nomads of the Present: Social Movements and Individual Needs in Contemporary Society*, Princeton: Princeton University Press

Melucci, A. (1995) 'The New Social Movements Revisited: Reflections on a Sociological Misunderstanding', in Maheu, *op. cit.*

Pakulski, J. (1995) 'Social Movements and Class: The Decline of the Marxist Paradigm', in Maheu, *op. cit.*

Parkin, F. (1979) *Marxism and Class Theory*, London: Tavistock

Robotham, S. (1997) *A Century of Women: the History of Women in Britain and the United States*, London: Viking

Rorty, R. (1993) *Contingency, Irony and Solidarity*, Oxford: Blackwell

Scott, G. (1998) *Feminism and the Politics of Working Women: the Women's Co-operative Guild, 1880s to the Second World War*, London: University College London

Scott, J. (1996) *Stratification and Power: Structures of Class, Status and Command*, Oxford: Polity

Scott, J.W. (1988) *Gender and the Politics of History*, Princeton: Princeton University Press

Segal, L. (1997) 'Generations of Feminism', *Radical Philosophy*, no.83, May/June pp. 6–16

Seidman, S. and D. Wagner (1992) *Postmodernism and Social Theory: The Debate over General Theory*, Oxford: Blackwell

Seidman, S. (1994) *Contested Knowledge: Social Theory in a Postmodern Era*, Oxford: Blackwell

Shawki, A. (1990) 'Black Liberation and Socialism in the United States', *International Socialism*, 47, pp. 3–62

Smith, S. (1994) 'Mistaken Identity – Or Can Identity Politics Liberate the Oppressed?', *International Socialism*, 62, pp. 3–50

Stedman Jones, G. (1983) *Languages of Class: Studies in English Working Class History*, Cambridge: Cambridge University Press

Therborn, G. (1976) *Science, Class and Society: on the foundation of Sociology and Historical Materialism*, London: New Left Books

Weber, M. (1948) 'Class, Status and Party', in *idem. Economy and Society*, in H. Gerth and C. Mills (eds) *From Max Weber: Essays in Sociology*, London: Routledge and Kegan Paul

Weber, M. (1964) *The Theory of Social and Economic Organization*, Glencoe: Free Press

White, S. (1991) *Political Theory and Postmodernism*, Cambridge: Cambridge University Press

Wright, E.O. (1978) *Class, Crisis and the State*, London: Verso

Wright, E.O. (1983) 'Giddens' Critique of Marxism', *New Left Review*, 138, pp. 11–35

Wright, E.O. (1989) 'Models of Historical Trajectory: An Assessment of Giddens' Critique of Marxism', in D. Held and J. Thompson *op. cit.*

10 Social Class and School

Relationships to knowledge

Richard Hatcher

Economic Inequality and School Achievement

Each year the United Nations publishes its Human Development Report. According to the 1998 report, Britain is one of the most unequal and poverty-stricken of the developed countries, standing fifteenth in a list of seventeen (*Guardian*, 9 September 1998). Wealth and income have always been very unequally distributed in Britain, but the gap has widened over the past twenty years.

Economic inequality has profound effects on education. There is a close correlation between how well off school students' families are and how well they do in the school system. Of course, some students from working-class backgrounds do well, and some students from middle- and upper-class backgrounds do badly (a point I will return to), but the overall pattern is very clear. At primary school, there is a strong correlation between Key Stage 2 Standard Attainment Targets (SATs) scores and the proportion of students eligible for free school meals (a commonly used indicator of family socio-economic status). The top ten local education authorities (LEAs) have on average 10 per cent of children eligible for free school meals, the lowest ten have an average of 51 per cent (*Times Educational Supplement*, 14 February 1997). Research by Ian McCallum into KS2 English, maths and science in London LEAs (reported in the *TES*, 18 April 1997) confirms that they are strongly influenced by social class. Average test scores range from Richmond, the wealthiest borough in London, at the top with over 220, to Hackney, the most deprived, with less than 120. McCallum's most recent research, into 5,000 students from age four through primary school confirms the crucial importance of social class in educational achievement (*TES*, 25 September 1998). McCallum has also demonstrated the strength of the relationship between social class and GCSE performance, using data comparing not only LEAs but individual students (*Education*, 19 February 1996). In a recent review of the evidence, Mortimore and Whitty (1997, p. 47) conclude that 'There remains a strong negative correlation between most measures of *social disadvantage and school achievement*, as even a cursory glance at the league tables of school by school results demonstrates.'

Just as economic inequality has widened in recent years, so has educational inequality: 'The flip side to the ever-rising proportion of 16-year-olds achieving GCSE grades A–C is that the number leaving school with no qualifications whatsoever is increasing at a faster rate' (*TES*, 17 October 1997).

Beyond Equality of Access

Working-class parents have always wanted a better education for their children. The long struggle for reform reaches from the introduction of universal state elementary schooling, through the opening up of secondary schooling to the working class, culminating in the 1944 Act, to the introduction in the 1960s (though still not completed today) of the common comprehensive school in place of the class-divided grammar–secondary modern system.[1] It was a struggle for equality defined as equality of access. However, it became clear that the achievement of the common school in itself did not guarantee equality of outcomes between the classes. Class differences in attainment, though less wide than before, remained substantial.

This poses fundamental questions for working-class education which have still not been satisfactorily answered. Equality of access alone is not enough – though it still remains to be achieved in post-compulsory education. The question of the *content* of the educational process becomes central. This was precisely the issue at the core of the movements for gender and racial equality in education which arose in the 1970s and transformed the debate about equality. They challenged the discriminatory content of schooling, in terms of curriculum content, pedagogy and relations between teachers and students. These developments also affected debates about social class, but in a much more limited way. Deficit models of working-class culture were challenged, and the voices and concerns of 'ordinary people' began to appear more prominently in the curriculum (in, for example, English and history). But these developments were limited, for two reasons. First, they were not driven by a powerful social movement like the Women's Movement or the black and anti-racist movements of the time. The working-class movement had no alternative agenda for education beyond that of access, which had been largely met by the introduction of comprehensive schools. Second, social class inequality seemed to be more intractable than race and gender inequality, more rooted in the fundamental economic arrangements of society, less amenable to practical political reform. Ellen Meiksins Wood (1990) invites us to imagine a democratic community which acknowledges all kinds of difference without them becoming relations of domination and oppression. We can imagine that for 'race' and gender, but not class. Though gender and 'race' are co-opted and reinforced under capitalism, they are not constitutive of capitalism in the way that class is. Class equality is a contradiction in terms. Social classes are constituted by relations of inequality of money and power. Thus 'while all oppressions may have equal *moral* claims, class exploitation has a different historical status, a more strategic location at the heart of capitalism' (*ibid.*, p. 77).

One consequence for education is that the equal opportunities agendas which have been developed since the 1970s and which have now become established in every LEA and every school, at least formally, concentrate on race and gender (and more recently disability), but rarely address issues of social-class inequality.

Social Class and 'School Improvement'

In the 1990s, the dominant agenda has become that of 'school improvement'. Issues of equality have been marginalized. There are targets and performance indicators for raising levels of attainment, but not for reducing inequality. But raising standards does not necessarily entail reducing inequality. Overall standards of achievement can rise while relative inequalities remain or even widen. According to Mortimore and Whitty (1997, p. 9), 'one of the depressing findings is the *relative* performance of the disadvantaged has remained similar even when the absolute performance of such groups has improved'. If the aim of 'school improvement' is to raise standards generally *without* also explicitly tackling inequality, then inequality will tend to *increase* as standards rise:

> if all schools performed as well as the best schools, the stratification of achievement by social class would be even more stark than it is now. This would happen because socially advantaged students in highly effective schools would achieve even more than they might do in a less conducive environment and the gap between them and their less advantaged peers would increase.
>
> (*ibid.*)

In fact there is some evidence that the class gap at GCSE level has widened as schools have focused on A–C grades at the expense of lower-attaining students. So, whether at the level of the classroom, the school, the local education authority or the national school system, it is essential to distinguish between two forms of 'improvement' with very different social meanings – 'polarizing improvement' and 'equalizing improvement'.

It is often argued by politicians and their educational advisers that schools with a similar class composition vary significantly in their results, and that therefore if working-class schools do less well than middle-class schools it is largely the fault of poor teaching. It is true that some schools are more effective with working-class students than other schools, but the relative weight of in-school factors compared to the weight of social class should not be exaggerated. McCallum, in the research referred to above, found that there were significant differences between LEAs with a similar class composition, but only 20 per cent of the differences in student performance could be attributed to other variables independent of social class (*TES*, 18 April 1997). Evidence of the weight of class compared to teaching methods is provided by a study published in 1991 by Mike Lake of the reading attainment of 18,000 seven- to eight-year-olds over a period of twelve years up to 1990. The factor that correlated most closely with poor reading was social disadvantage, not teaching methods or other school factors (*TES*, 21 June 1991). For Mortimore and Whitty (1997, pp. 8–9),

> it seems inevitable that schools will be affected by their role within a wider society which still maintains social divisions and a powerful sense of hierarchy. A particular criticism of school improvement work is that it has tended to exaggerate the extent to which individual schools can challenge such structural

inequalities. Whilst some schools can succeed against the odds, the possibility of them all doing so, year in and year out, still appears remote.

Rethinking Class and School

The most effective way to reduce educational inequality is to reduce the economic inequality in which it is rooted. This is the view of Peter Robinson in his recent study of class differences and educational achievement: 'a serious programme to alleviate child poverty might do far more for boosting attainment in literacy and numeracy than any modest interventions in schooling' (quoted in the *Guardian*, 8 September 1997). However, while it is important not to underplay the pervasive influence of social class on attainment in school, it is equally important not to fall into a sociological fatalism – the belief that educational outcomes are predetermined by social origin and that schools can make little or no difference while inequalities remain so great in the wider society. Significant inroads can be made into class inequality in schooling even in the context of a profoundly unequal economic system, but doing so requires more radical education policies than are presently countenanced in current governnment thinking on education or in the agenda of the mainstream 'school improvement' movement in Britain.

There is a very large body of writing on social class and school. The principal concern in the past forty years has been the relationship between social origins and educational outcomes. Earlier deficit models have been displaced, at least in the research literature, by a focus on how school processes interact with class cultures to reproduce patterns of inequality. More recently, attention has turned to the relationship between social class and parental and school choice in a quasi-market context. It is not my purpose in this chapter to attempt any comprehensive overview of research and debates. Nor do I want to focus on a critique of existing approaches and policies (see Hatcher, 1998a and b for a critique of Labour education policy and what I have called 'official school improvement'; see also Cole, 1998). I will propose an argument for a way of seeing social class and school and thinking about what seems to be at the core of the relationship, which can provide the basis for a more productive approach.

The first step is a redefinition of the concept of class.

Class as a Social Relationship

Thus far I have written of social class in terms of socio-economic status. Family wealth and occupation are the most common ways in which class is defined in relation to school. Class is seen as a location within a stratified and hierarchical social structure of distribution of jobs and income. It is certainly true that this correlates closely with educational attainment, but it is not helpful in explaining why this correlation exists. To do that we have to go beyond statistical correlations of social locations and educational outcomes and investigate the social processes which connect schooling to class. I want to draw here on the work of Ellen Meiksins Wood (1995) in her book *Democracy against Capitalism*.

She argues that there are two ways of thinking about class in society – as a structural location or as a social relation. The first treats class as a form of stratification which factors out relationships of power and exploitation between classes. The second (and Wood draws on E.P. Thompson here)

> presupposes that relations of production distribute people into class situations, that these situations entail essential antagonisms and conflicts of interest, and that they therefore create conditions of struggle. Class *formations* and the discovery of class consciousness grow out of the process of struggle, as people 'experience' and 'handle' their class situations.
>
> (Wood, 1995, p. 80)

School is one crucial social institution within which class relationships work themselves out. Schools produce the future occupants of positions in a class society – the future workers, managers and employers, the future rich and poor, powerful and powerless. The 'official' processes of school – what is taught, how it is taught, how students are selected and graded, and so on – are regulated by the state in accordance with the maintenance of the existing social and economic order. This desired correspondence is fraught with conflict and uncertainty, in large part because it continually encounters and engenders resistance and opposition. In this chapter I want to explore the 'experience' of schooling by working-class students and young people, which, I will argue, provides the key to understanding patterns of failure and the basis of an answer to it.

Before I do that, I want to deal briefly with two possible objections to an analysis in terms of social class. The first is the argument that class is no longer a decisive element in people's experience. There are two points to make in reply to this. The first is that class relationships powerfully shape experience whether people are aware of it or not. The second is that, even today when class mobilization is at a relatively low ebb in Britain, class relationships are in fact conscious parts of the experience of the large majority of people, as an article in *The Economist* (27 September 1997) entitled 'Fighting the Class War' confirms.

> Many commentators think that class is dying, but ordinary people are not convinced. In fact class antagonisms may even be worsening – the proportion of voters believing there is a 'class struggle' in Britain rose from around 60 per cent in the early 1960s to 81 per cent in the mid-1990s, according to Gallup.
>
> (cited in Leys and Panitch, 1998, p. 20)

The second objection is that class is just one of a number of structures of inequality and oppression, along with gender, 'race', disability and sexuality. I have already referred to Wood's argument that class does not have an equivalent conceptual status to 'race' and gender. This is also true with respect to disability and sexuality. It is not a question of creating a 'hierarchy of oppressions' but of recognizing that class is constitutive of capitalist society in a way that 'race', gender, sexuality and disability are not. Furthermore, class is not purely an economic category which leaves other areas of social life to other social identities alone. Capitalism is an overarching totalizing system which is constituted by class but which shapes all social oppressions. While it is indifferent to the identities of those it exploits, it also systematically co-opts and structures extra-economic oppressions (Wood, 1995, p. 266). Wood is critical both of liberal formal equality, which addresses the principles and procedures of social institutions but not the underlying patterns of class power, and 'identity politics', which believes that 'The social relations of capitalism can be dissolved into an unstructured and fragmented plurality of identities and differences' (*ibid.*, p. 78).

Class Relationships and Schooling: Bob Connell

Much of the writing about social class and school is based on a stratification model, typified by such terms as 'social disadvantaged' rather than 'working class'. This certainly demonstrates the substantial social inequalities that exist in education, but it does little to help us understand the processes at work connecting the world outside school to what happens to students and young people inside it. To understand that, it is necessary to see class, as Wood does, as a social relationship. The next step in my argument is to apply the conception of social class as a relationship to schooling. (In what follows I deal with class, for the sake of brevity and clarity, without taking account of how it is often intertwined with gender and 'race'.)

The work of Bob Connell, an Australian educationalist, and his colleagues is particularly helpful. In their book *Making the Difference: Schools, Families and Social Division* (Connell et al., 1982), they argue that we must change the terms of the discussion from a focus on inequalities of social class in terms of location to a focus on class as a 'complex association of activity, situation, and structure' (*ibid.*, p. 146).

> Educational inequality isn't a matter of factor piling upon factor, and cannot be understood by a kind of arithmetic of advantage and disadvantage . . . Of course some people have more money, more education, than others. But equally plainly there is a larger reality all around and underneath those differences – the social relations and practices in which they arise. Notions like 'inequality' are not much use when we try to grasp how people enter those relations, what they do to them, where they come from, and how they might be changed.
>
> (*ibid.*, p. 193)

For Connell and his co-authors, the core of the social relationships of schooling is the relationship between the student and knowledge. This is the key idea which I want to develop. They argue that social class positions people, including school students, in different relationships to knowledge. Class differences in relationships to knowledge are rooted in the social division of labour. Capitalism dispossesses the working class of knowledge, in both the economic and the political spheres, as worker and as citizen. This is not a mere distributional asymmetry, it is a social division of conception and execution; in other words knowledge is a function of power relationships. At the economic level, this functions largely as a mental/ manual distinction, though with some qualification. There is an increased intellectual element in manual labour, but because it operates at a low level of the hierarchy of power, it tends to be fragmentary, concrete, task-specific; divorced from the more abstract forms of knowledge involved in planning at the system level. The working class stresses practical learned-on-the-job knowledge, in contrast to abstract theoretical knowledge which takes the form of the manipulation of symbolic systems, principally language. It is abstract knowledge in this sense that characterizes school, and especially the high-status school knowledge on which academic success is based. Furthermore, entry to competitive careers entails the individual competitive appropriation of abstract knowledge in the form of credentials. This is a different relationship to knowledge to that of working-class families' experiences of practical knowledge as a means of co-operatively coping with real-life problems (Connell et al. 1982, pp. 66, 122; see also Ashendon et al., 1987, pp. 257–8).

I find this a powerful argument, but there is a problem with it. Not all working-class students fail at school, and not all middle- and upper-class students succeed academically. Students from the same family can have very different educational outcomes. This cannot be explained by determinist theories, whether of cultural deficit, cultural distance or social reproduction. Social origin structures educational outcomes but it does not determine them: they are mediated by individual identities and actions.

Class Relationships and Schooling: Bernard Charlot

This has been the theme explored by Bernard Charlot, a French sociologist of education, in a number of books. In *Ecole et savoir dans les banlieus . . . et ailleurs* (Charlot, Bautier and Rochex 1992), Charlot and his colleagues describe their large-scale ethnographic study of students at secondary and primary schools in both poor and relatively affluent districts of Paris. (The title of their book is difficult to translate into English because the words 'suburb' and 'inner city' have different class connotations in the two languages because of the different demographies of French and English cities.)

> Our problem was to understand the individual educational failure of individuals belonging to the same social categories. On the one hand, the undeniable statistical correlation between school failure and social origin; on the other, the experience of schooling as a singular history marked by events, by encounters, by the unforeseeable: the challenge is to understand how social inequality is transformed into educational differentiation through individual histories.
>
> (Charlot et al., 1992, p. 229; my translation)

On the basis of their empirical research they argue that differences in academic achievement are associated with different relationships to knowledge on the part of the student, and that academic achievement in school is dependent on developing a particular relationship to knowledge. They distinguish three epistemological processes which define relations to learning in school.

- In the first, knowledge is defined in terms of the learning situation in which the student is involved, and the student role is defined in terms of coping with that task.
- In the second, knowledge is seen as objectivized: abstracted from the learning task, decontextualized and external to the learner. The role of the student is seen as to appropriate it.
- In the third, the learner is engaged in a process not only of objectifying and appropriating knowledge but entering into it, interpreting it and relating it to the self in a process of consciously reflexive self-education.

The first process is typical of low-achieving students. It is a relationship to school rather than a relationship to knowledge. The other two processes, especially the third, are associated with higher academic attainment. These processes are highly class-differentiated. Working-class students tended to see learning much more in terms solely of the completion of tasks than as the entering into universes of knowledge. Many of them were motivated to succeed at school in order to get a good job, but they did not conceptualize this link between school and future destinations as mediated by intellectual work in the way that most middle-class students did. Middle-class students tended to give meaning and value to intellectual work both for intrinsic reasons – as interesting and enjoyable in itself – and for extrinsic ones – as the means to a good job.

Where do these different class relationships to knowledge come from? Charlot and his colleagues offer a similar explanation to that of Connell. They emphasize that working-class knowledge tends to be contextualized in the family and the street, and based on personal involvement.

A Meaningful Relationship to Knowledge

This argument has important consequences for teaching. First, it poses entry into intellectual universes as the key to academic success. Second, it poses, as the necessary condition of this relationship to knowledge, its *meaning* for the student. Without that, neither the presentation of an intellectually demanding curriculum nor hard work by the learner is enough. The student can work hard but ineffectively in terms of academic success. Charlot and his colleagues argue that teachers can help students to construct a meaningful relationship to knowledge and thus achieve greater academic success, but that teachers have often adopted one of two opposite, and ineffective, approaches. One is to present knowledge through an academic curriculum which has little meaning for working-class students, since it doesn't connect with their experiences and identities. The other is to make the curriculum 'relevant' to working-class students, but at the expense of diluting its intellectual demands. Charlot and his colleagues argue that teachers often use strategies with working-class students which are intended to facilitate learning, but which actually serve to exclude them from entry into abstract systems of knowledge which is necessary for academic success. They give examples: the focus on the local and the personal which tends to restrict students to the immediate context; the fragmentation of knowledge into small simple steps with little intellectual challenge, the slippage towards the affective at the expense of the cognitive.

The task is to bring the intellectual world and the world of the child or young person together in a meaningful way.

> This is only possible if the subject installs himself or herself in the relationship to the world which the constitution of this knowledge supposes. There is no knowledge without a *relationship* of the subject *to this knowledge*. However, the subject . . . is never a pure subject of knowledge: it maintains various kinds of relationships with the world. So a proposition which can be invested in a relationship to the world which might be a relationship of knowledge can also be invested in another type of relationship: the student will learn in order to avoid a bad mark or a smack, in order to go up to the next class, to have a good job in the future, to gain the approval of a sympathetic teacher, etc. In such a case, the appropriation of knowledge is fragile because this knowledge is not supported by the type of relationship to the world (decontextualization, objectification, argumentation . . .) which gives it a specific meaning . . .
>
> If knowledge is a relationship, the object of an intellectual education must be the process which leads to the adoption of a relationship of knowledge to the world – and not the accumulation of intellectual contents. But note: this process is not purely cognitive and didactic. It is a question of bringing a child to inscribe himself or herself in a certain type of relationship to the world, to the self and to others – which brings pleasure but which always entails the renunciation, provisional or profound, of other forms of relationship to the world, to the self and to others. In this sense, the question of knowledge is always also a question of identity
>
> (Charlot et al., 1992, pp. 73–5; my translation)

This should not be posed as a question of integrating theory and practice, or the abstract and the concrete. Charlot (1997, p. 83) is very insistent on this point. It is an error to translate epistemological relations into characteristics of the student or of 'reality'. The real question is of the student being able to use 'school knowledge' to organize understandings and actions in order to further his or her own meanings and purposes. In an earlier book (Charlot and Figeat, 1979, p. 245), Charlot and his co-author stress that the key relationship is the couple 'problem–knowledge'.

> All learning must start from problem situations, that is to say situations which have a meaning for the student, which pose a problem, which demand the elaboration of ideas to resolve this problem and which lead effectively to the mastery of rigorous concepts and language.

However, there is a fundamental problem for working-class students making use of 'school knowledge' to tackle meaningful problems. School knowledge, in terms of its cognitive content and the forms in which it is transmitted, is often experienced as alienating. As Connell (1994, p. 137) says:

> the experience of teachers in disadvantaged schools has persistently led them to question the curriculum. Conventional subject matter and texts and traditional teaching methods and assessment techniques turn out to be sources of systematic difficulty. They persistently produce boredom. Enforcing them heightens the problem of discipline, and so far as they are successfully enforced, they divide pupils between an academically successful minority and an academically discredited majority.

Empirical support in the British context comes from a survey carried out by Keele University of 30,000 eleven- to sixteen-year-old students at 200 secondary schools all over the country. 'Most worrying is the pattern that emerges of many youngsters steadily losing interest in their education as they go through secondary school. By the time they reach their crucial GCSE year, many are apparently bored by their work and disenchanted with their teachers, and do not want to stay on' (cited in *TES*, 5 April 1997).

Social Class and Student Grouping

Before I focus on the curriculum, let me explain what I mean by alienating modes of transmission in which knowledge is embedded. There are numerous aspects to this: relationships between teachers and students; modes of assessment; regimes of individual competitiveness; the language of schooling; and resourcing issues such as teacher–student ratios. By way of illustration, I will deal with only one here: the ways in which students are grouped. Ability grouping, the prevalent form of student grouping in British schools, is currently on the increase, encouraged by government policy. It has long been known that ability grouping both reflects and constructs social-class differentiation. The most recent research in Britain is Jo Boaler's (1997) study of maths classes in two secondary schools, both largely white working class in composition. Amber Hill is a traditional school which sets students by subjects, Phoenix Park is a 'progressive' school which favours mixed-ability grouping. Phoenix Park got significantly better GCSE grades, as a result at least in part of the negative effect of ability grouping on working-class students at Amber Hill, where there was a disproportionate allocation of working-class students to low sets, and where, Boaler suggests, working-class students are more likely to be negatively affected by the experience of setting than middle-class students. Boaler (1997, p. 590) says:

> at Amber Hill the disparity between initial mathematical capability and eventual achievement . . . is partly created by a small number of mainly middle-class students who achieved more than would be expected and a relatively

large number of mainly working-class students who achieved less than would be expected. Similar evidence of class polarisation is not apparent at Phoenix Park.

Yet the consequences of various forms of student grouping for issues of equality, and especially social-class equality, are scarcely considered either in the 'school improvement' literature or in the schools themselves. According to Benn and Chitty (1996, p. 473) in their study of over 1,500 comprehensive schools, only 10 per cent of them monitored student grouping in relation to social class.

Reconstructing School Knowledge

So in order to provide the most favourable conditions for working-class students to construct meaningful relationships to knowledge, the alienating aspects of its mode of transmission and appropriation need to be removed. But that is not enough: the content of much school knowledge is also alienating. The curriculum itself needs to be reconstructed. As Connell (1994, p. 140) says:

> Each particular way of constructing the curriculum (i.e. organizing the field of knowledge and defining how it is to be taught and learned) carries social effects. Curriculum empowers and disempowers, authorizes and de-authorizes, recognizes and mis-recognizes different social groups and their knowledge and identities.

At this point I want to introduce a new element into the argument. Thus far I have spoken of the aim of education for working-class students solely in terms of success within the academic curriculum in order to reduce inequality of 'outcomes'. This is a necessary aim but not the whole story. Connell in *Schools and Social Justice* argues for 'a broader conception of the "empowerment" of working-class students as the goal. Such a concept would embrace not only skills and knowledges required for success within the existing system but also skills and knowledges required for collective action' (Connell, 1993, p. 104). There is a tradition within working-class education of education as a means to social emancipation which stretches back to the early nineteenth century. Richard Johnson (1983, p. 22) describes the concept of 'really useful knowlege', which started out from everyday concerns, that broke down the distinctions betweeen learning and life, and between the theoretical and the applied:

> Really useful knowledge involved, then, a range of resources for overcoming daily difficulties. It involved self-respect and self-confidence which came from seeing that your oppressions were systematic and were shared. It included practical skills, but not just those wanted by employers. . . . Really useful knowledge was also a means to overcoming difficulties in the long term and more comprehensively. It taught people what social changes were necessary for real social ameliorations to occur.

Connell argues, on both social justice and epistemological grounds, for the replacement of the current mainstream hegemonic curriculum with a new common curriculum based on principles of social justice.

> This strategy accepts the need for a program of common learnings in the schools, but does not accept the basis on which common learnings are currently constructed. The strategy seeks a way of organizing content and method which builds on the experience of the disadvantaged, but generalizes that to the whole system, rather than confining it to an enclave. The strategy thus seeks a practical reconstruction of education which will yield relative advantage to the groups currently disadvantaged.
>
> (*ibid.*, p. 38)

Similarly, in their introduction to *Democratic Schools*, which contains four case studies of American schools, Michael Apple and James Beane (1995, p. 17) say: 'Our task is to reconstruct dominant knowledge and employ it to help, not hinder, those who are least privileged in this society.'

Meaningful Knowledge in Practice

We can find at least elements of a curriculum based on 'really useful knowledge' in some schools today, and see that they can provide the basis for a different relationship to knowledge by working-class students which can empower them in the ways that Connell suggests. The most fertile contexts in British schools in recent years are the anti-racist and anti-sexist movements in education, which have combined the aim of removing the obstacles to academic success within the system with wider goals of developing a critical understanding of race and gender oppressions in society. In recent years the advent of a centrally prescribed subject-based curriculum and more technicist models of teaching has tended to marginalize this tradition and prevent egalitarian initiatives, in spite of the continuing, though largely unacknowledged, efforts of many teachers in their own classrooms and schools (see, for example, Cole et al., 1997; Hill and Cole, 1999).[2] In the United States there is greater freedom to innovate, at least in some contexts, as the following brief case studies demonstrate.

A curriculum which combines being intellectually challenging and building on students' concerns and experiences in the wider society is one of the key features of Newmann's (1996) research into 'authentic achievement', based on the School Restructuring Study of twenty-four significantly restructured public schools in the United States. Newmann and his associates define 'authentic achievement' in terms of the following criteria: the construction of knowledge (rather than its reproduction); disciplined enquiry (comprising the use of a prior knowledge-base, in-depth understanding and elaborated communication); and value beyond school (that is, discourses, products and performances which have a meaning and purpose beyond the demonstration of competence to a teacher) (Wehlage et al., 1996). They single out four schools as most successful because of their concern for the intellectual quality of classroom practice. I will briefly describe one of them, an innovatory multiracial school, with around one-third of the students receiving free or reduced-fee lunch, governed by teachers and parents and based on a Deweyan concept of applied learning (Doane, 1996). The school's curriculum was built around enquiry-oriented activities that involved real-world application of knowledge' (Newmann et al., p. 166). Two consecutive 5th Grade lessons illustrate the school's emphasis on intellectual quality. A newspaper report of the killing of three high school students by rival gang members led to a discussion of the reasons why young people joined gangs, possible alternatives and solutions. The students worked in groups, writing letters to the local radio station and newspaper, creating slogans, posters, songs and leaflets persuading students to be independent, collecting data on gang crimes for the school newspaper, and producing and videotaping a role-play to show to the school. 'Consistent with [the school's] commitment to Applied Learning, the lessons connected school knowledge to situations outside the classroom and included specific attempts to influence audiences beyond their own classroom' (*ibid.*, p. 167).

A similar conception underlies the case studies in Apple and Beane's book *Democratic Schools*.

> The idea of a thematic curriculum dominates these schools, not simply as an effective methodology that keeps kids happy, but because this approach involves putting knowledge to use in relation to real life problems and issues . . . Rather than being lists of concepts, facts and skills that students master for standardized achievement tests (and then go on to forget, by and large), knowledge is that which is intimately connected to the communities and biographies of real people. Students learn that knowledge makes a difference in people's lives, including their own.
>
> (Apple and Beane, 1995, p. 102)

One of the case studies is of an innovatory two-way bilingual elementary school governed by teachers and parents in Milwaukee, Wisconsin. Approximately two-thirds of the students are eligible for free school lunches. Bob Peterson, a teacher at the school and one of its founders, begins his description of the school with an account of three 5th Graders on their own initiative devising a role-play based on anti-gay discrimination. In the class discussion that followed, other students related it to family experience, a recent gay rights demonstration and Martin Luther King's march for civil rights: 'the incident reminded me of the inherent links between classroom and society: how society influences the student who shows up in our classrooms for six hours a day and how broader movements for social reform affect daily classroom life' (Peterson, 1995, p. 59).

Another case study in *Democratic Schools* describes the 9th Grade programme at a school of technical arts in Cambridge, Massachusetts (Rosenstock and Steinberg, 1995, pp. 48, 47): 'The goal of CityWorks projects is to help students understand their community and its needs, and ultimately to see themselves as people who can affect that community and create new opportunities for others who live and work there . . . Cambridge is the "text" as students investigate the neighborhoods, the systems, the people, and the needs that compose an urban community . . . CityWorks combines key characteristics of vocational programmes . . . with the broader content and essential skills of academic education.'

These examples demonstrate that a curriculum which brings together 'school knowledge' and the real-life experiences and concerns of students is capable of enabling them to construct a meaningful problem-solving relationship to knowledge. As Apple and Beane (1995, p. 16) say:

> A democratic curriculum invites young people to shed the passive role of knowledge consumers and assume the active role of 'meaning makers'. It recognizes that people acquire knowledge by both studying external sources and engaging in complex activities that require them to construct their own knowledge.

Conclusion

Let me summarize briefly the outline of my argument.

- Social class correlates strongly with educational achievement.
- But individual educational trajectories are not socially predetermined, so we need an explanation which sees individuals as not reducible to incarnations of social groups.
- We need to start from the notion of class as a relationship, not a location.
- In school, the central relationship is between the student and knowledge.
- The key element in that relationship is the question of meaning.
- Different relationships to knowledge are causally related to differences in academic achievement.
- Those different relationships to knowledge are structured, but not determined, by social-class cultures.
- Changing students' relationships to knowledge needs to be the organizing principle of policies to raise working-class achievement and reduce educational inequality.
- Making school knowledge fully meaningful for working-class students entails integrating it into the knowledge the child uses to understand and act in the world.
- To do this requires both bringing the experiences and concerns of the child or young person into the curriculum and reconstructing the curriculum on a basis which combines high intellectual quality with the perspectives of the socially deprived and oppressed rather than those of the privileged and powerful.
- It also entails disembedding meaningful school knowledge from forms and processes of transmission and acquisition which are alienating to working-class students.
- This provides the basis both for high academic achievement within the system and wider goals of education for emancipation.

In this chapter I have tried to develop an argument for the central place occupied by the student's relationship to knowledge for academic success in school, and for the need to enable working-class students to transform school knowledge into meaningful real-life problem-solving knowledge. I am not claiming that this is the only issue, and that provided it is secured, everything else falls into place, for two reasons: first, because, as I have said, school knowledge is embedded in forms of transmission which may also be alienating, especially for working-class students (I gave the example of ability grouping, but there are a number of other equally important aspects); and second, because there is an element of technical effectiveness in teaching which has a certain partial autonomy. For example, take learning to read. While it is deeply involved with issues of meaning, identity and culture – that is, the social and personal meaning of reading for the student – it also entails questions of technical pedagogy – the effective teaching of 'phonics', for example. Other things being equal, some ways of teaching students how to perform computations are more effective than others, at a technical level. Nor am I claiming that the transformation of school knowledge into 'life-experience knowledge' is the only basis on which working-class students can enter into intellectual worlds. Clearly, some already do, and achieve academic success as a result, even 'against the stream'. What I would claim is that the question of the meaning of school knowledge is central to educational attainment, and that unless it is the organizing principle of school reform aimed at working-class students, what can be achieved will inevitably be limited. That seems to be the fundamental problem with education action zones.

EAZs are a new government initiative designed specifically to raise achievement in schools in socially disadvantaged areas. At the time of writing, the first phase of twelve zones was just starting, with a further thirteen to follow. It is too early to make any judgement based on evidence of practice about how successful they will be. Furthermore, there is considerable local variation among the zones. But it is possible to make some evaluation, in relation to the argument put forward in this chapter, of the government's brief for EAZs and the proposals which have been approved. Most of the comments about the zones published so far have focused on the role of the private sector in them, and in particular on the proposal that business should take the lead in some zones. The proposal to disapply teachers' national pay and conditions has also attracted comment. Much less attention has been paid to questioning whether the measures proposed, of which the above are two among many, will succeed in raising educational achievement among working-class students.

The first point to make is that the EAZ project, either at national or local level, is not based on a serious, all-embracing, research-based and theoretically informed analysis of low achievement in working-class areas. Of course, elements of an explanation underpin the choice of remedies, which include more effective 'parenting', more literacy, teaching longer school hours and a work-related curriculum. What is strikingly absent from this agenda is a willingness to place at the very centre a critical reappraisal of the relationship between the curriculum and the student's identity and experience, in order to make intellectual knowledge meaningful.

Without this, as Charlot and his colleagues (1992, p. 103) say, a strategy of strengthening the links between school and work reinforces the existing relations to knowledge – instrumental rather than 'intrinsic' – which working-class students already tend to have. This is especially so if the proposed work-related curriculum is an alternative to the 'academic' curriculum within a prevocational training perspective, not one either of developing critical understanding or of the integration of the 'world of work' dimension into high-quality intellectual education. They raise the same objection to a strategy of strengthening the links between school and home, if it is not based on a reconstruction of the educational experience in order to make it meaningful to working-class students. Similarly, homework clubs may reinforce students' relationship to knowledge simply as tasks to be completed.

Nor is there any critical appraisal of the ways in which the forms of transmission and acquisition of knowledge within schools may alienate working-class students. I have used the example of ability grouping, which is seen as a solution, not a potential problem, by the government.

The concept of an education action zone brings to the fore the 'territorial' dimension of school, as part of the locality, the community, the city. There is an opportunity here to raise fundamental questions about the nature of that relationship which is not being taken. In much EAZ discourse, there is an implicit deficit model, a tendency to see parents and community in terms of lacks and absences, rather than strengths which can be enhanced. There is a lot of emphasis on adults as mentors, coming into school and supporting students. This may be valuable, but it should be part of a much more far-reaching perspective in which students relate to adults, as a dimension of the curriculum, in their lives as workers and citizens in the real world outside school, as we have seen in the case studies of American schools. Real-life experience-based enquiry into social life and social institutions needs to be central to the school curriculum. That is what the concept of the 'learning zone', the 'learning society', should mean: that every social institution, every aspect of our society, is opened up to educational exploration and critical understanding, not just in terms of 'work experience' but as an integral dimension of the entire curriculum in primary and secondary schools, combining intellectual adventure and developr ent with active education in democratic citizenship, and making knowledge re ly meaningful for working-class students.

Notes

1 For some observations on the rise of mass schooling and its intersection with class and 'race', see Chapter 4.
2 These books deal with disability and sexuality *as well as* with the more conventional concerns of class, 'race' and gender.

References

Apple, M.W. and Beane, J.A. (eds) (1995) *Democratic Schools*, Washington, DC: Association for Supervision and Curriculum Development
Ashendon, D., Connell, B., Dowsett, G. and Kessler, S. (1987) 'Teachers and Working-class

Schooling', in Livingstone D.W. (ed.), *Critical Pedagogy and Cultural Power*, Basingstoke: Macmillan

Benn, C. and Chitty, C. (1996) *Thirty Years on: Is Comprehensive Education Alive and Well or Struggling to Survive?*, London: David Fulton

Boaler, J. (1997) 'Setting, Social Class and Survival of the Quickest', *British Educational Research Journal*, 23 (5), pp. 575–95

Charlot, B. (1997) *Du Rapport au Savoir*, Paris: Editions Economica

Charlot, B. and Figeat, M. (1979) *L'Ecole aux enchères*, Paris: Petite Bibliothèque Payot

Charlot, B., Bautier, E. and Rochex, J.-Y. (1992) *Ecole et savoir dans les banlieus . . . et ailleurs*, Paris: Armand Colin

Cole, M. (1998) 'Globalization, Modernization and Competitiveness: A Critique of the New Labour Project in Education', *International Studies in Sociology of Education*, 8 (3), pp. 315–32

Cole, M., Hill, D. and Shan, S. (eds) (1997) *Promoting Equality in Primary Schools*, London: Cassell

Connell, R.W. (1993) *Schools and Social Justice*, Philadelphia: Temple University Press

Connell, R.W. (1994) 'Poverty and Education', *Harvard Educational Review*, 64 (2), pp. 125–49

Connell, R.W., Ashenden, D.J., Kessler, S. and Dowsett, G.W. (1982) *Making the Difference: Schools, Families and Social Division* Sydney: Allen and Unwin

Doane, K.B. (1996) 'Careen and Lamar Elementary Schools', in Newmann, F.M. (ed.), *Authentic Achievement: Restructuring Schools for Intellectual Quality*, San Francisco: Jossey-Bass

Hatcher, R. (1998a) 'Labour, Official School Improvement and Equality', *Journal of Education Policy*, 13 (4), pp. 485–99

Hatcher, R. (1998b) 'The Politics of School Effectiveness and Improvement', *Race, Ethnicity and Education*, 1 (2), 267–89

Hill, D. and Cole, M. (eds) (1999) *Promoting Equality in Secondary Schools*, London: Cassell

Johnson, R. (1983) 'Educational Politics: The Old and the New', in Wolpe, A.M. and Donald, J. (eds), *Is There Anyone Here from Education?*, London: Pluto Press

Leys, C. and Panitch, L. (1998) 'The Political Legacy of the Manifesto', in Panitch, L. and Leys, C. (eds), *The Communist Manifesto Now: Socialist Register 1998*, Rendlesham: Merlin Press

Mortimore, P. and Whitty, G. (1997) *Can School Improvement Overcome the Effects of Disadvantage?*, London: Institute of Education, University of London

Newmann, F.M. (ed.) (1996) *Authentic Achievement: Restructuring Schools for Intellectual Quality*, San Francisco: Jossey-Bass

Newmann, F.M., King, M.B. and Secada, W.G. (1996) 'Intellectual Quality', in Newmann, F.M. (ed.), *Authentic Achievement: Restructuring Schools for Intellectual Quality*, San Francisco: Jossey-Bass

Peterson, B. (1995) 'La Escuela Fratney; A Journey toward Democracy', in Apple, M.W. and Beane, J.A. (eds), *Democratic Schools*, Washington, DC: Association for Supervision and Curriculum Development

Rosenstock, L. and Steinberg, A. (1995) 'Beyond the Shop: Reinventing Vocational Education', in Apple, M.W. and Beane, J.A. (eds), *Democratic Schools*, Washington, DC: Association for Supervision and Curriculum Development

Wehlage, G.G., Newmann, F.M. and Secada, W.G. (1996) 'Standards for Authentic

Achievement and Pedagogy', in Newmann, F.M. (1996) *Authentic Achievement: Restructuring Schools for Intellectual Quality*, San Francisco: Jossey-Bass

Wood, E.M. (1990) 'The Uses and Abuses of "Civil Society"', in Miliband, R. and Panitch, L. (eds), *The Retreat of the Intellectuals: Socialist Register 1990*, London: Merlin Press

Wood, E.M. (1995) *Democracy against Capitalism*, Cambridge: Cambridge University Press

Index